Racial Integration in the Church of Apartheid

Studies in Reformed Theology

Editor-in-Chief

Eddy van der Borght (*Vrije Universiteit Amsterdam*)

Editorial Board

Abraham van de Beek (*Vrije Universiteit Amsterdam*)
Martien Brinkman (*Vrije Universiteit Amsterdam*)
George Harinck (*Vrije Universiteit Amsterdam*)
Dirk van Keulen (*Theological University Kampen*)
Daniel Migliore (*Princeton Theological Seminary*)
Richard Mouw (*Fuller Theological Seminary, Pasadena*)
Emanuel Gerrit Singgih (*Duta Wacana Christian University, Yogjakarta*)
Pieter Vos (*Protestant Theological University, Amsterdam*)
Conrad Wethmar (*University of Pretoria*)

VOLUME 36

The titles published in this series are listed at *brill.com/srt*

Racial Integration in the Church of Apartheid

A Unity Only God Wants

By

Marthe Hesselmans

BRILL

LEIDEN | BOSTON

Cover illustration: The Dutch Reformed Church in Ladybrand, Free State, South Africa. Photo by Marthe Hesselmans.

The Library of Congress Cataloging-in-Publication Data is available online at http://catalog.loc.gov
LC record available at http://lccn.loc.gov/2018960513

Typeface for the Latin, Greek, and Cyrillic scripts: "Brill". See and download: brill.com/brill-typeface.

ISSN 1571-4799
ISBN 978-90-04-36463-9 (paperback)
ISBN 978-90-04-38501-6 (e-book)

This book is printed on acid-free paper and produced in a sustainable manner.

Printed by Printforce, the Netherlands

*To Rens, who showed me as a child that grown-ups
can actually change. Matjiesfontein!*

Contents

Preface

Sunday in South Africa is church day. Except perhaps on the beaches of Cape Town, you can barely escape the sounds of church bells ringing, clapping and singing. Researching religion in South Africa, I could surely not escape. Every Sunday, a different church visit was on my schedule as well as on that of my husband, mother and 7 month old daughter who accompanied me. This called for quite some flexibility on their part.

On certain Sundays, my husband would quietly take off his jacket during service, overdressed as he felt amidst sneakers, shorts and t-shirts. On others, he wished he brought a tie to match the shiny suits and hats of our fellow churchgoers. My mother made different breakfast plans depending on where the church would be located. Prior to praying in the suburbs, tea with toast sufficed. Service here usually would not take more than an hour. Contrarily, worshipping in the townships meant a hefty breakfast and a bag full of snacks to last us well into the afternoon. There were churches so quiet and spacious that our daughter could stay in her stroller and enjoy an extended morning nap. In others, she had no choice but to join the dancing and singing as she was passed from hand to hand throughout the packed church.

What made these diverse experiences all the more intriguing was that each took place within the same denomination: the Reformed Church. Apart from differences in confession – and quite significant ones as we will see – the above churches hold on to the same faith tradition. They have common roots in the Dutch Reformed Church that landed on South African shores in the sixteen hundreds. They also, willingly or unwillingly, share a contested history as bearers of apartheid. It was among the Reformed churches that racial segregation evolved from common practice to an official ruling and ultimately to a strict religious doctrine. Well before apartheid became government policy, Reformed churches held separate services for white, black, colored and Indian communities. Notably, an extensive religious-nationalist doctrine was used to justify racial separation. It would be the will of God to keep South Africa's diverse communities apart and protect what was claimed to be a divinely chosen people: the Afrikaners.

Challenging God's will is not an easy thing to do, unless you are convinced that God wants something else. This was the conclusion the Reformed churches drew by the late 1990s. They had misinterpreted the Bible. God did not desire division, but unity. Beliefs in chosenness and white superiority were replaced by discourses of unity and reconciliation. Instead of segregating, the Reformed churches vowed to integrate their communities into one multiracial church institution.

What has come of this apparent change of heart? How do religious communities move from a belief system of exclusion to one of inclusion? Visiting numerous Reformed churches made me skeptical at first. The differences between white suburban and black township churches just seemed too big to reconcile. However, as the communities in this book show, churches are but one place where people might experience faith together. They join in worship outside traditional religious institutions, while servicing a soup kitchen or building a new daycare for the community. Here, there is no expectation of certain rituals tied to certain group identities. People find common ground in their faith in a God who, above all, wants them to help each other.

Acknowledgments

When Peter Berger first advised me to do a short study on the Dutch Reformed Church in South Africa, I admit I had my doubts. Why study a fading church in South Africa? The minute I started reading how this church denounced its own apartheid history however, I realized why. This research would become a rare opportunity to learn about what it actually means to come to terms with a painful past and reconcile long divided communities. I hence thank Peter Berger for encouraging me to study this fascinating topic and for supporting me with profound insights, enthusiasm and confidence in my work.

Speaking of confidence, I wish to mention my family at the top of these acknowledgements rather than is commonly done at the end. This research would not have been possible without the trust my husband and mother have placed in me. They took turns in accompanying me to South Africa, helped take care of our baby daughter *and* critically evaluate my research findings.

At Boston University I owe great thanks to Nancy Ammerman. She crucially motivated me to concentrate on local faith communities and their stories of South Africa's post-apartheid transition rather than those of institutions alone. In addition, I thank Frank Korom for gracefully guiding me through my research trajectory, from the first fundraising proposal to the last chapter outline. I am also grateful for the academic support of Eddy Van der Borght and John Stone. Upon returning to the Netherlands, Eddy Van der Borght helped me find a new academic home at the Vrije Universiteit Amsterdam. Here I also owe much gratitude to Marina de Regt and to Peter Versteeg for welcoming me at the Social and Cultural Anthropology Department.

Many people participated in this research as interlocutors, interviewees and advisors. I am indebted to the Theology faculties at both Stellenbosch and the Free State universities. Many thanks to Robert Vosloo for inviting me to the seminar on the Reformed Churches in South Africa and the Struggle for Justice and making countless vital introductions. At Stellenbosch University, my special thanks go out to Mary-Ann Plaatjies Van Huffel, Nico Koopman, Christo Thesnaar and Monty Sahd. At the University of the Free State, I thank Anlene Taljaard for her extensive support in helping me set up my fieldwork in Bloemfontein and surroundings, as well as Dawid Mouton for introducing me to one of the most interesting case studies I encountered during my stay in South Africa. I also wish to express my great gratitude to Coenie Burger, Johan Botha and Gideon van der Watt for confiding in me and for so warmly inviting my family and me into your homes. Of the people who engaged with my research in South Africa, most did so out of deep commitment to the churches and with the hope for a better future for the involved communities. I admire their generosity and courage to share experiences with me despite the difficult memories this sometimes triggered.

Planning and conducting field research in South Africa while at the same time starting a family, came with numerous challenges that I could not have faced without many dear friends and family on both sides of the ocean. Special thanks to Dalene and Hendrik in Stellenbosch, Jenn and Rhoda in Boston, Dani, Hadas and Eva Maria in New York and to Kris, Johan, Lisa and Florieke in the Netherlands. Thank you for hosting me when I needed a couch to sleep on or a place to write, for making sure I got away from my computer, and back to it.

Tables

Abbreviations

AACC	All African Church Council
ANC	African National Congress
APK	Afrikaanse Protestantse Kerk (Afrikaans Protestant Church)
DA	Democratic Alliance
DRC	Dutch Reformed Church
DRCA	Dutch Reformed Church in Africa
CFW	Commission For Witness
EFF	Economic Freedom Fighters
IRA	Irish Republican Army
NP	National Party
RCA	Reformed Church in Africa
UPS	Uniting Presbytery of Stellenbosch
URCSA	Uniting Reformed Churches in Southern Africa
WARC	World Alliance of Reformed Churches
WCRC	World Council of Reformed Churches

Introduction: When Religion Unites or Divides

"We believe that the Lord demands from us to heal the old divisions as soon as possible and come together as the entire family of churches into one church association … We are afraid to say it, but we judge that failure to do so will not only mean we have failed the Lord, but also our South African society, and perhaps especially the children and youth."[1]

∵

In 2004, the Dutch Reformed Church (DRC)[2] thus reaffirmed its denouncement of the racial and ethnic divisions it once so fervently supported. The statement exemplifies the DRC's tortuous turnabout from being a major pillar of South Africa's apartheid regime to calling itself an advocate of the new rainbow nation. In 1990, the church had already admitted it made a mistake in endorsing the political system of racial separation "too uncritically."[3] Since then, the DRC has struggled to catch up with the country's post-apartheid transition. Despite the urge for unity, Reformed congregations remain de facto segregated. And they are not alone. Racial separation prevails across South Africa's religious landscape. Places of worship are often said to form last bastions of apartheid in this heavily Christian country. Why are the churches lagging behind in its post-apartheid transition and how far behind really are they?

---

1   *DRC 2004*, General Synod. Besluite. [Decisions]. 2.

2   The Dutch Reformed Church is the English translation that will be used in this book for the *Nederduitse Gereformeerde Kerk* (NGK) in South Africa. The church was established in 1652 and over time set up separate churches for different racial and ethnic communities. The historically segregated Dutch Reformed churches and their successors are today referred to under the umbrella term of Reformed Church family or family of Reformed churches in South Africa. See for more details on this history, chapter 2. According to the 2016 Community Survey, the family represented 5.4% of all Christian denominations counted in South Africa. This still puts the family in the top five largest single denominations in the country. *Community Survey 2016 In Brief.* Statistics South Africa, 2016, 42–43.

3   *Church and Society 1990: A Testimony of the Dutch Reformed Church (ned Geref Kerk).* Bloemfontein: General Synodical Commission, 1991. Paragraph 282.

Zooming in on the Reformed churches, we see a complex story. Indeed, 11 a.m. on Sunday seems to be South Africa's most segregated hour of the week.[4] But not for lack of effort. Over the past decades, Reformed churches have undertaken numerous initiatives to overcome racial differences. Simply stating their failure to do so discards the intricate dynamics at play here. How does a former pillar of apartheid seek to transcend its controversial past? What does successful integration mean and why has it been so difficult? This book seeks to uncover capacities within South Africa's Reformed churches to bridge their own deeply embedded divisions. Focus is given to faith communities themselves. Why and how do ordinary churchgoers join or rather resist the reconciliation their leaders now decree?

The very term reconciliation is contested here. It implies hope for more cohesion among communities torn by an apartheid past and disparate present. Concretely, it has become associated with the visible unification of the black, white, colored and Indian sections by which the Reformed churches have remained separated.[5] The past two decades reveal an extensive trajectory through which these churches pursue their structural merger into one multiracial institution, thus far with little success. The Reformed Church family is still subdivided between the predominantly white DRC on the one hand, and the black, colored and Indian churches on the other hand. The DRC long claimed the position of 'mother church' within the family. It considered its white Afrikaner constituency a unique nation chosen by God to rule South Africa. After apartheid the DRC might have abandoned this doctrine. Its congregations remain largely white and Afrikaans speaking. Related is the Uniting Reformed Church in Southern Africa (URCSA). With roots in the DRC's mission churches, it now functions as an independent institution that harbors mostly colored and black Reformed communities. Additionally, there is the Dutch Reformed Church in

---

4   Eddy Van der Borght has written an insightful article on this topic for his inauguration speech at the Free University of Amsterdam, see: Eddy Van der Borght, *Sunday Morning – the Most Segregated Hour: On Racial Reconciliation As Unfinished Business for Theology in South Africa and Beyond* (Amsterdam: Faculty of Theology, VU University, 2009).

5   These contentious terms reflect the racial categories of South Africa's apartheid regime. African and black remain prevalent terms to indicate its indigenous African population groups whereas white refers to European heritage, colored to communities with mixed African, European and Asian backgrounds, and Indian or Asian to those with origins in especially India. The terms are still commonly used in South Africa to describe one's own and others' group identities. Their employment in a study like this is problematic and can contribute to further stigmatization, as will be addressed in section 1.2. It should be clear that wherever used in this book, the terms are considered as complex social and political constructs that are neither fixed nor static. None capture South Africa's immense diversity or the hybrid forms of identification that have evolved over time.

Africa (DRCA) that serves a small black section, and the Reformed Church in Africa (RCA) representing the few Indian congregations left in the church family.

Unifying these ethnically, racially and socially divided churches appears a mission impossible. What motivates their efforts and what hinders them? With a critical analysis of religious discourse and practice, this book explores what it means to try and break entrenched patterns of separateness. The Reformed churches provide a highly relevant perspective here. Their segregated realities might make them unusual suspects in South Africa's ongoing reconciliation process. Yet, they exhibit all too familiar challenges with diversity, and sometimes surprising responses. Reformed congregants wrestle, as communities throughout the country do, with the pressure to adapt to the new norm of integration while trying to hold on to their specific identities. How to cross boundaries without losing the language, traditions and solidarity of one's own community?

South Africa's post-apartheid reconstruction forms the backdrop to the story of the Reformed churches in this book as well as a central theme in itself. Underlying the church struggle with integration is the larger question of how to live together in a divided society. Alienated from each other by decades of forced segregation, South Africans today face the challenge to build a sense of common belonging. Most still live separated lives due to the race policies of the past, but also because of the vast social-economic disparity of the present. Divisions are deepened further by persistent beliefs in the existence of and necessity to preserve distinct identities. This reality contributes to increasing disillusion with the rainbow nation Bishop Desmond Tutu envisaged in 1994. Promises of reconciliation, justice and equality have faltered on immense inequality, outbursts of xenophobia and crises of unemployment, crime and sexual violence. None of these difficulties can be grasped without considering their roots in the apartheid era. With an in-depth analysis into the efforts of one major protagonist of the old system to change course, this book seeks to offer one more piece of the puzzle that constitutes South Africa's enduring transformation towards greater unity.

Religious Responses to Social Upheaval

The post-apartheid context of South Africa lays out two key dilemmas for its Reformed church communities. On the one hand, they wish to join the country's trajectory towards greater national unity, justice and reconciliation. At the same time, they are desperate to maintain what is left of their own groups and protect supposedly distinct cultures, languages and church traditions against erosion. Visions of inclusivity furthermore clash with a persistent reality of segregation and inequality. The pursuit of racial integration is perceived as threatening to the communal solidarity necessary to face the country's enduring insecurity, a solidarity that the churches have historically bolstered through their separated structures.

These juxtapositions, wider unity versus particular identity preservation, and inclusivity versus exclusivist group solidarity, are far from unique to South Africa or its Reformed churches. Worldwide, we see a persistent tendency among religious traditions to form around one distinct national or ethnic group.[6] That is nothing new. In contemporary societies however, exclusivity is increasingly difficult to sustain. From Spain to Indonesia, societies are becoming more diverse as a result of globalizing economies, rapid urbanization and mass migration. It raises critical questions for faith communities. They see the need to open up to diversity, but fear the loss of their own identity. How faith communities confront this dilemma will be a key topic throughout the following chapters. What makes communities embrace diversity, or resist it? Is there a middle road?

These are questions that require an interdisciplinary approach. At stake here are matters of religion, social change as well as identity conflicts. The theoretical frame chosen in this book hence combines insights from both religious and identity studies. From the first field it particularly draws on the shift denoted by religious scholars from secularization to pluralization: societies are not becoming less religious, but rather more religiously diverse. Regarding the second field, focus is given to religious-nationalist movements. Studies into such movements importantly show how religious, national, racial and ethnic identities become entangled and contribute to intransigent community divisions, if not violent conflict. A question that tends to remain unanswered is what happens after a conflict ends. How do communities themselves – especially faith communities – seek to overcome their divisions?

Personal and Social Religion

For answering the above questions, it needs to be clear how religion is understood in this book. Central here is the social scientific conception of religion as an embedded function in society. It is constructed and manipulated, historic, personal, collective and, notably, fundamental to the lives of people in diverse ways. It implies a constant tension between on the one hand the notion of religion as shaped through particular circumstances, and on the other hand the tendency of believers to perceive their religious beliefs, values and traditions

---

6 Peter Beyer usefully discusses this tendency and how it is currently under pressure by forces of globalization. See: Peter Beyer, *Religion and Globalization* (London, U.K: Sage Publications, 1994).

as static, deriving directly from the transcendent. Emile Durkheim addressed this tension when he stressed religion to be both an image of and function in society.[7] It would build on communities' collective consciousness and simultaneously help develop this consciousness by providing key categories for shared understanding of the social world.

Religion should thus be perceived as perhaps a human construct, but real in the observers' minds and lives and arising from actual life experiences.[8] The Reformed churches were forced to deal with this paradox as they navigated their way out of apartheid in the 1990s. Claiming the idea of God ordained segregation as a mistaken interpretation of the Bible, the churches undermined a belief many congregants had long taken for granted. By discontinuing a community's once sacred perception, they thus weakened, using Peter Berger's terms, their own plausibility structure.[9]

The fact that the Reformed churches have nonetheless remained influential in post-apartheid South Africa points at another key social scientific view of religion as a historically determined power construct. Thousands of members left the Dutch Reformed Church after 1990, but few completely relinquished their attachment to the institution of their childhood and community, or the perceptions disseminated through this institution. Beyond a way to help explain the world, the church had been part of what Pierre Bourdieu famously called *habitus*. It involves systems of perceptions and beliefs about one's surroundings that are internalized from early childhood and shaped according to the reality of daily life.[10] The habitus operates largely beyond people's consciousness. Without realizing, people come to understand their social reality, particularly their class identity and the power relations involved, as the way it is.

Religion, according to Bourdieu, plays a crucial role in feeding such understanding. It presents the world around us as a natural, if not supernatural, state of being. In the South African context, it was and still is highly instrumental in justifying the social hierarchy that has remained a reality for (ex-)

---

7   Émile Durkheim, *The Elementary Forms of the Religious Life* (New York: Free Press. [1912] 1965).

8   See also Peter L. Berger and Thomas Luckmann, *The Social Construction of Reality: A Treatise in the Sociology of Knowledge* (Garden City, N.Y: Doubleday 1966) in which the authors denote the paradox of a social world that is created and constantly recreated by people, but experienced as as an objective reality.

9   Peter L. Berger, *The Sacred Canopy: Elements of a Sociological Theory of Religion* (New York: Anchor Books. [1967] 1990), 46–51.

10   Pierre Bourdieu *Outline of a Theory of Practice* (Cambridge, U.K: Cambridge University Press, 1977). 76–78.

Reformed church members well after the dismantling of apartheid. The elites of the country long manipulated religious dispositions in such a way that they explained their power and the subordinate position of others as in accordance with divine order. Through religious practice, these dispositions became self-reproducing. They fostered the recognition or rather misrecognition of inequality as normal. Throughout this book we will see the prevailing influence of such dispositions among Reformed communities.

A risk of looking at religion in terms of power though, is that it dismisses perspectives from within these communities. While a significant number of people have given up on the Reformed churches, many others stayed. For the past two decades, church members have seen vast changes in society as well as their religious experience. They necessarily constitute a key vantage point throughout this book. It follows the interpretive sociology propagated by Max Weber and expanded in the anthropology of Clifford Geertz. Their focus on the 'participants of religion' is relevant here in that it calls for a close analysis of perspectives among the women and men inside Reformed Church communities on processes of unification. Ordinary churchgoers tell different stories about why they pursue interracial connections, or not, than does the institution itself. Their stories need to be considered against the details of their specific surroundings. Is a congregation situated in a rural or urban area, with a homogeneous or heterogeneous demography, characterized by a rigid social hierarchy or changing mobility?

It should be clear that such circumstances define only part of people's religious experience. A final social-scientific perspective featured here, concentrates on the highly personal nature in which people perform their faith, in and outside designated institutions. It builds on theories of William James and Martin Riesebrodt among others. Both stressed that any conceptualization of religion should start with people's individual encounters with the divine.[11] Faith is expressed, or rather *performed*, in many different ways with the ultimate goal to help deal with life. Some people find faith in Buddhist meditation, but do not consider themselves adherents of a particular religion. Others mix different religious acts and beliefs, whether or not associated with a monotheistic god. We will also perceive this in South Africa's Reformed churches. Practices of worship form pillars around which their communities evolve. Not seldom however, do members attribute greater significance to faith inspired performances outside the church, while praying for water at a town hall

---

11   William James, *The Varieties of Religious Experience: A Study in Human Nature* (New York: Modern library, 1936); Martin Riesebrodt, *The Promise of Salvation: A Theory of Religion* (Chicago: University of Chicago Press. 2010).

meeting or joining a neighborhood initiative to build day care facilities. What happens at these instances is well captured by Nancy Ammerman's concept of "everyday religion."[12] Religion is personal *and* socially embedded. As people's social and political contexts change, the ways in which people live their own religious experience change as well.

Once Taken for Granted, Now a Personal Choice

In the case of South Africa's Reformed churches, vast and pretty much simultaneous changes have taken place in both the social context and personal experience of religion. Besides the transition away from apartheid, churches today are confronted with vast individualization and pluralization. Religion is not in decline as secularization theorists long claimed. It has rather become a matter of choice amidst a diverse landscape of religious *and* secular worldviews. This shift can be seen globally. It holds significant consequences for traditional religious institutions, not in the least for the Reformed churches.

To gain insight on what is happening here, calls for a closer look at the changing position of religion in contemporary societies. S.N. Eisenstadt's theory of multiple modernities offers a good starting point. It challenges the notion of modernization as a Western-style process of industrialization and differentiation combined with a strong separation between state and religion. Eisenstadt rather sees different interpretations of modernity worldwide and stresses its ongoing construction and reconstruction. What modern societies do have in common is the tension between pluralistic and universal visions, between allowing differences and the urge to subdue them under one totalizing worldview. Eisenstadt's theory has been highly influential among scholars defying secularization theories. José Casanova notably speaks of multiple roads to modernity when it comes to church-state relations. Some modernizing countries have indeed separated faith from governance and experience a decline in religious life. Many others however, show a closer alignment between political and religious functions as well as a persistently strong position of religion in society.[13]

South Africa exemplifies one such alternative road to modernity. Since the end of apartheid, it has been balancing a rapidly changing society, including separation of church and state firmly consolidated in the new constitution, with deeply religious public life. It was not without reason that the state initiated Truth and Reconciliation Commission relied heavily on Christian discourse.

---

12   Nancy T. Ammerman, ed, *Everyday Religion: Observing Modern Religious Lives* (Oxford: Oxford University Press, 2007).

13   Casanova, "Rethinking Secularization," 13.

Notions of reconciliation and forgiveness through Jesus Christ resonated with at least 80 percent of the country's population, across racial and ethnic divisions. Churches have over the past two decades consistently enjoyed higher levels of trust than any public institution in the country.[14] Christianity in general has grown rather than decreased, especially with the rapid rise of Pentecostalism that, between the years of 1996 and 2001 alone, increased by 55 percent.[15]

Beyond the persistent public influence of religion, South Africa displays the shift scholars note towards an increasingly individualized experience of religion. Among the exploding number of Pentecostals, for instance, are many South Africans who decided to leave the churches of their childhood to join this global movement and its emphasis on one's personal relationship with God. Notwithstanding the many other factors leading to such decisions, they signal a global trend towards increasingly diverse market spaces in which people can choose from a range of religious and secular worldviews. This trend of pluralization forms, in Berger's view, the perhaps most salient consequence of modernization processes. It entails the increased exposure of people to the competition of different convictions, values and lifestyles.[16] In megacities and through the spread of mass culture and communication, we are nowadays bound to encounter others with different beliefs, religious or not, in constantly and rapidly evolving social interactions. Rather than following institutional guidelines, Steve Bruce argues in the same line, individuals thus determine ever more their own sense of meaning.[17]

Pluralization as outcome of modernity raises significant questions for the study of religion, and for religion in general. In his last book, *The Many Altars of Modernity*, Berger shows how plurality turns religious beliefs into but one option out of many and thus takes away their long taken for granted stature.[18]

---

14   E. Fakir, "Politics, state and society in South Africa: Between leadership, trust and technocrats," *Development Planning Division Working Paper Series No.1* (DBSA: Midrand. 2009). For recent statistics, see also: Steven Gordon, Benjamin Roberts and Jarè Struwig, "The state of the union? Attitudes to South African trade," *Human Science Research Council,* (March 2013). Accessed at 19 November 2015. http://www.hsrc.ac.za/en/review/hsrc-review-march-2013/the-state-of-the-union#sthash.omwZUabq.

15   "Under the Radar. Pentecostalism in South Africa and its potential social and economic role, " *Center for Development and Enterprise,* March 2008. Accessed 18 October 2015, http://www.cde.org.za/wp-content/uploads/2013/02/Under%20the%20radar%20-%20 Pentecostalism%20in%20SA.pdf.

16   Peter L. Berger, *The Many Altars of Modernity. Towards a Paradigm of Religion in a Pluralist Age* (Berlin: De Gruyter. 2014), 20.

17   Steve Bruce, "Cathedrals to cults: the evolving forms of the religious life," in Paul Heelas, David Martin, and Paul Morris, *Religion, Modernity, and Postmodernity* (Oxford, UK: Blackwell Publishers, 1998), 23–24.

18   Berger, *The Many Altars of Modernity*, 37.

It does not necessarily imply a weakening of religion though. Above all, Berger stresses the increasing influence of secular discourses and the tendency among believers to go back and forth between both religious and non-religious perceptions of the world around them as they navigate diverse realities. Ammerman also notes this back and forth, especially in respect to the everyday experience of religion in people's lives. She explains how people in modern differentiated societies tend to locate themselves within various structures at the same time.[19] The rules they experience in one, say the church, may be different from those at home or at work. Few are able to keep them separate at all times. As a result, individuals take different rules from one sphere into another, across institutional and social boundaries.

While this might not hurt religion per se, it affects religious institutions that seek to impose one particular rule, the rule of God, on all aspects of life. The Dutch Reformed Church has, as we saw earlier, already struggled with supplanting one aspect of its long dominant rule, apartheid, for a less exclusive belief system. Ultimately, this struggle relates to larger questions on how to balance the idea of one universal truth with the rising availability of other proclaimed truths. It comes back to the inherently modern tension Eisenstadt indicates between pluralistic and universal visions. The Reformed churches since the collapse of the previous regime confront the challenge of having to adapt once totalizing worldviews to a reality of difference.

Difference here not only pertains to greater racial and ethnic diversity and the ensuing variety in styles of worshipping, norms and beliefs. It also encompasses divergent attitudes towards the role of religion as guardian of a certain social morality. The Reformed churches, and many other denominations in South Africa, wrestle with questions about homosexuality, divorce and premarital sex, or the inclusion of women in leadership. Particularly difficult in this respect are the internal debates that have been splitting congregations, presbyteries and synods apart. Those favoring more openness of the church towards racial, ethnic, gender or sexual differences stand opposite to those pursuing a rather exclusive church that firmly stands for a distinct moral framework as well as group identity.

In between these opposites however, a majority of Reformed churchgoers are more likely to walk a middle path that perhaps builds on a specific religious tradition, but keeps the door open to other options. They might be conservative on social matters, but open to racial diversity. For these members, pluralization amounts rather to the expansion of grey areas between

---

19   Ammerman, *Everyday Religion*, 228.

religion and secularity. People feel attached to a religious institution, but may hardly practice their faith, or the other way around. Grace Davie explains this with the term "vicarious". Especially in Europe's supposedly secular societies, she perceives active minorities performing religion on behalf of a largely approving but non-believing majority.[20] Few Swedish for instance, would describe themselves as practitioners of a particular church tradition these days. Many do retain, at least on paper, their membership to the Lutheran Church of Sweden. They may not believe, but still feel they belong to the church of their parents or grandparents, and are willing to pay taxes to help preserve it. For Davie, such belonging without believing exhibits the persistent influence of religious institutions, even when they appear in decline. Traditional churches – whether in Sweden or in South Africa – may no longer count on claiming authority or expect large numbers of actual believers. They still find overall support on the basis of the social and historic affiliations they represent for people, whether or not they consider themselves religious.

One last perspective that deserves mentioning here is that of Danièle Hervieu-Léger. The French sociologist perceives a rising need for belief as a way to deal with the insecurities of contemporary society. Believing can help people (re)connect with a collective sense of lineage. It provides a sense of shared memory and identity that appears lost amidst today's individualization and pluralization. Religion is but one mode of believing here. In what Hervieu-Léger calls religious "bricolage", it interacts with other secular ways of believing manifested through for instance cult groups, sports or ethnic identities.[21] The latter borrow from existing religious institutions whereas these institutions increasingly incorporate secular features. Hervieu-Léger emphasizes the revival of ethnic religious groups in this respect. People draw from otherwise fading institutions to bolster claims of belonging to a specific ethnic community. The public exploitation of their symbols meanwhile proves crucial to sustain the involved religions. This last point appears especially true for some of the Reformed churches discussed in this book. They refuse to relinquish the historic

---

20   Grace Davie, "From believing without belonging to vicarious religion: understanding the patterns of religion in modern Europe," in Detlef Pollack and Daniel V. A. Olson, *The Role of Religion in Modern Societies* (New York: Routledge, 2008), 165–176.

21   Danièle Hervieu-Léger, "Bricolage Vaut-Il Dissémination? Quelques Réflexions Sur L'Opérationnalite Sociologique D'une Métaphore Problématique" ['Tinkering' Should Be Disseminated? Some Reflections on the Sociological Implications of a Problematic Metaphor] *Social Compass* 52.3 (2005): 295–308.

racial or ethnic attachments they believe are vital to safeguarding their presence within a certain community.

Throughout this book we will see a constant blurring of the lines between religious and secular experiences, and between believing and belonging. Outside the immediate worship area, close interactions emerge among people with vastly different traditions. Some adapted rigid beliefs to fit changing realities while others adopted alternative beliefs to handle the lack of change. We will see church members who stress their historic affiliations with the Reformed institution as part of their group identity and who simultaneously disconnect their beliefs from this institution, stating them instead in merely general Christian terms.

As for the institutions themselves, the Reformed churches show both decline and revitalization. Religious life in South Africa at large, with all the choices people nowadays make, continues to be organized chiefly through church institutions. Ammerman's argument – that people still get most of their religious cues from institutional traditions[22] – seems all too applicable here. These institutions meanwhile, are changing their own cues. Under pressure of the upsurge of Pentecostalism across the continent, traditional South African churches including the Reformed ones, have started to incorporate more charismatic features, healing practices and gospel music in their services. Simultaneously, they seek to battle decreasing membership numbers among the rising middle class with shorter supposedly Western style worship that focuses on individual meditation and intellectual reflection.

Thinking of such dynamics as one of multiple roads to modernity is essential, though only the first step to help grasp the many layers on which South Africans build their religious identity today. South Africa, one could say, defies any distinction between the religious and the secular. In the presented case studies, communities not merely go back and forth, but interweave spiritual with mundane discourses and practices to make sense of their surroundings and help shape them. Ample tensions emerge here, and not necessarily between the usual suspects. Beyond controversies over race, doctrines or morality, church members clash over what they perceive as the best survival strategy amidst the country's daunting inequalities, crime and political mismanagement. In these clashes, religion tends to play an ambiguous role as a factor of both reconciliation and conflict, notably when it comes to the preservation of communal identities.

---

22   Nancy T. Ammerman, *Sacred Stories, Spiritual Tribes: Finding Religion in Everyday Life* (Oxford; New York: Oxford University Press. 2014), 299–304.

Entangled Religious-Nationalist Identities

To communities that wish to hold on to particular beliefs and traditions, pluralization often appears a threat. Especially religious communities with strong ethnic or national identity claims tend to respond with resistance, if not aggression. Instead of choice, they emphasize the absolute truth of their tradition. Diversity presents an immediate danger to the supposed exclusive bond between the divine and their distinct group identity. It is a response that scholars like Mark Juergensmeyer and Catarina Kinnval perceive to be on the rise. Worldwide, they see the emergence of religious-nationalist movements that assert a deep spiritual connection with one essential territorial or group identity. These movements are often willing to defend this identity at high costs, even with extreme violence. What to make of this entanglement of religious, ethnic, national or – as in South Africa – racial identities?

Let us first take a closer look at some of the major terms involved here. In her essay "Essentialising Essentialism," Pnina Werbner states that, "to essentialize is to impute a fundamental, basic, absolutely necessary constitutive quality to a person, social category, ethnic group, religious community or nation."[23] Immediately, Werbner stresses the deceptiveness of such essentialist forms of representation. They imply a false sense of timelessness and homogeneity that often results in the rigid distinction between those considered inside or outside the group. Werbner clarifies however that not all collectivities or self-representations are necessarily essentialist. She makes an important distinction between the kind of ethnic and racialized identities so prevalent in countries like South Africa. Ethnicity points at a group distinction with potential for being essentialized. Still, this essentialization can very well take place from within an ethnic community and its fluid surroundings. Race on the other hand always involves an identity fixed by others and is often violently imposed upon opposite groups.[24]

Nation constitutes yet another often essentialized form of identification. Similar to race and ethnicity, it tends to comprise strong beliefs in separateness and un-changeability. Nationalists claim distinct features of different national communities that ought to be sustained and reinforced by ensuring strict boundaries between them. Kinnvall moreover emphasizes the strong interplay between essentialist identities like race and nation.[25] They mutually reinforce each other and help construct perceptions of internal similarity and negative

---

23   Pnina Werbner and Tariq Modood, *Debating Cultural Hybridity: Multi-cultural Identities and the Politics of Anti-Racism* (London: Zed Books, 1997). 228.

24   Werbner and Modood, *Debating Cultural Hybridity,* 248.

25   Kinnvall, "Globalization and Religious Nationalism," 760–762.

prejudice towards outsiders. South Africa's apartheid story is exemplary of this interplay. The notion of an Afrikaner people or 'nation' was deeply intertwined with the idea of absolute race categories that had to be kept in place by this distinct ethnic group. South Africa also displays the centrality of religion as a factor in the entanglement of identities. As chapter 1 will elaborate, church doctrines and practices were key in building, maintaining and justifying the apartheid system and its essentialized racial, ethnic and national identities.

To understand how religion can fortify these identities, it helps to distinguish three levels of religious identity entanglement. First is the function of religion as rallying point in times of crisis. It returns to the tendency of religions to provide fundamental tools to deal with life and suffering. Especially when surroundings change rapidly due to war, forces of globalization or the collapse of authority, people look for such tools and often turn to faith. In the words of Juergensmeyer, "religion is the language of ultimate order."[26] It provides clear answers and gives a sense of control in a world of disorder. This often happens along with a rise of nationalist sentiments. The idea of one strong nation offers a similar sense of security as religion. George Dreyfus illustrates this in his study on Hindu Nationalism.[27] The latter emerged as a movement resisting the economic and cultural changes affecting India such as the spread of global consumer goods or American movies and music. Fearing the intrusion of foreign influences, Hindu Nationalists emphasized the need for purity. Both the land and its major religion ought to be protected against outside interference. A threat to Hinduism was perceived a threat to the nation while each could only be kept pure as long as the nation's true religious traditions were maintained.

A second level of entanglement involves the role of religion in legitimating national and racial distinctions and their preservation as exclusive categories. It supplies core beliefs and rationale for the notion of peoplehood. These beliefs often pertain to the profound relation felt between a certain people, race or ethnicity and the sacred. Afrikaner communities were told they had been chosen by God and ordered to protect their distinctiveness. According to Smith and Van der Veer such sentiments of chosenness have been fundamental to many past and current nationalist movements. They see it among Dutch and British Protestants in the 19th century or political Zionists in Israel today. For

---

26   Juergensmeyer, "The Worldwide Rise of Religious Nationalism," 15.

27   Georges Dreyfus, "The end of the Saeculum and global capitalism. Should we be scared? The return of the sacred and the rise of religious nationalism in South Asia," in Miguel E. Vatter. *Crediting God: Sovereignty and Religion in the Age of Global Capitalism* (New York: Fordham University Press, 2011), 131–141.

Van der Veer, the belief in an elected people tends to be connected with a view of the nation as awaiting spiritual rebirth.[28] Smith in turn speaks of the nation as a sacred communion of the people. It aligns notions of a shared ethnic ancestry with the search for cultural distinction and a moral-legal framework that lines out the duties and rights all members have in common.[29] Goldschmidt draws comparable connections between religion and race. The narrative of a chosen people has in his view been vital for producing racial identities in the United States. Christian notions of peoplehood would have fostered a deep belief in unchangeable identities that strongly affected American discourse on race up until recent times.[30]

In a third intersection, religion operates as a cultural reservoir from which communities draw images and ceremonies to fortify self-perceptions. Roger Friedland underscores religion's institutional space to give actual content to a group's collective representation.[31] Through rituals of blessings and services at core moments in a nation's history, religious actors nurture people's sense of belonging to the community. Once their religious tradition becomes tied to a specific nation, it acts as a national unifier. It brings different individuals together for an all-encompassing cause: to preserve the nation in the eyes of God. Conversely, the nation is understood as a source of political power that can and should carry out the divine will on earth.

Parallel arguments have been made towards racial communities. In the South of the United States as much as in South Africa, white churches claimed it in accordance with God's plan to separate the races and ensure white hegemony. While this argument has lost much of its appeal in contemporary America, racial segregation remains a reality among many churches here. Emerson and Smith explain this by pointing at the organization of American religion today.[32] Congregations across society have been fostering internal similarity and cultural homogeneity as a way to carve out their own space in a pluralized religious field. The resulting segmentation builds upon and fuels racial differences outside the churches. As churches continue to create meaning and a sense of belonging for their members in separate ways, it is barely surprising that racial boundaries persevere.

---

28   Peter van der Veer and Hartmut Lehmann, *Nation and Religion: Perspectives on Europe and Asia* (Princeton, N.J: Princeton University Press, 1999), 6.

29   Anthony D. Smith, *Chosen Peoples* (Oxford: Oxford University Press, 2003), 24–35.

30   Goldschmidt, "Introduction: Race, Nation and Religion," 10–11.

31   Friedland. "Religious Nationalism and the Problem of Collective Representation," 138.

32   Michael O. Emerson and Christian Smith, *Divided by Faith: Evangelical Religion and the Problem of Race in America* (Oxford: Oxford University Press, 2000), 136–141.

Mapping these and other levels of religious-ethnic entanglement offers insight into religious responses to increased diversity. It draws a bigger picture of South Africa's Reformed churches as part of a global trend among religious communities to stress the absolute character of their identity and the need to ward off external threats that undermine its supposed purity. Often missing in such analyses however, are the vast intricacies inherent to the identity categories at issue. Indicating their constructedness does not suffice.

This becomes especially apparent with the term race. Critical race theorists such as Philomena Essed and Anoop Nayak warn against the reproduction of power constructs underlying the term through its constant use in research and public discourse. With the term "everyday racism," Essed explains how race and racism are being internalized and often considered part of routine situations and practices without acknowledging the ways in which they continue to serve power interest of certain groups of people, particularly whites.[33] Nayak specifies the position of researchers in keeping the notions alive by perhaps dismissing it as constructed, but still referring to racial constructions as key categories in their interviews, surveys and questionnaires.[34] He also notes the paradox of indicating the power structures underneath identity categories on the one hand, and seeking to avoid the stigmatization of any particular group, dominant or not, on the other hand.

To evade this paradox, studies on identity often employ notions such as hybridity and fluidity.[35] They imply processes of mixing in which people integrate elements from various identity groups. Rather than perceiving them as static, emphasis is put on the agency of groups and individuals in continuously shaping and reshaping their own sense of belonging. Such terms are definitely applicable to South Africa's post-apartheid landscape. Still, this book also detects challenges with the hybridity paradigm. Pointing out the multiple and shifting layers on which identities are built is necessary to undercut their persistent essentialization but rarely welcomed or recognized by communities themselves. Pressed to acknowledge cultural mixing, they might resort with social closure and disengagement. Key is then to recognize how hybridization is being experienced. Often, people barely notice how language or traditions

---

33   Philomena Essed, *Understanding Everyday Racism: An Interdisciplinary Theory* (Newbury Park: Sage Publications, 1991), 43

34   Anoop Nayak, "After Race: Ethnography, Race and Post-Race Theory," *Ethnic and Racial Studies* 29.3 (2006): 415.

35   See for instance: Frank J. Korom. *Hosay Trinidad: Muharram Performances in an Indo-Caribbean Diaspora.* Philadelphia: University of Pennsylvania Press, 2003; Werbner and Modood, *Debating Cultural Hybridity.*

over time merge with those of others.[36] Problems do emerge – and need addressing – when such mixing is imposed or felt as such. Throughout this book it will hence be important to distinguish between conscious and unconscious processes of mixing and carefully consider what drives people's (self-)identifications as well as how they play out in reality.

A Northern Irish Perspective

Not all religious communities resist the increase of diversity or cultural mixing. Few translate their resistance into violence while many others rather seek a mediating role between opposing parties. What makes the difference? When and how does religion become a factor of conflict between identity groups, or when might it help bridge differences? This is an important question for the Reformed churches. The DRC constituted a protagonist of apartheid that for decades openly nourished divisions between South Africa's diverse communities. Today, the church likes to portray itself as an advocate of unity and reconciliation. Most of the time though, the influence of religion in intercommunal conflict is far more subtle. To tease out these subtleties it serves to look beyond South Africa at another case of religious-nationalist entanglement: Northern Ireland.

However different, the Northern Irish conflict presents some notable parallels with South Africa's apartheid story. It involved opposing identity groups that borrowed heavily from their religions as they engaged in a prolonged power conflict. Northern Ireland has also seen a quite peaceful end to its conflict in which parties modified positions, though not their separate structures. Analyses of the conflict tend to speak of the political opportunism and the pursuit of nation building that drove the fighting Ulster Protestants and Catholic Republicans, rather than their religious ideologies. Similar arguments have been made concerning apartheid as an Afrikaner nationalism project rather than a church driven doctrine. But the role of religion here was not only one of ideology. In both Northern Ireland and South Africa, religion crucially helped build, deepen and maintain the communal divisions at the heart of the conflict. Concurrently, religious actors in both countries also played a role in dismantling these divisions, be it in unsuspected ways.

Claire Mitchell's work is particularly perceptive here. Mitchell emphasizes the multiple ways in which religion supplies thick fabric to the usually thin boundaries along which identity conflicts tend to be defined.[37] It gives

---

36   Werbner and Modood, *Debating Cultural Hybridity*, 4–5

37   Claire Mitchell, *Religion, Identity and Politics in Northern Ireland: Boundaries of Belonging and Belief* (Aldershot, Hants, England: Ashgate Pub, 2006).

meaning to existing differences and helps consolidate them. Religion was indeed a central dividing line in Northern Irish politics and society at large. Well after the Good Friday Accords made a formal end to the armed conflict in 1998, it continued to fuel prejudice and suspicion among the involved communities. It did so however not merely as an indicator of ethno-national boundaries, but by providing concrete content through ideas and values, ceremonies, institutions and space for community gathering.

Among Northern Irish Protestants, ideas first of all constituted a key element in their narrative of the conflict. It centered on the notion of liberty. In an effort to distinguish their own group from what they viewed as submissive Catholics, Protestants often highlighted traditions of free thought. Many claimed their religion a personal choice, stressing its contrast with the authoritarianism of the Catholic Church. Another influential religious idea often perceived among Protestants related to the covenant concept.[38] It entailed the belief in the Protestants of Ulster being a chosen people. In an exclusive contract with God, they agreed to follow the divine rule on earth in exchange for blessings on their promised land of Northern Ireland. The covenant belief moreover implied a deep sense of loyalty from Ulster towards the British Protestant Crown and expectation that the British would intervene on behalf of their fellow people of faith. While the idea of a covenant has little appeal these days, it left a powerful legacy. For many Protestants, religion and politics remain deeply intertwined. Even though the British are scorned for having done little to reward their devotion, many Ulster Protestants still nurture a sense of affiliation with their neighbors across the Irish Sea. Mitchell moreover notes that covenant beliefs could easily resurface in case of crisis or in protest towards further British disengagement.[39]

Catholics in Northern Ireland have generally been held to attach less value to religious ideas than Protestants did. Mitchell as well as Gladys Ganiel and Paul Dixon nonetheless note the significance of notions of victimhood and sacrifice in shaping Catholic attitudes towards the conflict. These often involved powerful images of Christ as an innocent victim of oppression who died for the sake of others. Catholics' identification with this image reinforced their sense of discrimination and suffering. Where this led some to withdraw in a mode of passivity, others took to extreme action, embracing martyrdom for instance during the Hunger Strikes in the early eighties.[40] Besides these

---

38   Akenson, *God's Peoples*, 183–202.
39   Mitchell, *Religion, Identity and Politics in Northern Ireland*, 125.
40   Gladys Ganiel and Paul Dixon, "Religion, Pragmatic Fundamentalism and the Transformation of the Northern Ireland Conflict," *Journal of Peace Research* 45.3 (2008): 424.

images, religion was influential in offering Catholics a platform for community gathering and ritual. The Catholic Church throughout the Troubles functioned as a vital space for its members to voice concerns, organize politically and bolster communal solidarity with powerful spiritual symbols and ceremony. Notably, the church has continued in this function for many Catholics, including those who claim to no longer believe.

As such, we arrive at a key issue. Deeply embedded in society, religion has persisted in affecting Northern Irish communities regardless of their level of religious commitment. In interviews Mitchell conducted throughout her studies, many indicated that they felt little affiliation with the church, hardly attended any services, but still identified as either Protestant or Catholic. This identification tended to correlate with profound sentiments of belonging and social boundaries. Protestants said they did not hang out with Catholics, let alone intermarry. Schools have remained largely segregated along religious lines, as have sports clubs, media, political or voluntary organizations. Religion thus deeply pervades everyday life, often more than class or national identities.[41] It moreover continues to do so in antagonist ways, promoting a discourse of Catholic victimhood, or notions of moral superiority among Protestants.

Mostly however, religion has served as a cultural reservoir. Still today, it offers imagery and ideas about the communities and their preset differences. Socialized early in life, these differences have become commonsensical for most of the Northern Irish population. Recent years do see some gradual changes in this respect and a slow development towards more hybridized identities, for instance among Catholics who have moved to the cities. Many now tend towards the more individualized worshipping that used to be associated exclusively with Protestants.[42] Also among Protestants a shift in focus is being perceived from resisting a specific group – Catholics – to concerns about more general moral issues such as abortion or homosexuality.[43]

Besides the deep and often troublesome intertwining of religion and ethnicity, Northern Ireland displays some relevant insights into how religion might help untangle these identities. Scott Appleby notes the various dialogue efforts of Catholic and Protestant institutions to overcome sectarianism and their value in in terms of long-term attitudinal change.[44] Ganiel and Dixon similarly identify the social capital of the religious actors at play in fostering harmonious

---

41   Mitchell, *Religion, Identity and Politics in Northern Ireland*, 136–138.

42   Mitchell, *Religion, Identity and Politics in Northern Ireland*, 141–142.

43   Ganiel and Dixon, "Religion, Pragmatic Fundamentalism and the Transformation of the Northern Ireland Conflict," 429.

44   Appleby, *The Ambivalence of the Sacred*, 191–3

relationships between communities by offering physical platforms, discourses of reconciliation as well as resources for civic activism.

Typically, such religious reconciliation efforts involve only a small group of people who already consider themselves as open to diversity. Ganiel and Dixon however also draw attention to the rather unsuspected role of fundamentalist Protestants in Northern Ireland. Known for its attachment to an exclusive religious-ethnic identity, this group made a significant turnabout in its attitudes towards the conflict. By the mid-nineties most fundamentalist Protestants had moved away from the idea of belonging to a chosen people.[45] The earlier mentioned covenant concept had encountered increasing critique. Evangelical groups most notably were casting the belief in a special relation between God, Ulster and Britain as idolatry. They thus undermined a key argument in the resistance against Catholics. This resistance was further weakened by the situation on the ground in which decades of violence for God's cause had rendered little but deprivation and isolation. As their position became increasingly unsustainable, anti-Catholic fundamentalists gradually moved towards engagement across long held divides. This engagement appeared more pragmatic than anything else. Realizing that they were losing public support for their narratives of chosenness, church actors and their political representatives not only agreed to enter the negotiations they had so long refused, but also turned out to be quite malleable towards the demands of their once despised Catholic neighbors.

What becomes clear from this limited discussion on Northern Ireland is that religion had an important, yet elusive position in the conflict. Religious actors on both sides may have at times advocated extreme religious ideas as they called followers to fight for God and nation. Churches across the board however, were most influential in the way they maintained and reinforced community boundaries. Providing separate gathering spaces, rituals and religious ideas and values for believers as well as non-believers, Protestant and Catholic churches greatly contributed to the divisions that allowed the conflict to linger for so long and that continue to characterize Northern Irish society today.

Still, the role of religion was not only a negative one. Religious actors on either side also engaged in reconciliation efforts, though not necessarily on the basis of their faith. The Protestant leaders who finally moved away from their covenant beliefs and towards negotiations above all hoped to retain their own base of support. This reconciliation out of necessity returns among the South

---

45 Gladys and Dixon, "Religion, Pragmatic Fundamentalism and the Transformation of the Northern Ireland Conflict," 429–430.

African church actors studied in this book. Many present strong religious rationale for untangling their old ethnic-nationalist attachments. In the end
though, they seem most concerned with the survival of their church amidst a
reality of vast social and religious change.

Mixed Methods

South Africa's contested reconciliation process leaves few untouched. Under
every stone one finds a different story. Stories of victimhood and heroism, of
deep despair and, at times surprising, humanity. To uncover the many stories
at stake here, this book incorporates diverse methods of discourse analysis,
archival research and qualitative field research.

Disguised Discourse

With regard to discourse and archival research, focus was given to written
documents contributing to both formal and informal discussions about a future unification of the Reformed churches in South Africa. Sources range from
minutes of meetings by the churches' respective leaderships, their reports and
statements, to official church magazines. Also included are debates in various
social media outlets. I limited the time period to discourse on church unity
after 2006 as this year constituted a major breakthrough in debates about a
possible merger between the DRC and URCSA. To gain insight into the long
path towards unity, I furthermore researched major church statements in the
late 1980s and early 1990s about the need to break with apartheid. The *Belhar
Confession* and its *Accompanying Letter* of 1982 are prime among them.

The over three hundred gathered documents revealed important threads
in the discourse as well as omissions. Prominent for instance were the intense
and constantly reoccurring debates about the identity of the churches in South
Africa today, especially in terms of social engagement. Church actors across
the various communities indicated the tremendous importance of outreach
for their religious identity. Opinions differed though on how far the churches
should reach and who deserved priority: the immediate congregation, people
from other communities, or even other countries.

Notably little attention was paid to notions of Afrikaner ethnicity or ethnicity in general. Language meanwhile, especially Afrikaans language, figured
high in almost any debate on church unification. It signaled something I was
warned about during my field research. Public debates on church unification,
however hostile they appear, tend to disguise some of the real concerns inside the communities as contributors are mindful of the need to be politically

correct and refrain from any direct references to race or Afrikaner identity. To detect sentiments concerning these matters, it was helpful to watch some of the more general discussions about South Africa's post-apartheid transition.[46] Here, anger about persistent white domination or reverse black on white racism, was often expressed in much sharper terms than in church unity talks, especially when the latter talks involved religious elites.

Careful Conversations

The judiciousness with which many inside the Reformed churches approached topics of unification also affected my congregational field research in South Africa. During two visits in 2012 and 2014, I conducted conversations with church members, ministers and theologians across the various communities and with the staff of several non-profit organizations. Some were set up as semi-structured interviews. Others took place in informal settings, after church service, during lunch breaks at seminars of the Stellenbosch or Free State theology faculties, or at the kitchen table at people's homes. They involved public church actors who were comfortable to have their names mentioned. Many others preferred to remain anonymous. References in this study distinguish between conversations and interviews, and mention, depending on the level of anonymity preferred by the participant, his or her name, church affiliation and position in the church. In addition to these interactions, I incorporated field notes from my visits with Reformed congregations across the country. This included regular Sunday services as well as special events such as church bazaars, evening gatherings during Pentecost or even a full Passion Play at one of the URCSA congregations in the Free State. All were crucial to gain a better understanding of the main concerns and changes inside these congregations and how they tie into greater questions about religious, ethnic and national belonging in South Africa today.

Perspectives of grounded theory and oral history[47] informed the way I conducted the field research. This meant above all that I took the participants and

---

46   For more on implicit biases in especially leadership discourse, see sections 3.1 and 3.2, and for instance in the literature: Deborah De Fina, Deborah Schiffrin and Michael G. W. Bamberg, *Discourse and Identity* (Cambridge. UK: Cambridge University Press, 2006); Teun van Dijk, *Discourse and Power* (Houndmills, Basingstoke, Hampshire: Palgrave Macmillan. 2008); Ruth Wodak and Teun A. Dijk, *Racism at the Top: Parliamentary Discourses on Ethnic Issues in Six European States* (Klagenfurt: Drava Verlag. 2000).

47   See for instance: Juliet M. Corbin and Anselm Strauss, "Grounded Theory Research: Procedures, Canons, and Evaluative Criteria," *Qualitative Sociology*. 13.1 (1990): 3–21; Patricia Leavy, *Oral History* (Oxford: Oxford University Press, 2011); Jan Vansina, *Oral Tradition As History* (Madison, Wis: University of Wisconsin Press, 1985); Kathy Charmaz, *Constructing*

their stories as the starting point. It enabled me to distinguish between issues which most concerned churchgoers, and those of less immediate relevance. Organizing these issues in a data exercise by congregation, church affiliation and position in the church gave a captivating overview of how various actors in the Reformed family differently perceived their churches' post-apartheid transition.[48] It for instance exhibited profoundly negative attitudes among ministers about merging the two churches' organizational structures. Members generally held more esteem for their national leaderships' official unity talks. Church elites, top leaders and academics, meanwhile indicated close to zero interest in the bottom-up exchanges most ordinary members tended to prefer as first step in any integration process. The data exercise also pointed at a remarkable consensus across the different congregations, and regardless of people's position in the church, on the value of unity for God and the nation. Former religious-nationalist notions appeared to be recycled here, this time to bolster ideals of integration rather than segregation.

For a deeper understanding of the dynamics at play here I selected a few in-depth case studies of Reformed communities. The selected cases exhibit typical differences between urban and rural communities and between the wealthier region of the Western Cape and the struggling Free State. Their stories are evidently unique and cannot be taken outside of their specific contexts. They do not stand on their own though. Many of the integration problems emerging in Stellenbosch or Bloemfontein or Philippolis paralleled those I encountered during my visits with other communities. The stories of the social works mentioned in chapter four also found resonance among the experience of various actors I met with. Put together, the distinct case studies thus allow for broader conclusions about the trajectory of the entire Reformed church family with post-apartheid reconstruction.

Insider/Outsider

Limitations remain. Significantly, it was difficult to adequately address the perspective of black African churches in this book. Most of the examples I discuss involve congregations with largely white, colored or slightly mixed memberships. A relatively straightforward explanation can be found in the fact that so few black African Reformed congregations are currently involved in interactions with white churches beyond traditional charity initiatives.[49] There

---

Grounded Theory: A Practical Guide Through Qualitative Analysis (London: Sage Publications, 2006).

48   See the Appendix for an overview of the main outcomes of this data exercise.

49   See also in this book the introduction to Chapter 4 and section 4.4.

certainly exist cases in which black and colored communities have begun to form alliances, as will be discussed in section 4.3 on the Free State. For this study however, I was most interested in learning about situations in which white congregations engaged with unity attempts, as they historically resisted such attempts far more strongly than colored and black congregations.

A more complex account of the choices I made here relates to my own background as white researcher speaking a language, Dutch, with great affinity to Afrikaans. This background made me an insider in and facilitated access to white churches and colored communities with Afrikaans as mother tongue. Among the latter it was often even more significant that I could communicate in Afrikaans than in the higher educated white communities where members were also comfortable with English. Conversely, in black communities access was harder. Language constituted a major barrier as well a relative lack of connections, especially compared to the other churches. The conversations and visits I had in these communities have been essential in gaining deeper understanding of the many layers of South Africa's prolonged post-apartheid transformation. That does not take away this dearth in my research though, something that, to say the least, calls for further reflection.

Structure and Organization

Investigating South Africa's church struggles with racial diversity requires a close look at what is happening inside the congregations, how churchgoers balance big questions about unity and disparity with small-scale coping strategies. Their predicaments are affected by past and current social disruptions, national identity politics and global religious change. The following chapters will exhibit the constant intertwining of religious, political, social-economic interests and personal motivations on matters of belief and belonging. What this book will not do, is offer a comprehensive overview of church institutional change nor a detailed investigation into one single congregation or theological doctrine. Coupling a number of short case studies to the bigger transition story of South Africa and its Reformed churches, it is rather meant to show the deep intersections between the local, the national and the global.

For this purpose, the book is divided into two parts, of which the first begins with the national context of a country still in the midst of its post-apartheid transformation. Chapter one outlines what has been described as the Afrikaner civil religion that helped build apartheid. Central to this historic discussion is the extensive reach of a religious-nationalist doctrine of segregation in 20th century South Africa and its remarkable unraveling towards the end. It draws a pivotal backdrop to the vast challenges the country faces in the present century. No longer segregated by law, the second part of this chapter deliberates, South African society remains partitioned by class, culture and race. These interwoven cleavages derive from old and new failures to deal with the country's immense diversity. Reaching unity among the officially recognized eleven different language communities, four population groups and their countless divergences in customs, interests, memories of the past and visions of the future, is hard enough in areas of education or labor. At a space as intimate as the church, it appears almost impossible.

As chapter two discusses, the Reformed churches have formed a controversial front line in the pursuit of unity well before South Africa's break with apartheid. Throughout the previous century, the Reformed church family wrestled with the question of how to find unity amidst diversity. Their strictly segregated institutions each in their own way sought to balance dilemmas of belonging, solidarity and independence. Powerful narratives were at play here. The white churches historically presented the Reformed family as spiritually one, but segregated in its worldly organization. It was considered the best way to sustain cultural differences and allow for the now notorious claim on separate but equal development. Black and colored Reformed churches conversely challenged this claim and its far from equal implications in reality. They urged the uniting of segregated church structures, albeit with significant ambiguity. Despised as the segregation system was, it also offered opportunities for these churches to foster distinct identities and a certain level of autonomy from the dominant white minority. The churches constituted one of the few safe havens where suppressed communities felt relatively secure from the long arm of the apartheid regime. Striving for the integration of white and black churches thus presented at once an act of resistance to the regime, and a threat to internal solidarity.

Part one thus lays out the main pieces of the conundrum this book seeks to decipher: where and how does religion enter the playing field of South Africa's post-apartheid reconstruction, especially considering its long detrimental influence in reinforcing the country's divisions? This conundrum still pervades debates on church unification today, the central topic of part two of this book. Chapter three closely follows discourse inside the Reformed family about its position in contemporary South Africa. To discern what it means to break with a religious-nationalist past, it looks at leadership and popular discussions inside the predominantly white DRC and black and colored URCSA congregations. Which arguments are used to defend, or still resist, the churches' shift towards racial reconciliation instead of segregation? We will see heated debates between proponents and critics of unifying the churches into one multiracial institution. They touch on problems within congregations seeking to adapt to the vast social and political transformations around them, as well as national tensions about the direction in which South Africa is heading. Religious arguments clash into pragmatic concerns regarding language preservation, and into politicized disagreements about the current government. A red thread comprises the churches' divergent perspectives on their history. Culminating in debates about a Reformed statement of faith, the *Belhar Confession*, they show engrained notions of victimhood on either side of the color line. Such notions turn every talk of racial integration into conflicts over who bears responsibility for the past and how justice should be done. Unity thus becomes a source of division itself.

What happens with the unity talk in daily church practices will be addressed in the fourth and final chapter of this book. It investigates tangible attempts to integrate congregations, church structures and organizations. What and who drove these attempts and what has hampered their implementation? Vast contrasts become visible here between the expectations of the so-called white, colored and black churches regarding a future unity and whether it could advance their own respective struggles for survival. The perhaps greatest tension still pertains to the matching of the churches' fairly recently embraced unity ideal with a persistent reality of segregation and disparity. Critics and opponents of church unification, elites and ordinary churchgoers, DRC and URCSA, tend to agree these days on the integral value of racial unity in the eyes of God. Difficulties emerge when they have to find consensus on its real life implications in the current South African context.

Chapter four explores these implications on the basis of five communities in Stellenbosch, Wynberg, Bloemfontein, Ladybrand and Philippolis. Each of these sites comprise DRC and URCSA congregations that have been engaged in racial integration efforts, some intentional, some unintentional, and most with little visible success. Their stories show alternative routes towards the untangling of once rigid religious-ethnic and racial identities, each with their own challenges for the communities involved. The chapter furthermore exposes the intriguing perspective of church related social organizations. Operating on the threshold between the churches and the non-profit world, these organizations have become increasingly active in forging intergroup collaborations towards common societal goals of poverty relief, HIV AIDS awareness or youth employment. They point at the potential of such collaborations to build trust within and between communities, but also signal the immense difficulty of overcoming entrenched patterns of paternalism and dependency.

Throughout these various efforts to foster unity, profound resistance hence appears inevitable. Church discourse shows controversies about the dangers of unification for each church's individual identity. A sense of belonging to one's own community still matters highly. Local initiatives towards integration falter on lack of commitment and resources while joint social programs collapse in the face of organizational differences. Power and how it is exercised in these local religious struggles mirrors South Africa's larger struggle to transcend its divided past. Underneath the presenting issues linger deep mutual suspicions, contrasting memories and concerns about the country's future. How such diverging narratives are inhibiting unity processes is a central question throughout this book. Focus is given to motivations of church actors confronting these challenges and their effectiveness in facilitating integration. What drives unification efforts against so many odds? Faith in a God of unity and reconciliation in Christ are reoccurring themes among supporters of unity on all sides. Are these beliefs, so lately adapted to the changing world, strong enough though to overcome both the divisions of the past and the challenges of today? Can they help put into effect the remarkable transition these churches embarked on in the 1990s from evading to engaging with difference?

PART 1

Divine Divisions

∵

The South African Context: A Torn (Hi)story

"I sometimes ask myself when I'm alone, why did God make me black when a lot can happen in a good way when you're otherwise?"[1] With this quote the documentary *Luister* [listen] commences its account of racism experienced by students at the prestigious University of Stellenbosch. Within weeks after its release in August 2015, the documentary triggered a storm of protests, culminating in a parliamentary meeting asking the rector of the university to explain the allegations. The students railed against the Afrikaans language still prevalent at Stellenbosch, but even more so against the failure of the new South Africa to bring equality. Their actions comprise only the most recent episode in the country's ongoing struggle to come to terms with the racial divisions of both the past and the present. It returns to the violently crushed Soweto Uprising in 1976 in which students protested against the Afrikaans language imposed on their schools, and connects to a long string of civil protests and infinite public discussions about the legacy of apartheid.

Over twenty years since the first open elections in 1994, this struggle has become exceedingly complex. Black leaders rule the country and official segregation has long been abolished. Yet, the lion's share of South Africa's black population continues to live in poverty, far removed from the well-established white elites and a slight black upper class. The Constitution proclaims unity in the country's diversity, but many of its citizens appear to have withdrawn in communal enclaves, apart from each other. That this present is inextricably linked with the past is not surprising. What traces the apartheid era left behind in contemporary South Africa however, remains a subject of contention, and a relevant topic when studying one of the major pillars of this era, the Dutch Reformed Church. Today's persistent segregation of neighborhoods, social-economic disparities and white privilege are often attributed to the policies of the former regime. Those critical of the current government rather point at the incompetence of ANC politicians to properly dismantle these policies. In either narrative, emphasis tends to be put on the acute situation then and now, but rarely on which belief framework the old system rested on, and what happened to it.

---

1 Quoted in Greg Nelson, "Luister: the viral film exposing South Africa's ongoing racism problem," *The Guardian,* 7 September 2015. Accessed 10 September 2-15, http://www.theguardian .com/world/2015/sep/07/luister-south-africa-film-racism-stellenbosch.

A closer look at the premises of South Africa's civil religion of apartheid, the first section of this chapter, is crucial for a better understanding of what seems to be a relentless tendency among South Africans towards communalism and cultural essentialism. This tendency can also hardly be separated from the vast economic, social and political transitions of the past two decades, as will be addressed in the second section. The recent Stellenbosch controversy has everything to do with South Africa's enduring racialization, reinforced through a deep unemployment crisis and ethnic mobilization by leaders across the political spectrum. It points at a convoluted context in which South Africans, their political, educational and religious institutions, have to balance between traumas of the past, dreams of unity and a reality of discord.

1.1 Afrikaner Civil Religion and the Road to and from Apartheid

Few doubt that religion played a part in the emergence and consolidation of South Africa's apartheid regime in 1948. The churches, above all the Dutch Reformed Church, crucially helped justify its system of racial segregation as the will of God. But religion did more than justification alone. T. Dunbar Moodie famously described the DRC endorsed apartheid doctrine as a Christian-nationalist civil religion that came to dominate the country throughout much of the 20th century.[2] Its carriers not only comprised the church, but also the policy makers of the ruling National Party as well as the secretive and highly influential association of the Afrikaner *Broederbond*. Together, they made sure that apartheid ideology, its theological legitimation and practical implementation, permeated nearly every aspect of South African life for close to four decades. By 1994 it nonetheless turned out to be unsustainable. In the face of mounting national and international critique, internal divisions, protests and violence, the three major carriers each in their own way chose to leave apartheid's sinking ship. How can we understand the Afrikaner civil religion of Christian-nationalism and its role in making and ultimately breaking the former regime?

1.1.1 *A Christian-Nationalist Alliance: Church, Party and Broederbond*

Robert Bellah famously described the term civil religion within the American context as a "collection of beliefs, symbols, and rituals with respect to sacred things and institutionalized in a collectivity."[3] It is public and geared towards

---

2 Moodie, *The Rise of Afrikanerdom*.

3 Robert Bellah, "Civil Religion in America," *Daedalus.* 96 (Winter 1967), 8.

national self-understanding. Civil religion, according to Bellah, shapes individual and collective views of oneself and of the nation. Importantly, the sociologist discussed the potential advantages as well as dangers of abusing civil religion. While it might serve to build common understanding and bolster universal values, civil religion is also often manipulated in the interest of power politics, to further imperialist expansion and, to quote Bellah, employed as a "cloak for petty interests and ugly passions."[4] This last description appears particularly apt for the Afrikaner version of civil religion as discussed by T. Dunbar Moodie in *The Rise of Afrikanerdom*.[5] Deeply influenced by Bellah's essay, Moodie was among the first scholars to employ the term civil religion in the South African context. While later studies by for instance Charles Bloomberg, Rebecca Davies and Johann Kinghorn rather employ the notion of Christian-nationalism,[6] civil religion is still widely held as an appropriate term to describe the belief system shaping Afrikaner society for much of the twentieth century.

Across the board, these scholars agree on several key features. First among them was a deep sense of nationhood. The white Afrikaans speaking communities that descended from European immigrants to South Africa would belong to an exclusive Afrikaner nation, with its own history, language and culture. A central element of this history constituted farming. Afrikaners long described themselves above all as *Boers* or "farmers" with a markedly rural lifestyle and devout commitment to their main church, the Dutch Reformed Church. They notably distinguished themselves from the English speaking whites who had dominated South Africa since 1806 and were thought of as an oppressing colonial force. In addition to the sense of a unique Afrikaner nationhood, the belief in a sacred Afrikaner mission to bring Christianity to South Africa comprised another key feature of the civil religion. God had elected the Afrikaners to civilize the country. One aspect of this civilization was the separation of different communities according to race and ethnicity. The intermingling of communities was considered a sin against God's explicit will to preserve distinct cultures, particularly the Afrikaner one. In this respect Christian-nationalists moreover claimed God to be authoritarian and opposed

---

4 Bellah, "Civil Religion in America," 19.

5 Moodie, *The Rise of Afrikanerdom*.

6 Bloomberg and Dubow, *Christian Nationalism*; Rebecca Davies, *Afrikaners in the New South Africa: Identity Politics in a Globalised Economy* (London: Tauris Academic Studies, 2009); Johann Kinghorn, "Modernization and Apartheid: The Afrikaner Churches," in: Richard Elphick and T R. H. Davenport. *Christianity in South Africa: A Political, Social, and Cultural History. Perspectives on Southern Africa* (Berkeley, Calif: University of California Press, 1997), 135–154.

to an egalitarian treatment of different communities. Racial hierarchy, with whites on top, would be divinely ordained and help foster peace and security in South Africa. Besides these fundamental doctrines, Afrikaner civil religion has been characterized by its highly public presence. Civil rituals, imagery and liturgy propagating Christian-nationalist ideals dominated sectors across South African society. They returned in schools, at work and during political campaigns. Above all, Christian-nationalist ideals shaped Afrikaners' extensive church life.

Central to the latter was the Dutch Reformed Church. The DRC not merely fostered Christian-nationalist beliefs, but also sustained them with crucial theological resources. Most importantly perhaps, the DRC presented itself as the *volkskerk* or People's[7] church of the Afrikaner nation, with Reformed Christianity as the nation's primary belief system. In Moodie's words this entailed a "sophisticated theological interpretation of God's acts in Afrikaner history with an explicitly republican eschatology [and] a generalized feeling of 'Afrikanerness.' "[8] As a *volkskerk* the DRC became intrinsically tied to the Afrikaner people. It implied a profound engagement with every aspect of life, from education to care for the poor to politics. All for one purpose: the preservation and further advancement of a united Afrikanerdom.

Besides the DRC, Christian-nationalist ideology was ardently propagated by the *Afrikaner Broederbond,* or Brother Bond. A secret all male Protestant society, the *Broederbond* had been established in the 1920s solely to foster Afrikaners' ethnic identity. As its chief secretary claimed: "The Afrikaner nation was planned by God's hand in this country and is destined to continue existing as a nation with its own character and calling."[9] Over time, the Brother Bond developed a vast professional network to which membership appeared almost inevitable for anyone who wished to accomplish something within the Afrikaner community or society at large. It sustained powerful ties with both the church and the government, particularly the governing National Party. *Broederbond* members employed Reformed theology to bolster their nationalist ideals and

---

7   The Afrikaans term *volk* literally translates to "people" but is according to Moodie best understood as "People" with its capitalization indicating the crucial value attached to the notion in the context of Christian-nationalism. Nation and *volk* were often intertwined in this context, both referring to the belief in Afrikaners as a distinct ethnic group. Throughout this essay I will be employing the term "People" whenever the term *volk* or *volks* would have been used in Afrikaans. See also: Moodie, *The Rise of Afrikanerdom,* xi.

8   Moodie, *The Rise of Afrikanerdom,* 79.

9   Text by I.M. Lombard, secretary of the *Afrikaner Broederbond,* in *Die Transvaler,* December 1944-January 1945. Quoted in Bloomberg and Dubow, *Christian Nationalism and the Rise of the Afrikaner Broederbond in South Africa, 1918–48,* 41.

did not shy from using their elite connections to pressure local authorities, educators or businesses into policies favoring Afrikaner culture, language and corporate interests.

With the National Party (NP) we arrive at a third major carrier of Christian-nationalism. Founded in 1914 shortly after the establishment of the Union of South Africa, the NP advocated a rigorous ethno-nationalist agenda. Its major aim was to overcome Afrikaners' social, cultural and economic marginalization by strengthening their common identity. Key to this identity was first and fore-most the Afrikaans language. It not only symbolized Afrikaners' culture and history, but also presented a crucial tool for the latter to distinguish themselves from English speakers and carve out their own place in South Africa away from despised British influences. Throughout the early 20th century the National Party increasingly incorporated religious elements in its nationalist program. Similar to the *Broederbond*, it justified the need to preserve and foster the na-tion by stressing Afrikaner's special mission to serve as God's instruments in South Africa. By 1934 the party had formally adopted Christian-nationalism, stating in the first article of its Constitution that "all black people must be kept 'under the Christian trusteeship of the European race.' "[10]

Together, the DRC, *Broederbond* and National Party shaped Christian-nationalism into an influential, pervasive civil religion that formed the basis for the apartheid regime formally established after the National Party's 1948 election victory. The party had won the elections with an unambiguous racial outlook. It proclaimed to once and for all establish the white Afrikaner nation and defend it against both the English and black population.[11] This victory did not appear out of thin air. What allowed the Afrikaner civil religion to gain such popularity and how did it evolve into the notorious system of racial seg-regation South Africa ultimately became known for?

1.1.2   *From a Movement for Unity to a System of Separation*

Considering its successes later on, Afrikaner Christian-nationalism started out as a rather marginal movement. It focused primarily on language issues and still had to invent much of the Afrikanerdom it would come to propagate so ve-hemently. Both the National Party and the *Broederbond* built their initial pro-grams around the common effort to bolster Afrikaans as opposed to English speaking in schools, public institutions and at home. This language battle soon appeared rather a means to an end though. Central for both actors became the

---

10   Quoted in Bloomberg, *Christian Nationalism*, xxiii.

11   Moodie, *The Rise of Afrikanerdom*, 251.

rehabilitation of their key constituency, the Afrikaners, after the devastating South African or "Anglo-Boer" wars.[12] Interestingly, the term Afrikaner was still quite new at the time. Even today, its meaning remains contentious. According to Hermann Giliomee, the term only came into use by the late 1800's in strong competition with other modes of identification such as *Boer* or *Burgher*, "citizen." While "Afrikaner" generally referred to white Afrikaans speakers with European ancestry, efforts have throughout history been made to include white English and more recently, colored Afrikaans speakers.[13] For the Christian-nationalists however, it comprised a highly exclusive ethno-national and racial identity that had to be protected against external influences, whether English, black, liberal or communist.

Support for this position appeared limited at first. The unique Afrikaner community that the *Broederbond* and National Party sought to speak to was far from homogeneous at the beginning of the 20th century. Many shared membership to the Dutch Reformed Church. Other than that they encompassed a highly diverse mix of backgrounds though, with different European ancestries and a wide variety of dialects, local customs and trades. Few perceived themselves in terms of one common identity, let alone as a unique nation.

By 1938 this had changed drastically. In this year the hundredth anniversary took place of what was presented as the *Great Trek,* or the long journey of the Afrikaner pioneers, the so-called *Voortrekkers*, who halfway through the 19th century traveled from the coast into South Africa's mainland in search of autonomy from the British. It entailed a mystic narrative in which the *Voortrekkers* were portrayed as the heroes of the Afrikaner people. In December 1838, the legend told, they conquered the indigenous population with help from God and established free republics in the Northeast. On the eve of the battle, the *Voortrekkers* were said to have made a vow for establishing a new Reformed church should they win. This vow became known as the covenant

---

12   The South African or Anglo-Boer wars took place from 1880 to 1881 and again from 1899 to 1902, and involved an often gruesome power struggle between Boer communities and the ruling British. The Boers suffered vast losses in what they considered an epic battle for independence, not in the least through the notorious concentration camps in which mostly women and children were placed. Among Afrikaner communities, the wars thus became associated with both heroism and victimhood. Often overlooked is the contribution of black South Africans who fought and lost lives especially on the side of the Boers. The term "South African wars" tends to be considered more appropriate to indicate their broader impact on the entire South African population and not only the Boer and English communities, and will therefore be used throughout this book.

13   Hermann B. Giliomee, *The Afrikaners: Biography of a People*, (Charlottesville: University of Virginia Press, 2003), xix.

between God and the Afrikaners as a divinely chosen nation destined to bring Christianity to South Africa. Drawing vast crowds of people, the centenary of this covenant and the so-called Blood River Battle became a historic feat in itself, a perfect symbol of the Christian-nationalist myth of Afrikanerdom, its sacred mission and ethnic unity.[14] Reverend J. D. Vorster during the centenary explained the mission as such: "In answer to prayer and covenant, God Almighty confirmed on 16 December 1838 that it is his will that the Afrikaner volk shall live ... And on December 16 the Almighty gave his approval to the volk's direction and our fathers bound us with a holy, unimpeachable covenant never to be untrue to the Volk and God."[15]

What drew Afrikaans speaking communities to this myth? At stake here was above all the search for a common unifying identity to help stave off what appeared to be a conglomeration of social-economic and political crises. The search for Afrikaner unity first emerged in the 19th century primarily as an expression of anger over British domination. The Boers staunchly resented the British colonization of what they considered as their lands. After the Great Trek, they had finally founded their independent Boer Republics, only to lose much of their autonomy by the end of the South African wars a few decades later. Giliomee closely relates the wars' tremendous impact on Afrikaans speaking whites to their rising urge for a common identity. Women and children had died *en masse* in concentration camps, communities had been uprooted and farmlands burned and lost. Only in unity, it was believed, could the deeply impoverished population survive and strengthen their position versus the English.[16] Simultaneously, the country was changing significantly. As elsewhere in the world, South Africa experienced the emergence of industries, an expansion of its cities and the impact of global politics and commerce. Together, these developments roused a profound sense of calamity. Already a minority among a vast black population, Afrikaans speakers feared the undermining of their farmer lifestyle as much as the loss of control over their own communities and lands due to urbanization. Unity also amidst these tribulations became imperative.

---

14   Moodie, *The Rise of Afrikanerdom,* 175–196.

15   1938 Text by Rev. J.D. Vorster. Quoted in Anton Ehlers, "Desegregating History in South Africa: The Case of the Covenant and the Battle of Blood River/Ncome," *Conference on Desegregating History.* Cape Town. 5–9 July 2000. 9. Accessed at 12 October 2015, http://sun025.sun.ac.za/portal/page/portal/Arts/Departemente1/geskiedenis/docs/desegregating_history.pdf.

16   Giliomee, *The Afrikaner,* 355–364.

Nevertheless, the so-called Afrikaner communities had still to be convinced of what actually tied them together. For this purpose, the *Broederbond*, in joint effort with DRC clergy and National Party members, launched an extensive campaign to spread its ideas. As Davies argues, this occurred in quite a pragmatic manner.[17] Rather than converting people to its Christian-nationalist ideology, the *Broederbond* primarily sought to build consensus among Afrikaans speakers and convince them of the need to stick together and help advance their own nation. Along with the church, it developed extensive development programs meant to uplift the Afrikaner from deprivation. Key activities included networking events, poverty relief and education. Most importantly, such activities helped institutionalize Christian-nationalism as a civil religion, with its belief in a sacred Afrikanerdom increasingly entrenched in Afrikaner institutions, schools, hearts and minds.

For the hearts and minds, Christian-nationalists claimed more than the pragmatic urge for unity and survival. They crucially appealed to already present sentiments about race as shaped through complex historic relationships between the Boers and black South Africans, and, notably, through the Dutch Reformed Church. Bloomberg refers to the early days of the Afrikaans speaking farmer communities and their struggle to maintain a strict racial hierarchy.[18] The sense of inequality between the races and the need for whites to rule over blacks was in the author's view deeply engrained in the farmers' psyche. The enslavement of black and colored population groups had formed a vital part of their economy and way of life for centuries. Its abolishment in the coastal areas in 1834 would have driven many of the *Voortrekkers* to move further inland and establish autonomous republics in which they did not have to comply with the changing rules. It should be noted that the Afrikaans speaking farmer communities shared the preference for hierarchal race relations with many of their white contemporaries. The farmers however received significant encouragement for their position from one of the country's main churches, the DRC. In practice as well as through its beliefs, the DRC developed throughout the nineteenth century an extensive system of racial segregation in the church. It ensured separate worship services for black and white communities and motivated this with theological discourse about the need to preserve the racial and cultural diversity God created. With this discourse, the church did not so much design apartheid. Rather, the DRC tuned in with existing attitudes and offered important rationale to help sustain practical measures already in place.[19]

---

17   Davies, *Afrikaners in the New South Africa*, 20–26.

18   Bloomberg, *Christian Nationalism*, 204, 228.

19   Saul Dubow, "Afrikaner Nationalism, Apartheid and the Conceptualization of 'race'," *Journal of African History*. 33.2 (1992): 212.

The DRC however did not limit itself to the initially rather haphazard Bible statements endorsing common practices. As the Christian-nationalist movement picked up steam in the 1920s, it proceeded towards an actual doctrine on divinely ordered group distinctions that in turn came to define the movement and its Afrikaner civil religion. Essential here were neo-Calvinist ideas on 'pluriformity' and the order of creation.[20] According to Abraham Kuyper, an early 20th century theologian and statesman from the Netherlands, God had not only divided humanity into different nations. The various nations were also meant to retain their sovereignty. God's desired world was a pluriform one, in which every community should be allowed to set its own rules and protect its distinct traditions. Equally important was the belief in God's presence in the totality of a nation's life as well as politics. The South African Dutch Reformed philosopher H.G. Stoker further developed this belief as the Skeppingsidee, or Idea of Creation. All of creation in his view had the obligation to follow divine laws. These were first and foremost geared towards maintaining order. Any disobedience comprised a sin in the eyes of God.

The DRC appropriated, or as some would say rather misappropriated, the neo-Calvinist teachings to the South African context. It asserted that as God was everywhere, it was suitable for the church to support political authorities and ideologies, especially when those benefited the Afrikaner nation it was most concerned with. While the Christian-nationalists of the National Party and the *Broederbond* employed the DRC's theology to justify their earthly interests, the church hence found a way to legitimate its own support for the political implementation of its pluriformity ideal, the soon to be formed apartheid regime.

In the civil religion the DRC, the National Party and the *Broederbond* jointly shaped, the idea that God desired segregation took on another role in convincing Afrikaner communities to join their nationalist movement. Conflating the term nation with race, ethnicity or any other supposedly distinct community, the three institutions presented the separation, or more specifically the separate development of South Africa's many population groups, as a just panacea for handling the country's diverse reality. In accordance with God's will, each community was to have the chance to develop itself, its culture, language and lifestyle, separately but equally. Separation became "the Christian way" and any intermingling of nations, ethnicities or races a sin.[21] This provided the

---

20   J.C. Pauw, *Anti-apartheid Theology in the Dutch Reformed Family of Churches: A Depth-Hermeneutical Analysi* (PhD. Dissertation, Vrije Universiteit Amsterdam, 2007), 112–114; Eugene M. Klaaren, "Creation and Apartheid: South African Theology Since 1948," in Elphick and Davenport. *Christianity in South Africa,* 372–374.

21   Kinghorn, "Modernization and Apartheid," 145.

Afrikaans speaking communities an important sense of moral justness. It fostered optimism and the belief that they were engaged in an ethically sound project to help all of South Africa's communities advance. Kinghorn perceives this optimism particularly in the 1950s when an upsurge took place in mission activities.[22] White DRC missionaries as well as ordinary members saw it as their special task to support black and colored churches in education and leadership. It fitted well within the Christian-nationalist ideal of bringing civilization to South Africa and was widely viewed as respectable.

Moodie describes the above views about separate development with the term "positive apartheid."[23] It helps explain the appeal of Christian-nationalist ideology among the DRC's white Afrikaans speaking constituency. The emphasis on equal development did not only provide the ideology with an image of respectability. It also resonated with Afrikaners' personal experience. Many felt their community had benefitted from the development programs set up under the auspices of nationalism and Christian guidance. They had elevated the Afrikaner people from decades of poverty and marginalization. Now the same could be done for other South African populations.

Besides this optimistic reasoning, Moodie offers a far more negative interpretation of the Christian-nationalists' allure. Their segregation ideal also tuned in with deep anxieties within white Afrikaner communities about the so-called "black threat." The 1930s and 1940s had seen an influx of Africans into cities long dominated by white population groups, leading to fears among the latter for their jobs as well as for the mixing of cultures. Concerns about social disruption further mounted after the Second World War in response to independence movements elsewhere on the continent. Also the increasing popularity of the communist party among the black population was considered a threat to social order and stability. Moodie as well as Bloomberg and Davies leave little doubt about the true origins of these fears.[24] While triggered perhaps by an indeed changing reality, they were cultivated through the Christian-nationalist movement. Especially the National Party, under the strong influence of the *Broederbond*, consciously nurtured the idea of a "black invasion," casting itself as the only real party that could protect the Afrikaner *volk*, its culture and welfare. Apartheid formed a key strategy to do so. Presented in both pragmatic and idealistic terms, it became the glue for the Christian-nationalist order about to be consolidated. Racial segregation would help safeguard Afrikaner

---

22   Kinghorn, "Modernization and Apartheid," 146–7

23   Moodie, *The Rise of Afrikanerdom,* 263–267.

24   Moodie, *The Rise of Afrikanerdom,* 251; Bloomberg, *Christian-Nationalism,* 228; Davies, *Afrikaners in the New South Africa,* 29

interests and could meanwhile be sold to the broader public as a moral and sensible approach to manage South Africa's plural society.

The Christian-nationalist civil religion could hence gain a strong foothold among Afrikaner DRC communities. It provided the latter with an image of the nation they desired, an image of national survival, unity and morality. While clearly manipulated to serve power interests, the Afrikaner civil religion also built on existing sentiments and was shaped through the socio-political context of the time. When this climate changed, so did some of these sentiments. Four decades after the establishment of the National Party regime, few Afrikaners could still be mobilized for the Christian-nationalist ideology. Today, it has become a source of embarrassment rather than pride.

1.1.3   *A Changing World, an Untenable Idea*

Thinking of the end of South Africa's apartheid era, the first images that come to mind are Nelson Mandela and the African National Congress (ANC). They represent, among many others, the protagonists of South Africa's prolonged anti-apartheid movement who persisted their struggle, through demonstrations, civil disobedience and at times violent protests, despite the government's harsh crackdown. In 1994, Mandela and his ANC party broke white minority rule and came to power after remarkably peaceful negotiations and the country's first fully open democratic elections. This part of the story is well known. Far less attention tends to be given to the other side of what is now often abbreviated to the Struggle. What happened to the Afrikaner civil religion on which the apartheid regime had based itself? And what role did its three main carriers play in the dismantling of their own system? On this side of the coin we discern once again an accumulation of economic, social and political factors. The rising national protests, severe trade sanctions and pressure from the international community pushed the *Broederbond*, the National Party and ultimately even the Dutch Reformed Church to change course and gradually allow for a departure from systemized racial segregation. At the heart of this change was the near complete deflation of the once so carefully contrived Christian-nationalist ideology.

This deflation occurred gradually and with much ambivalence. In a 1988 survey among prominent Afrikaner businessmen, politicians and clergy, 81.1 % said they viewed the political system of separate development as somewhat or a serious threat.[25] A significant majority moreover preferred a federal state

---

25   Kate Manzo and Pat McGowan, "Afrikaner Fears and the Politics of Despair: Understanding Change in South Africa," *International Studies Quarterly* 36.1 (1992): 11, 20.

with power sharing and no group domination as an alternative to the apartheid system. While representing only a small section of the population, the survey showed a steep decline of support for the Christian-nationalist order and its underlying premise of segregation as a morally just way to organize society. At the same time, scholars have pointed at the exceedingly slow change of attitudes among the broader white Afrikaans speaking public. In *Afrikaner Identity after Nationalism*, Thomas Blaser describes a "conflicting picture of the 'state of mind' of the Afrikaners in the 1980s."[26] Many appeared aware of the increasing problems with apartheid, but refused to let go of the pillars supporting this system. A 1984 survey described by Donald Akenson indicated their steadfast commitment to major institutions of Afrikaner nationalism, especially the National Party, even while these institutions were losing ground amidst the country's increasing chaos. A majority of respondents also expressed continued support for key segregation policies such as the Mixed Marriages Act, separate education and separate amenities.[27]

The institutions that used to propagate such policies meanwhile had begun to retract some of their own doctrines. The National Party and the *Broederbond* both faced deep internal divisions towards the final years of the apartheid regime. While moderates sought to open up the system, hardliners threatened to split off if any reform took place. During P.W. Botha's government in the 1980s, careful steps were taken to alleviate some of the harshest measures, including the highly discriminative Group Areas Act. Inside the *Broederbond* the so-called moderates gained such influence that they managed to reorient the organization towards a more balanced outlook. In her extensive study on the *Broederbond*, Annette Knecht discusses how it ultimately began to push NP elites to work towards power sharing with black leaders and a gradual dismantling of apartheid laws. In 1993 the organization decided to alter its name into *Afrikanerbond*, open its membership and end its insistence on secrecy. Key to these transformations was the increasing awareness within the *Broederbond* as well as the National Party leadership with which it was deeply intertwined, that apartheid had become a liability. With the mounting international boycott and internal upheaval, it seemed that the only way to ensure Afrikaner survival was to release the Christian-nationalist ideal of Afrikaner hegemony and enter negotiations with the ANC. While such negotiations were considered hazardous

---

26 Thomas Blaser, *Afrikaner Identity After Nationalism* (Basel, Switzerland: Basler Afrika Bibliographien, 2006), 4.

27 Donald H. Akenson, *God's Peoples: Covenant and Land in South Africa, Israel, and Ulster* (Ithaca: Cornell University Press, 1992), 300.

and met with steep resistance, Afrikaner political elites increasingly thought it to be a "greater risk to take no risk at all."[28]

The church elites ran into quite different deliberations. Inside the DRC, similar divisions occurred as in the NP and the *Broederbond* between those wishing to maintain rigid segregation and rising voices for change.[29] Where the political and business elites focused increasingly on the pragmatic aspects of this debate, the DRC however ran into intricate matters of principle. Abandoning apartheid meant it would have to admit the church had falsely interpreted the Bible about God ordained segregation. This triggered an extremely sensitive debate within the DRC as well as among other Christian communities in and outside South Africa. Supporters of the church's Christian-nationalist apartheid doctrine stood in sharp opposition to a growing group of theologians, clergy and ordinary members claiming that God desired unity among all human beings rather than division.

As early as the 1960's, dissidents like Beyers Naudé, had indicated the inconsistency between the church's alliance with the NP government and the Christian faith it asserted. Back then, the DRC minister and theologian could count on little support and was even expelled from his own church. By the 1980's however, theological critique on segregation had amounted to a storm raging at the DRC's doors from across the Christian world. The World Alliance of Reformed Churches[30] along with various black and colored Reformed churches in South Africa as well as individual white theologians responded to the increasing atrocities against the black population with vehement statements denouncing apartheid as a heretic affront to the gospel. The Kairos Document of 1985 was particularly antagonistic. It urged the church to actively challenge the system and spread the Bible's message for justice and liberation "not only in words and sermons and statements but also through its actions, programmes, campaigns and divine services."[31] De facto, Kairos called upon Christians to join the anti-apartheid struggle.

---

28   Annette Knecht, *Ein Geheimbund Als Akteur Des Wandels: Der Afrikaner Broederbond Und Seine Rolle Im Transformationsprozess Südafrikas* [A Secret Organization as Actor of Change: The Afrikaner Brotherhood and its role in South Africa's Transition Process] (Frankfurt am Main: Peter Lang, 2007), 306–8.

29   These internal divisions are further elaborated in Chapter 2.

30   The World Alliance for Reformed Churches (WARC) is an international fellowship of churches rooted in largely Calvinist traditions that after expressing strong critique on the DRC's apartheid theology suspended the DRC's membership in 1982. In 2010 the WARC merged with the Reformed Ecumenical Council into the World Communion of Reformed Churches (WCRC).

31   *Kairos Document* 1985. https://kairossouthernafrica.wordpress.com/2011/05/08/the-south-africa-kairos-document-1985/. Retrieved at 12 August 2015.

For many DRC leaders and members, Kairos and the accusation of heresy implied a direct threat to everything the church stood for. Those on the defense notably abandoned much of the Scriptural rationale for apartheid, but maintained their overall support for the regime even after the NP had begun serious talks about power sharing. In the course of the 1980's focus among DRC proponents of segregation shifted from the Afrikaner duty to preserve divinely created distinctions to broad arguments of order and morality. They claimed it above all as a way to ensure stability among the various population groups and a just social strategy to allow for each group's equal but separate development.

Ultimately, the DRC national leadership chose for the side of anti-apartheid voices, albeit with a quite ambiguous safety clause. First, in 1986, the church national leadership declared open membership for all, ending decades of official prohibition for black and colored church members to attend white services. Then, in 1990, the DRC formally acknowledged it had for too long "adjudged the policy of apartheid ... too abstractly and theoretically, and therefore too uncritically."[32] Nonetheless, the significant *Church and Society* document issuing this statement made a point of noting the well-meant principles with which the DRC had endorsed apartheid. It never wished to impose discrimination in the name of God, but rather provide for the "optimum development of all groups."[33] That the implementation turned out to be so detrimental for the vast majority of South Africans was now recognized as an unfortunate reality, but not for lack of good intentions.

As the institutions began to waver in their support for apartheid, their Afrikaner constituency underwent a perhaps far more drastic development. It did not so much involve debates about the system, but rather about lifestyles and, subsequently, worldviews. The 1970s had seen the emergence of an Afrikaner middle class that cherished a more globally oriented secular identity. It watched American TV series, listened to BBC news, and bought commercial produce from all over the world in brand new shopping malls. Christian-nationalist notions of white superiority, Afrikanerdom and divine election appeared scarcely compatible with this new lifestyle.[34] Eager to partake in the rapidly globalizing markets and mass culture, Afrikaners became more sensitive to foreign

---

32 *Church and Society 1990: A Testimony of the Dutch Reformed Church (ned Geref Kerk)*. Bloemfontein: General Synodical Commission, 1991. Paragraph 282.

33 *Church and Society 1990.* Quoted and discussed in Johann Kinghorn. "On the theology of Church and society in the DRC." *Journal of Theology for Southern Africa* 70 (March 1990): 21–36. 21.

34 J. Hyslop, "Why Did Apartheid's Supporters Capitulate? 'Whiteness', Class and Consumption in Urban South Africa, 1985–1995," *Society in Transition.* 31 (2000): 36–44.

critique and ever less willing to defend their leaders' ideologies, whether at home or abroad. This was especially the case among Afrikaner businessmen. With little affinity to the traditional farmer or *Boer* identity, they sought to unlock the country's racist economy and foster connections with the rest of the world. Secularization also played its part here. Following Western European trends, Afrikaners attached ever less value to their churches. The DRC retained a key historic position in society, much more so than in many European countries today. Still, it could no longer count on having as central a position in people's lives as in previous decades.

Hyslop and Davies perceive the changes in Afrikaner mentality as crucial factors pressuring institutions like the NP and the DRC to shift gears. Davies particularly notes the disintegration of the once so celebrated Afrikaner unity as highly detrimental to the Christian-nationalist mindset.[35] Compliance with collective Afrikaner norms and culture made way for a growing emphasis on individualistic expression, whereas the urge to be accepted by the larger international community ate at notions of national solidarity and sacrifice. The fact that the pillars of the Christian-nationalist movement themselves were being torn apart by internal divisions about how to move forward did little to reinforce such notions. The very idea of a unified Afrikaner nation increasingly turned out to be a farce for which few of its members could still be mobilized.

The civil religion of Christian-nationalism thus entered a downward spiral. Its fading public support generated doubts about Afrikaner unity, which in turn damaged the ideal of a homogenous nation. Socio-political developments meanwhile helped accelerate the downhill trend. The international boycott strengthened the plea of Afrikaner businessmen, usually also powerful *Broederbond* members, to dismantle discriminative economic policies. It moreover tuned in with public fears for the isolation of South Africa from the rest of the world. Another important factor here pertains to Afrikaners' nagging conscience. Many had supported apartheid under the pretext of equal but separate development. This pretext was becoming increasingly hard to sustain against the background of escalating protest and its harsh suppression by the regime. Foreign media brought the images of violence right into South African living rooms, making it almost impossible to deny the anything but equal impact of racial segregation.

The issue of conscience was particularly important for the DRC's white Afrikaans speaking constituency.[36] For decades they had been told that as loyal

---

35   Davies, *Afrikaners in the New South Africa*, 40.
36   Kinghorn, "Modernization and Apartheid," 153.

church members they were doing the right thing in supporting apartheid. Now, Christians from around the world accused them of heresy, and their leaders actually admitted they had made a mistake. Illustrative for the extent of this concession was the 1989 statement the prominent DRC theologian Willie Jonker made at a conference in the South African city of Rustenburg. Here, Jonker confessed in the name of himself, the DRC and the Afrikaner people, the "sin and guilt, and my personal responsibility for the political, social, economical and structural wrongs that have been done to many of you, and the results of which you and our whole country are still suffering from."[37] The argument of having done so with the best of intentions did little to minimize members' disillusion with the DRC and the entire Christian-nationalist belief system it had propagated. In the 1990's they responded by leaving the church in vast numbers. Those who remained withdrew in their congregations, seeking minimal public presence in South Africa's quickly changing society. Scholars generally agree that the DRC did not lead these communities in the country's transition towards democracy.[38] It did however end up removing the moral basis that had been so crucial in fostering public support for the civil religion underlying apartheid.

Although hesitant, all three major carriers hence took steps in undermining the Afrikaner civil religion with which they had buttressed the apartheid system. The *Broederbond* and NP turned from an Afrikaner survival strategy of exclusion and suppression to a policy of careful engagement to help save what could be saved of Afrikaner interests. The Dutch Reformed Church slowly but surely shifted from a white *volkskerk* to an, at least on paper, open church that welcomed all South Africans. It however acknowledged that segregation did not always work out as well as hoped for. To the critical international community and anti-apartheid movement, these changes, not surprisingly, seemed minimal at best. Yet, they shook up the belief framework that had long prevailed among the broader Afrikaner public. The divisions running through their three major institutions not only signaled the near collapse of their social and political system. It exposed the perhaps greatest flaw in the Christian-nationalist ideology of the supposed sacredness of Afrikaner unity.

---

37   1990 Text by Willie Jonker. Quoted in Louw Alberts and Frank Chikane, *The Road to Rustenburg: The Church Looking Forward to a New South Africa*, (Cape Town: Struik Christian Books, 1991), 92.

38   See for instance: Kuperus, *State, Civil Society, and Apartheid in South Africa*; and Wolfram Weisse and C.A. Anthonissen, *Maintaining Apartheid or Promoting Change?: The Role of Dutch Reformed Church in a Phase of Increasing Conflict in South Africa. Religion and society in transition*, Volume 5 (Munster: Waxmann, 2004).

At the end of the 1990s little was left of this Afrikaner civil religion. Its major institutions all three suffered significant losses in membership. In the new South Africa of Nelson Mandela they retreated from society, taking the public aspects of their once rampant segregation doctrine with them. Its image of a distinct Afrikaner nation had received tremendous blows. Still, this idea remained a powerful motive for the former carriers of Christian-nationalism to, in their own limited ways, join in South Africa's transition. The survival of the Afrikaners as group, the protection of their language, culture and economic welfare had the highest priority. To safeguard their position, Afrikaner leaders appeared willing to go to great lengths, even if that meant negotiations with the "black threat." It showed once again how much of the Christian-nationalist order was based on pragmatic concerns rather than a deep-seated ideology of sacred missions and segregation.

This ideology however was of central importance to the Afrikaner communities at which it had been directed, particularly those who affiliated themselves with the DRC. The church had held on to much of its segregation doctrines up until the very end, convincing itself and others of the fundamentally well-meant principle of separate development. It is this belief in good intentions that continues to reemerge in debates about apartheid in contemporary South Africa. While we may never know the depths or genuineness of these intentions, they present a key to understanding South Africa's convoluted past.

Communities are not mobilized for the sake of political or economic interests alone. They need ideas, and a sense of moral right and wrong. For the Afrikaner DRC constituency, apartheid formed a system they had become an intricate part of, as much as an idea many felt they could honorably support. It was indeed a civil religion, deeply institutionalized, decidedly public and engrained in individual and collective self-perceptions. Its collapse was generated by a complex confluence of factors. Leaders moved away from the belief in separate development to protect the interests of the Afrikaner nation. For many of their constituents however, this nationalist ideal in the end did not appear strong enough to sustain the required unity. In that sense, the ideology of separate development turned out to be a harder nut to crack. It would demand "a great deal of soul-searching" to acknowledge that the churches had helped legitimate an oppressive system by presenting it as the Christian way.[39] While still far from completed, the fact that this soul-searching has been taking place remains a remarkable development in and of itself.

---

39   John W. De Gruchy, *The Church Struggle in South Africa* (London: Collins, 2005), 226.

1.2   South Africa Today: Class, Race, Culture

When Desmond Tutu coined the term "rainbow nation" in 1994, he envisioned a country in which South Africa's communities could live together peacefully, without one dominating the other. Implicit in this metaphor is the very presence of communal differences, whether on the basis of color, ethnicity, culture or otherwise. It symbolizes the diversity of a society with eleven official languages and a wide range of population groups,[40] including the Zulu and the Xhosa, colored[41] and Indian people, Afrikaners and English. For long, apartheid politics rendered these groups culturally distinct and sought to guarantee their strict separation. This essentialist identity approach has left deep marks on South African society. Scholars such as Adam Habib, Cees van der Waal and Christoph Marx discern it in ANC affirmation policies, the Afrikaans language battles or the changing interpretation of South Africa's famed constitution.

What local, national and global forces are shaping South Africans' perceptions of group identity today? To what extent are these perceptions a remnant of the apartheid past, or rather a product of more recent identity politics in addition to a globalizing and increasingly disparate economy? The following pages aim to set out the pervasive cleavages along which post-apartheid South Africa has come to be organized in terms of class, race and culture. The three categories intersect and overlap, and are above all deeply contentious as they counter the dream South Africans have continued to foster, against many odds, of a unified, just and equal nation.

---

40   The term "population group" is a regularly used term in official documents describing South Africa's population. Generally, the term refers to four major groups classified as African, Colored, Indian/Asian, and White. Within these groups the South African government site distinguishes between "the Nguni (comprising the Zulu, Xhosa, Ndebele and Swazi people); Sotho-Tswana, who include the Southern, Northern and Western Sotho (Tswana people); Tsonga; Venda; Afrikaners; English; Coloured people; Indian people; and those who have immigrated to South Africa from the rest of Africa, Europe and Asia and who maintain a strong cultural identity." It says that "members of the Khoi and the San also live in South Africa." *South African Government Information. South Africa's People.* http://www.info.gov.za/aboutsa/people.htm. Accessed at 6 February 2013.

41   Whether or not to use capitals here is debatable. For this book I have chosen not to use capitals for the group descriptions of black, white and colored. While contested in themselves, these terms are still among the most common descriptions used by South Africans to identify themselves and others. It should be clear that all three terms carry a heavy load from the past and are considered here as fluid social-political constructions rather than static racial categories.

1.2.1   *A Divided Nation, Once Again*

Over two decades since the end of apartheid, South Africa faces deep economic, social and political challenges. Despite declining poverty rates, income disparities have worsened over the past years to such an extent that South Africa is considered one the world's most consistently unequal countries.[42] The disparities in wealth coincide with high levels of crime, an escalating HIV epidemic and rising political instability. The ANC government is widely perceived to be underachieving as pervasive corruption and inefficiency hamper its service delivery. Labor conflicts have been culminating in violent protests, with the miner strikes of recent years as just one example of South Africa's brewing social unrest. Amidst these challenges, race remains a major source of controversy. Across the board, black South Africans are still far worse off than the relatively prosperous white population. The latter tends to have the highest incomes and enjoys better health and higher education levels than any other population group. Especially in education the numbers are striking. Among whites, 36.5% have gained a degree beyond the twelfth grade, compared to only 8.3% of black and 7.4% of colored South Africans.[43]

It is tempting to attribute the divisions in South Africa today chiefly to the apartheid past. Its legacy of segregation and inequality still pervades the country's geography, education system and economy. Much of the farmland and major corporations remain in the hands of a white minority who live in wealthy suburbs and benefit from a historically privileged position in society. Black Africans meanwhile continue to reside by and large in the impoverished townships and native lands the National Party regime once ordered them to live in, with insufficient schooling, health services and employment opportunities.

There is more at play here however. The ANC led post-apartheid transition generated its own challenges, notably through the economic model it chose to work with. Maserumule describes how the ANC immediately after 1994 "committed the country to a neo-liberal agenda."[44] It opened South Africa's economy to international markets and ran a policy that loosened labor laws, reduced trade barriers and advanced big foreign and national corporations over small businesses. Formally, the ANC sought to combine its open market approach with social development programs aimed at elevating the country's

---

42   Haroon Bhorat and Carlene van der Westhuizen, "Poverty, Inequality and the Nature of Economic Growth in South Africa," *DPRU Working Paper 12/151*. November 2012.

43   *Census 2011. Statistical Release* (Statistics South Africa, 2012), 30.

44   M.H. Maserumule, "Politics of Transition in South Africa and the Post-1994 Democratic State," *Journal of Asian and African Studies*. 47.3 (2012), 310.

excruciating poverty. But few of these programs mustered the efficiency and support required to take on this humongous task. In negotiations with the National Party, the ANC moreover conceded significant economic control to still powerful white elites by allowing them to run the central bank and the treasury.[45] These steps appeared at the time a sensible strategy to facilitate South Africa's calm transition towards liberal democracy. Twenty years later, the ANC's neoliberalism has generated economic growth for a few "haves" at the cost of a vast majority of "have-nots." Unemployment currently stands at a quarter of the labor force. Half of all South Africans under the age of 24 are looking for work.[46] Those who do work often make minimal wages while lacking workers' protection or prospects for better paying jobs.

The "haves" these days do include a growing number of black South Africans. In 2009, they made up 31% of the core middle class as compared to 15% in 2004.[47] The emergence of this black middle class also raises questions though. It has profited from a mixture of privatization and the development policies the ANC was able to push through despite the market-driven economy. Among these development policies are a range of economic empowerment and affirmative action measures established in the late 1990s and early 2000s. They demand companies to hire black employees or set quotas for government agencies to ensure a diverse pool of civil servants and their equal treatment. According to Ratuva, momentous strides have thus been made for the incorporation of blacks in the corporate and public sector.[48] The government regulations nonetheless tended to benefit only a small group of people who were more often used as tokens in an organization rather than actually involved in policy making or management. They crucially failed to reach the large mass of poverty-stricken South Africans. Notably, the Black Economic Empowerment or BEE policies as they came to be called, created new patterns of patronage and discrimination. While directed at the entire non-white population, the policies often favored black Africans over colored or Asian communities, and notably, ANC members over non-ANC members. The policies have been denounced for pushing underskilled workers into high positions, reducing production quality

---

45   Jason Hickel, *Democracy As Death: The Moral Order of Anti-Liberal Politics in South Africa* (Oakland, California: University of California Press. 2015), 119–120.

46   Hickel, *Democracy As Death,* 120–121.

47   Steven Ratuva, *The Politics of Preferential Development: Trans-global Study of Affirmative Action and Ethnic Conflict in Fiji, Malaysia and South Africa* (Acton: A.C.T. ANU E Press, 2013), 236.

48   Ratuva, *The Politics of Preferential Development,* 239–240.

and eliciting widespread corruption as companies have sought to circumvent the imposed quotas.[49]

The issue of corruption takes us to another key challenge in contemporary South Africa. After twenty years of single party rule, the country's political landscape has become a myriad of personal vendettas, fraud and negligence.[50] The ANC remains a powerful player in this landscape. A symbol of the anti-apartheid struggle and of the country's democratic achievements, the party has long been beyond reproach for many South Africans. Mounting scandals about mismanagement and the extravagant spending of its leaders did not prevent the ANC from winning another majority during the general elections of 2014. Still, political tensions have been on the rise for years now. Opposition parties such as the Democratic Alliance (DA) and the Economic Freedom Fighters (EFF) are tearing at the ANC's supporters' base. Although the DA primarily draws voters from white and colored communities, it has managed to gain control of at least one province, the Western Cape, and increasing popularity in the equally if not more important Northern region of Gauteng. The self-described Marxist EFF meanwhile has been pulling black voters away from the ANC, often through ferocious campaigns against the once untouchable liberation party. It tunes in with the social protests spreading across the country. The Civic Protest Barometer sets these protests at an all-time-high of 218 in 2014.[51] They involve organized actions through which citizens express their anger, increasingly with violence, at local governments for their failure to provide proper pubic services, from water to electricity or infrastructure.

The civic protests signal a deepening sense of disillusion with the new South Africa. The high hopes and promises of the mid-nineties have been shattered, especially for the many black South Africans whose living standards barely improved. The continued discrepancies among different population groups feed into both old and new social tensions as well as violence. It is no surprise that the income divides between black and white South Africans remain particularly sensitive. They remind blacks of the many forms of oppression suffered at the hands of whites during apartheid, while white South Africans themselves fear for revenge through for instance labor discrimination or targeted attacks on their farms.[52] Additional frictions have emerged towards newly arriving

---

49   Ratuva, *The Politics of Preferential Development*, 239–240.

50   Hein Marais, *South Africa Pushed to the Limit: The Political Economy of Change* (London: Zed, 2011), 4–5.

51   D.M. Powell, M. O'Donovan and J. De Visser, *Civic Protest Barometer 2007–2014* (Cape Town MLGI. 2014).

52   Opinions about the extent of so-called farm attacks in South Africa differ widely. The Afrikaner musician Steve Hofmeyr is known for claiming that whites are being killed

immigrants from other African countries like Zimbabwe, Malawi and Mozambique. 2008 saw a series of severe attacks on immigrants who were blamed for taking away jobs from the local population.[53] Although the violence has abated somewhat since then, hostilities still flare up regularly such as in early 2015 when troops were deployed to stem the anti-immigrant attacks after seven had been killed.

By far the most violence occurs elsewhere however, in the form of crime. South Africa had a murder rate of four and a half times the international average in 2012.[54] Armed burglaries, rape, gang and drugs related violence have become inherent features of the lives of millions of South Africans. Those with money live behind the fences of gated communities and hire private security agencies to protect themselves. Those without money are often left to their own devices as authorities lack resources to police their areas or simply refuse to venture into the gang-run townships.

On all sides one thing appears clear. The key source of division today is class, as deeply intertwined as ever with race.[55] Income groups broadly parallel the various racial groups formalized during apartheid and are often decisive for the extent to which someone has access to facilities, employment, education and health services. What should we make of these group identities and their position in the so-called rainbow nation?

1.2.2 *Post-Apartheid but Not Post-Race*

Christoph Marx states it unambiguously in his article "Ubu and Ubuntu." Ever since the early twentieth century South Africans have in his view "suffered

---

"like flies" on their farms and that one white farmer dies every five days. A report by the NGO Africa Check reveals a more nuanced story of around 70 attacks annually in which farmers and farmworkers from across the different population groups have died. *Africa Check*, "Are SA whites really being killed 'like flies'? Why Steve Hofmeyr is wrong." 24 June 2013. Accessed at 28 June 2014. https://africacheck.org/reports/are-white-afrikaners-really-being-killed-like-flies/.

53   More on this topic can for instance be found in: Loren B. Landau, *Exorcising the Demons Within: Xenophobia, Violence and Statecraft in Contemporary South Africa* (Tokyo: United Nations University Press, 2012).

54   Alexander Johnston, *Reinventing the Nation. South Africa* (London / New York: Bloomsbury. 2014), 267.

55   In the yearly polls conducted by the Institute for Justice and Reconciliation, income or class have come out consistently as the number one dividing issue in the country, followed by political parties and race. See: Institute for Justice and Reconciliation, *Confronting Exclusion. Time for Radical Reconciliation. SA Reconciliation Barometer Survey: 2013 Report*, (Cape Town. South Africa. 2013).

under an obsession with 'national identity.' "[56] It is an obsession that surfaces in the profound racialization of society. Whether in terms of politics, culture or economics, South Africa remains largely organized by racial or ethnic background. Such communal distinctions are being nurtured through a constant referral to the different population groups in media, political and public discourse. This was the case before the apartheid regime was established in 1948 and has continued well after its demise in the 1990s.

The early transition years did mark a significant break in the trend that has left its footprints on the current society. A crucial element of the negotiated end to apartheid comprised the development of constitutional patriotism as an alternative to the ethno-racial nationalism that had characterized the NP regime and that also surfaced among some of the anti-apartheid parties.[57] Notably, the ANC itself long considered African nationalism, a perhaps more open but still deeply ethnic version of nationalism, as the cornerstone of its identity. The constitutional patriotism constitutional patriotism's party ended up promoting after 1994 entailed an inclusive perspective on who belonged to the nation, a clear rejection of any form of ethnic or racial superiority thinking and, above all, a commitment to the values embodied in the new South African Constitution as primary binding force. Central among these values were and still are "human dignity, non-racialism, non-sexism and the rule of law."[58] Davies and Giliomee similarly perceive some relief in South Africa's ethnic preoccupation for the brief period after Nelson Mandela's election. They note the multiple efforts made to overcome former divides, most famously through the Truth and Reconciliation Commission headed by Archbishop Desmond Tutu. Most of all, Mandela himself emphasized throughout his presidency the need to build nonracial alliances in an inclusive nation that welcomes everyone regardless of their history, background or color.

Before the decade ended however, racial and ethnic differences seemed to reemerge on the political agenda. For Giliomee, this shift became apparent with the "two nations" speech made by Mandela's successor Thabo Mbeki in 1998. Here Mbeki claimed that South Africa was not becoming one but rather two different nations, including one white and relatively prosperous, and the other black and poor.[59] While often denounced for its divisive tone, the

---

56   Christoph Marx, "Ubu and Ubuntu: on the Dialectics of Apartheid and Nation Building," *Politikon: South African Journal of Political Studies* 29.1 (2002): 55.

57   Johnston, *Reinventing the Nation.*

58   National Planning Committee June 2011, 464. Quoted in Johnston, *Reinventing the Nation,* 7.

59   Giliomee, *The Afrikaners,* 683.

speech did reflect a threatening reality. Most of all, it reflected a deep inclination among South Africans to continue to view oneself and others in terms of essential group identities, regardless of the non-racialism values of the Constitution to which they now subscribed.

The returned or rather continued racialization of South African society is, just like the chronic economic inequalities, often first and foremost attributed to its apartheid past. Decades of forced separation not merely left a strong awareness of group identities.[60] It also engrained an anxiety among the various populations for prejudice and oppression on the basis of color or ethnicity. In response, many South Africans have been seeking to build layers of protection around their own community, its culture, lifestyle and language.[61] Any new policy or law tends to be interpreted in terms of how it may benefit either black or colored people, whites or Indians. Politicians strategically tune in with people's fear of being discriminated against as they seek support among their constituencies. They promise to defend supposedly typical African or Afrikaans traditions while blaming socio-economic ills on the lack or failure of affirmative action policies. What follows is a racially divided public debate, whether on the topic of civic protests, matters of immigration or, to name one famous example, a painting depicting a nude President.

This painting surfaced in 2012 and is in many ways emblematic of discussions around race in South African media. Showing an image of former President Zuma with exposed genitals, the painting triggered great contention and a strong reaction from the ANC and its President at the time. The latter filed a court case against the painter who is white. Where some, particularly ANC supporters, saw the painting as indicative of whites' arrogance and their mockery of black leadership and culture, others accused the President of having put his sexuality in the limelight by openly practicing polygamy as an expression of his Zulu background. Above all, references were made to the past. The painting and ensuing controversy would show that South Africans were still struggling with their prejudice and cultural differences. As the ANC's secretary general at

---

60 Paul Maylam, "Unraveling South Africa's Racial Order: The Historiography of Racism, Segregation, and Apartheid," in Jo-Anne Lee and John S. Lutz, *Situating "race" and Racisms in Time, Space, and Theory: Critical Essays for Activists and Scholars* (Montréal [Que.: McGill-Queen's University Press, 2005), 155.

61 Zimitri Erasmus, "Undoing the Yoke of Race," in David Chidester, Abdulkader Tayob, and Wolfram Weisse. *Religion, Politics, and Identity in a Changing South Africa* (Munchen: Waxmann Munster, 2004), 89–95.

the time said about the painting: "It's crude … we have not outgrown racism in our 18 years [of democracy]."[62]

Referring to the conflicted memory of apartheid does not suffice as an explanation for the above trends though. They are fostered through the ways in which South Africa has been dealing with both past and present challenges of diversity. Regarding the past, scholars such as Marx, Shore and Chapman remark on the problematic nature of the Truth and Reconciliation Commission (TRC).[63] Established in 1995, the TRC was mandated to advance national unity and bear witness to the atrocities and human rights violations of the apartheid era. Between 1996 and 1998 it held extensive hearings in which victims and perpetrators could express their grievances, forgive, repent and in some cases be granted amnesty. The Commission received extensive praise for serving as a unique platform to expose and reflect on a deeply contested period in South Africa's history. With its strong focus on individual reconciliation however, the TRC has been faulted for not addressing the structural ills of the system.[64] It failed to recover historical facts and hampered investigations into the role of business or apartheid's many silent beneficiaries. Significantly, critics point out the exclusivist African-Christian style of reconciliation that dominated TRC hearings.[65] Emphasizing a unique tradition among African Christians to forgive, often referenced with the term *Ubuntu*, Bishop Desmond Tutu and his fellow commissioners would have fostered an essentialist understanding of black African culture. This not only ignored the country's vast religious and cultural diversity, but also put pressure on participants to act accordingly.

While the Commission significantly reduced its work in the late nineties, the idea of Ubuntu and of a distinct African tradition of forgiveness carried on.[66] It has come to symbolize a rather controversial (re-)appreciation of tribal African cultures, their supposed focus on chiefdom and communalism versus the individualism associated with white Western culture. Recent years have seen a rising trend among ANC politicians to talk about the need to Africanize

---

62   David Smith, "Jacob Zuma goes to court over painting depicting his genitals," *The Guardian,* 21 May 2012. Accessed at 28 August 2015, http://www.theguardian.com/world/2012/may/21/jacob-zuma-court-painting-genitals.

63   Marx, "Ubu and Ubuntu;" Megan Shore, *Religion and Conflict Resolution: Christianity and South Africa's Truth and Reconciliation Commission* (Farnham, England: Ashgate Pub. Ltd, 2009); Audrey R. Chapman and Bernard Spong, *Religion & Reconciliation in South Africa: Voices of Religious Leaders* (Philadelphia, Pa: Templeton Foundation Press, 2003).

64   Davies, *Afrikaners in the New South Africa,* 65; Chapman. *Religion & Reconciliation in South Africa,* 286–288; Marx, "Ubu and Ubuntu," 50–52.

65   Shore, *Religion and Conflict Resolution,* 59–74.

66   Marx, "Ubu and Ubuntu," 53–9.

South Africa by promoting its specific black African cultures and traditions. The emphasis on African communalism also surfaces in the post-apartheid legal system. According to Davies, this system has increasingly been geared towards the protection of particular South African cultures, languages and customs. It implies in the Davies' view a further institutionalization of ethnicity politics.[67] Even the Constitution that was once praised for its nonracial outlook has become a tool towards advancing particular community rights and ethnic differences over a broader sense of belonging. One remarkable consequence has been the apparent benefits of these ethnicity politics for Afrikaner communities. As a major minority, the latter have claimed special rights to for instance educate their children in the Afrikaans language or retain certain monuments commemorating Afrikaner history. While contentious, several of these rights were granted in recent years. Davies and Giliomee attribute this lenience primarily to the desire of ANC politicians to court the Afrikaner establishment and ensure the vital investments of its business sector.[68]

South Africa today then displays a rather schizophrenic image when it comes to issues of race. On the one hand, it touts a democratic triumph over apartheid and pride in a constitution based on non-racialism. The national reconciliation process as conducted through the TRC is perhaps controversial, but also a symbol of this triumph, showing to the world and themselves South Africans' ability to end an oppressive system of segregation without turning to revenge towards any particular group. Simultaneously, the country continues to embrace the former regime's despised group categories. Skepticism regarding the post-apartheid transition into a so-called rainbow nation has mounted in recent years. The very term reconciliation now holds for South Africans across the population groups a negative association with failed justice and increasing chaos rather than the stability people had hoped for after the violent struggle years.

The employment of racial categories appears in this context primarily as response to a taken for granted reality. In a study on public debates and daily interactions, Whitehead finds that the old apartheid categories seldom emerge to reproduce race on purpose, but rather as a matter of pragmatism.[69] Depending on the situation, people claim their black- or whiteness in order to clarify why they might critique or support the current government. In other

---

67   Davies, *Afrikaners in the New South Africa*, 76–8.

68   Giliomee, *The Afrikaners*, 683–687; Davies, *Afrikaners in the New South Africa*, 48–49.

69   K.A. Whitehead, "Racial Categories As Resources and Constraints in Everyday Interactions: Implications for Racialism and Non-Racialism in Post-Apartheid South Africa," *Ethnic and Racial Studies* 35.7 (2012): 1248–1265.

cases, race is dismissed as irrelevant, a non-factor in discussions about for instance the suffering of small businesses across the country. The categories help explain as much as sustain a divided reality that few desire, but from which even fewer people perceive a possibility to escape. Adhikari perceives this sentiment in the deepening identification among colored communities with their racial identity in post-apartheid South Africa. "For many, racial thinking is so deeply entrenched that racially unifying approaches to politics or inter-group relations are automatically discounted as unrealistic, even delusional. (...) Even among those who profess to subscribe to multi-cultural values, there is fear that Coloured interests will be lost sight of within any broadly South Africanist or non-racial outlook."[70]

South Africa thus appears stuck in a chicken and egg story. Communities claim to require strong racial identities to survive, whilst the constant buttressing of these identities, whether through politics, public debate or in everyday life, preserves and reinforces the organization of South African society along racial cleavages. On all sides frustrations abound. Even though South Africans largely claim to have lost faith in the new nation pronounced after apartheid, the idea that the promises of equality and non-racialism should one day be fulfilled remains very much alive. It returns prominently among the younger generations, the so-called "born-frees," who are growing up without having had any personal experiences with the former regime. In what is for them an undoubtedly post-apartheid South Africa, they are shaping new alliances within, between and beyond the country's tenacious racial boundaries. How far are they able to push these boundaries?

1.2.3 Global Citizens Caught in Cultural Identities

In her valuable study *Constructing Race*, Nadine Dolby tells the story of high school students in Durban who in the post-apartheid era have increasingly come to identify themselves in terms of taste and culture.[71] Their self-perceptions are no longer formed through ethnic or communal backgrounds alone, but through global flows of pop music, fashion and other cultural expressions that have been flooding South African markets ever since they were fully opened up to rest of the world after 1994. With youth from various backgrounds listening to the same English rap, watching the same American TV

---

70 Mohamed Adhikari. " 'Not Black Enough': Changing Expressions of Coloured Identity in Post-Apartheid South Africa." *South African Historical Journal* 51:1. (2004): 176.

71 Nadine Dolby, "Rethinking Selves: Identity and Change." *Constructing Race: Youth, Identity, and Popular Culture in South Africa* (Albany: State University of New York Press, 2001), 7–18.

programs and following the same social media, boundaries have been crossed in a way unthinkable twenty years ago. They find common ground in the brand of jeans they wear or blogging trend they follow. Differences are conspicuously no longer attributed to race, but rather to diverse cultural preferences. Yet, Dolby and other scholars conducting similar studies, observe that these younger generations often end up making the same group distinctions as their parents. Schools and universities show an awkward mixture of integration in the classrooms, and segregation on the schoolyards, along the well-known color lines of the past. As Wale puts it in her discussion on university students in Johannesburg and Cape Town: "While this discourse [of cultural differences] might allow respondents to feel as if they are presenting themselves in a non-racial light, it in fact works to reproduce, legitimate and police racial boundaries."[72]

The challenge of these boundaries is particularly visible at those institutions that were once exclusively white or Afrikaner. Officially integrated today, these institutions still carry the remnants of the old regime with predominantly white leadership, prioritization of the Afrikaans language and Western literature and culture. In order to function in this environment, black students necessarily adapt to the existing traditions. They are referred to as Model C students after the label given to previously white schools that became multiracial after the transition. Wale describes these students as "black South Africans who have become well versed in white ways of being, knowing and speaking, and thus occupy an in-between racial position."[73] It is a complex position in which the students run into accusations of having betrayed their own group, and into persistent social-economic barriers with other groups. They can seldom afford the same type of entertainment as their white peers. Meanwhile the latter appear unable, or unwilling, to connect with the cultural expressions common among their black, colored or Indian classmates.

The students are not alone in this dynamic. The argument that South Africans belong to distinctly different cultural groups emerges across the generations as a way to account for their persistent separation in social life. As soon as people leave their gradually integrating work places, schools or public institutions, they return to group settings that broadly reflect their racial or ethnic backgrounds, with the churches as the perhaps most notorious example of such self-segregation. One could say this is neither surprising nor unique to South Africa. Problematic however is the extent to which group differences

---

72 Kim Wale, "Policing Racial Boundaries: University Students' Interpretations of Race Relations in South Africa," *MMG Working Paper 10-10* (Göttingen: Max Planck Institute for the Study of Religious and Ethnic Diversity, 2010), 17.

73 Wale, "Policing Racial Boundaries," 9.

continue to be essentialized. Where race might have become a rather pragmatic self-description for many South Africans, culture and the way it is expressed especially through language, has increasingly taken on the role of absolute identity marker. This involves a thorough policing of group boundaries to ensure its cultural authenticity is preserved.[74] Whoever crosses the boundaries, whether in social or dating life, or in worship, risks being cast aside as traitor. It returns to the embedded anxiety indicated above for the oppression of one's own group by other culturally or politically dominant groups. Amidst these anxieties it is often overlooked how the various group cultures are tied to the despised apartheid categories and how both entail social-political constructions that are far from static but constantly shaped and reshaped in alternating circumstances. The rest of this section will illuminate these dynamics by taking a closer look at some of the communities at stake. South Africans especially with Indian and Afrikaner heritage have been struggling to carve out a spot in a country that increasingly stresses its black African identity above anything else. How and to what extent do these communities seek to adapt to, or rather withdraw from society?

To begin with Indian communities it is important to first elucidate matters of terminology. "Indian" in South Africa generally refers to those segments of the population whose ancestors came from the Indian subcontinent in the late 19th and early 20th century. Between 1860 and 1911 an estimated 150,000 Indians arrived in South Africa to work as migrant laborers.[75] They were part of an arrangement by the government in Natal to supply workers for its sugar industry. Today, the Indian population makes up 2.5% of the total population, with the majority still living in the eastern region of KwaZulu-Natal according to the 2016 Community Survey.[76] Notably, the survey denotes this population group with both the terms Indian and Asian. The latter would also include more recent immigrants from areas such as Bangladesh and Pakistan. Both terms remain contentious for their association with the racial categories of apartheid and for their dismissal of the group's immense internal diversity. As an alternative, some prefer to speak of Indian South African or South African with Indian descent. The author Pallavi Rastogi has offered the term "Afrindian," implying that "Indianness exists in South Africa in an *Africanized* state."[77]

---

74   Wale, "Policing Racial Boundaries," 25–26

75   Patrick Maxwell, Alleyn Diesel and Thillay Naidoo, "Hinduism in South Africa," in Martin Prozesky and J. W. De Gruchy, *Living Faiths in South Africa* (New York: St. Martin's Press, 1995), 178–9.

76   *Community Survey 2016.* 20.

77   Pallavi Rastogi, *Afrindian Fictions: Diaspora, Race, and National Desire in South Africa* (Columbus: Ohio State University Press, 2008),18.

"Afrindian" may not be a prevalent self-description in present South Africa. It does raise some relevant issues. Rastogi first of all employs the term to indicate the fusing of African and Indian identities as she perceives it particularly in Indian-South African fiction.[78] Over time, Indians have come to make up an intricate part of South Africa. They have shared its burden of apartheid, the struggle to overthrow the system and transition towards democracy. This history has affected Indian communities, just as these communities have helped shape South African society into what it is today. They contributed by bringing different traditions and cultures to the country, as well as through their involvement in the anti-apartheid movement. This involvement is often dismissed, not in the least by Indian South Africans themselves. Many have rather felt guilt over their relatively privileged position during the National Party regime when they were often granted a special position in terms of for instance housing and education, allowing them to be just slightly better off than black South Africans. With the collapse of apartheid, fears rose about new forms of discrimination in a society that would now favor the latter population. These fears subsided during the first decade of the ANC government as it made an effort to reach out to Indian communities and stress their inclusion in the new non-racial rainbow nation.[79]

This brings us to a second element of Rastogi's Afrindianness. At its center is the desire for a citizenship in which Indians can maintain their traditions while being fully recognized as South Africans. Rastogi thus touches upon two key issues. Her emphasis on citizenship on the one hand reveals the importance for Indians to not only be acknowledged as a cultural community, but also in their social, political and economic position as equal citizens. In Ramsamy's view, the latter has become pertinent since the ANC's apparent shift from its non-racial rainbow discourse to a new form of "Africanism."

Especially disquieting for Indians have been policies introduced during President Mbeki's term to boost the position of African population groups such as Black Economic Empowerment. While intended for all "non-whites," the BEE policies in reality seem to focus primarily on African communities, raising Indians' fear of becoming second-rate citizens, simply because they are not "black enough." Meanwhile, Rastogi discerns a strong sense of affiliation among Indians with African communities. Implicit in her concept of Afrindianness is the former's identification with black African culture and history.

---

78   Rastogi, *Afrindian Fictions*, 23–40.

79   Edward Ramsamy, "Between Non-Racialism and Multiculturalism: Indian Identity and Nation Building in South Africa," *Tijdschrift Voor Economische En Sociale Geografie* 98.4 (2007): 475.

In the novels she studied, Indians appear to move beyond and between different races, revealing what Rastogi calls a "hybridization of national consciousness."[80] Especially younger generations seem to join in this hybridization, merging their parents' traditions with both African and global cultural expressions. For many youth, being Indian or not appears less of an issue today. Their prime identity is South African.

Moving on to Afrikaner communities again first requires some clarification with regard to terminology. As the previous section indicated, "Afrikaner" has been and remains a highly controversial identity category. If we look at the 2011 census, there is no mentioning of Afrikaners as a distinct population group. Instead, the document speaks of "Afrikaans speakers" that make up 13.5% of the population.[81] It signals the near complete deflation of what once constituted South Africa's most dominant population group. What is left can according to Davies be captured with three definitions. For some, the term Afrikaner refers merely to those with Afrikaans as their mother tongue. Others claim it to include chiefly Afrikaans speaking whites, or thirdly, those who describe themselves as Afrikaner and claim a distinct culturally homogeneous identity.[82] As such, Davies allows for the inclusion of black, colored and Indian Afrikaans speakers, while recognizing the tendency among many self-identified Afrikaners to think of their community as white Afrikaans speaking only. Having been most engaged in a range of heated identity debates over the past years, this last group will be of particular interest here.

At the heart of the mentioned debates lies the issue of language. The Afrikaans mother tongue has become a core symbol for white Afrikaans speakers as something many fear will disappear unless its use in South African society is safeguarded. Cees van der Waal describes an intense struggle over the presence of Afrikaans at Stellenbosch University, traditionally a major Afrikaner institute. The author understands the struggle as 'moral panic' in response to a deep sense of threat.[83] For conservative Afrikaners, the language tends to form a last stronghold. It is all their community has left after almost everything that used to define them is perceived to be lost in a society increasingly focused on African culture and English as primary language. Reminiscent of similar

---

80   Rastogi, *Afrindian Fictions*, 18.

81   *Census 2011 Key results*, Statistics South Africa, 6.

82   Davies, *Afrikaners in the New South Africa*, 8.

83   Cees van der Waal, "Essentialism in a South African discussion of language and culture;" Adrian Hadland, *Power, Politics and Identity in South African Media: Selected Seminar Papers. Cape Town, South Africa* (HSRC Press, 2008), 65–70.

struggles at the dawn of the 20th century, the recent language debates tune in well with South Africa's current political climate. Afrikaans language enthusiasts strategically refer to the ANC's ethnicity politics and claim equal minority rights for their cause. Emphasis has been put on the racial neutrality of their demands and the involvement of Afrikaans speaking colored communities. This does not take away the primarily white orientation of many pro-Afrikaans statements though, as well as their tendency to embrace essentialist perceptions of Afrikaner ethnic identity.[84]

The language debates reveal more than concern for the Afrikaans mother tongue. They reflect a broader struggle among those who think of themselves as Afrikaners. Davies speaks about their lack of a clear joint group ethos.[85] There may be some who speak out strongly to advance the Afrikaans language. For the most part however, the community is riven with deep internal divisions over their position in the new South Africa. How can they claim an identity and language so profoundly connected with the apartheid past, so manipulated and used to justify the oppression of millions? At the same time, what would happen if they do not request social, cultural and political space for what many still perceive as their community? After initial support for policies that sought to compensate victims of apartheid, Afrikaners have grown impatient with the ANC's affirmation laws and now fear for reverse discrimination if they do not stand up for their rights. Large numbers of white Afrikaans speaking youth have already left the country in search for opportunities elsewhere. Others have withdrawn in small enclaves, seeking as little contact with the rest of the country as possible. The latter however appears scarcely possible in today's increasingly connected world. National and international media reach deep into the most remote corners of the country, while sons and daughters bring home different cultures and ideas they have picked up abroad. For these youth, Afrikaner identity has become but one of many modes of identification. It competes with the English language of their work places, African-American hip-hop music, Pentecostal spirituality, and most of all with a global self-perception.[86] Their passports say they are South African, but many reside elsewhere and have family and friends all over the world. They have become global citizens.

Obviously, much more can be said about the two described communities in addition to the other designated "African" or "black" and so-called "colored" population groups. The former is so diverse that one can hardly speak of a

84   Waal, "Essentialism in a South African discussion of language and culture," 63–65
85   Davis, *Afrikaners in the New South Africa,* 106
86   Blaser, *Afrikaner Identity After Nationalism,* 13–16.

single community. Black South Africans often first identify themselves as Zulu or Xhosa and draw sharp boundaries around what are perceived as distinctly different cultures, traditions and languages. The description of "colored" is equally complex in that it indicates an Afrikaans speaking community that descended mostly from enslaved people and people from African, Asian as well as European descent. Over time, colored South Africans obtained a separate status within the country's racial hierarchy as a "mixed race" group, also referred to as "brown," that was considered superior to blacks but inferior to whites.[87] Similar to Indian communities, colored South Africans struggle with not being black enough for current affirmative action policies. They also carry an ambiguous luggage of the apartheid past in which they enjoyed certain advantages over black Africans but still endured vast discrimination at the hand of the white minority regime. Withdrawing into a distinct group identity has long been a strategy for colored communities to protect themselves against either black or white domination. It involves strong emphasis on the Afrikaans language and a certain pride in feeling comfortable to mix African, Eastern and Western cultures. Recent years have however seen contradictory developments in which some colored communities replace Afrikaans with English as their home language and try to identify more strongly with the black elements of their heritage, whereas others have been drawing closer alliances with white Afrikaans speakers, stressing their common language and, as we will see later, common Dutch Reformed tradition.

Within each of the four official population groups communal identities retain an unrelenting significance. Having an Indian or Afrikaner background strongly affects a person's position in society, chances for work, education and social standing. Ethnicity and color remain central issues in South African public discourse and are carefully considered as well as manipulated in policy making and legislation. Nonetheless, it seems as if the country's long prevalent communalism is gradually losing its rigidity. A changing economy, increased migration flows and global culture tear at the once so firm ethnic and racial boundaries. While it is mostly the younger generations who are at the forefront of this change, their hybridizing identities affect broader society. It is an impact that cuts in two ways. It forces schools, parents and public institutions to engage with different population groups and slowly break down their divisions as they see their youth and businesses crossing borders. Simultaneously, it triggers reverse responses. Across the various communities, people are seen

---

87   Mohamed Adhikari, "Contending Approaches to Coloured Identity and the History of Coloured people in South Africa," *History Compass* 3. AF 177 (2005): 1–16.

to retract within their own cultural fortresses to shield themselves from outside influences. It appears partly a response to the resistance perceived among communities that feel forced into a quickly globalizing world.[88] Even more so, South Africa's persistent communalism can be seen as a reaction to the country's identity politics.

The ANC's drift towards "Africanism" has done little to relieve such responses. Its sporadic support for communities' cultural or economic demands runs the risk of pushing them further into the specified population categories. This leaves the younger generations in a difficult position. They engage with diversity in the classroom, while sharing Facebook posts or traveling abroad. As soon as they wish to settle down in their own country though, many may see little choice but to turn to the communities of their upbringing for support, networking, political protection and social life. As long as South Africa remains as thoroughly racialized as it is now, this is unlikely to change soon. It nonetheless does not mean that group perceptions and relations remain stagnant. Considering the country's tortuous past, much has already changed. South Africans today are bound to engage with each other at work, in schools or in sports more than they were ever before. It takes time before the effects of such a transition become apparent.

1.3   Conclusion

Upon a visit to the national capital of Pretoria in 2012, the city was still in the process of replacing the old street names for ones that refer to heroes of the liberation struggle. Beatrix / Voortrekker Street became Steve Biko Street whilst Vermeulen Street turned into Madiba Drive. The fact that this process took place as late as 18 years after the collapse of the former regime is telling of South Africa's prolonged journey with apartheid. Many of the system's core traits have prevailed, albeit often in a revised format. Most visible are the racially segregated neighborhoods and the discrepancy between predominantly black townships and wealthy white suburbs. Besides the white suburbs however, one can today find gated communities for the black elites, as well as inner city areas inhabited by an interracial mix of impoverished people. Race continues to be a pivotal identity marker, but is no longer perceived as the central line of division in society. Social-economic inequalities appear to have come

---

88   Korom. *Hosay Trinidad: Muharram Performances in an Indo-Caribbean Diaspora*; Werbner and Modood, *Debating Cultural Hybridity*).

in its place, besides cultural differences, both of which remaining deeply intertwined with race.

Most reminiscent of the apartheid days is the continued emphasis on the preservation of supposedly distinct ethnic communities. Throughout the population groups, these distinctions often receive priority over ideals of national unity. Disappointed with the unfulfilled promises of the rainbow nation, South Africans are returning to the default option of self-segregation. Retreating within one's own group appears the best out of the worst strategies to deal with the many insecurities of the post-apartheid era, especially for those who consider themselves cultural minorities such as the Afrikaner, Indian and colored communities.

This is not to say that South Africans lack any sense of common national belonging. Johnston perceives a minimum but still highly functional nationhood in the new South Africa that binds the various communities together on the basis of a broadly agreed upon set of secular democratic values as expounded in the Constitution. Simultaneously however, Johnston points at a shadow nation in which alternative religious and tribal value systems with often exclusivist or even outright discriminatory traditions are existing alongside, and clashing with, the official discourse of inclusiveness.[89] In these shadows, which frequently end up in the limelight as we saw with Zuma's painting controversy, the old mindset of apartheid appears to resurface. The idea of the intrinsic value of particular group cultures and of the separate functioning of these groups in society as a sound way to protect their cultures remains a particularly obstinate legacy of this mindset.

The difficulty to overcome such ideas becomes apparent when younger generations venture into the few areas where South Africa's population groups interact on a somewhat equal level. Central to the recent grievances of black students in Stellenbosch was the sense that they were ultimately expected to behave "white" and that there was insufficient space at the university for their "blackness." What these two terms encompass is far from clear, and hardly the point. More noteworthy is that these students experienced the small in-between space they could occupy at a supposedly multiracial university to still be dominated by one single group. Their sentiments are important to take into account. They signal the impact of the ongoing racialization of public debates in South Africa, as well as the direction in which these debates have been heading for a number of years now. The country's post-apartheid search for reconciliation is increasingly considered a doomed project. Instead of interracial

---

89   Johnston, *Reinventing the Nation,* 319–326.

engagement and integration, South Africans want their authorities to first focus on social-economic justice, especially for the poor black majority.

It is a setting that presents grave difficulties for the religious institution at the center of this research. Leaders of the Reformed churches are after decades of internal discussions gradually reaching a point of agreement that they should unify into one multiracial institution. Their talks of unity and reconciliation however correspond little with the reality of congregations on the ground and their daily challenges to survive. It is a survival struggle that still takes place largely along racial and ethnic lines. Breaking such patterns is hard enough in general, let alone for a religious institution that once made separateness into a principal doctrine.

Once We Were One: Church (Dis)unity from 1948 until Today

Among the many points of contention within South Africa's family of Reformed churches is, ironically, whether it is working towards unification or rather reunification. The former term, to be used also throughout this book, has become a relatively neutral way of indicating a future unity of the four Reformed churches long segregated by race. Reunification however implies a narrative of a united past that was broken and that needs to be restored. Proponents of this term refer to the early Dutch Reformed Church of the seventeenth and eighteenth century in which racial and ethnic communities worshipped together in the only church allowed in Dutch controlled South Africa. This narrative has been criticized for ignoring a historic reality in which non-white congregants formed only a small minority, often seated in the back of the church far removed from white congregants. It would also ignore the de facto segregation of the DRC into white congregations and mission posts for black and colored communities, each developing its own distinct church identity.

Still, the narrative of a united past remains a central motive for processes of unification today, particularly within the DRC. At the heart of these processes is the ideal to structurally integrate the Reformed churches into one multiracial institution. It would signal the ultimate proof that the churches have changed and adapted to their post-apartheid reality. Conversely, the fact that they have thus far remained largely segregated on the basis of the old apartheid categories, appears to indicate the churches' failure to overcome their past. Often forgotten however, is the complex and ambiguous history of the relationships among the so-called black and white Reformed churches. Both have been pursuing some form of church unity throughout the apartheid era and ever since, be it in often sharply divergent ways. Their story displays dilemmas of belonging, of separation and the ability to maintain your own culture versus unity and the risk of being overwhelmed by others. Significantly, the churches' struggle with unity shows the controversial role of religion, and the symbolic power of a confession of faith named after the South African town of *Belhar*, in simultaneously bridging and simultaneously deepening divisions.

2.1 Pre-1994: Modeling Apartheid

2.1.1 *A Family Story*

The Reformed churches' search for unity, one could say, starts as early as 1652, when the Dutch established their outpost at the Cape to provide fresh supplies for ships on the way to the Far East. Along with these supplies, the Dutch trading company offered Dutch Reformed services for its early immigrants settling in South Africa. In the following decades, the Dutch Reformed Church established a monopoly in the colony, banning all other churches and indigenous faiths. It would maintain this position until the British gained control of the Cape by the end of the eighteenth century. Throughout this period the DRC tended mostly to white communities of Northern European descent. This however did not make the DRC an exclusively white church.[1] Farmers provided services to their non-white farmworkers, while children from mixed backgrounds could be baptized and attend worship. This brief and often contentious history of joint worshipping has up until today formed a key element in the DRC's claim on a united past. It came to an end halfway through the nineteenth century when the DRC began to extend evangelization efforts throughout the country. Early onwards, the mission posts and ultimately mission churches were set up to serve indigenous communities separately from their neighboring white congregations.

In 1857 the DRC secured these missionary practices by formally legitimizing its church organization on the basis of race. The church leadership claimed that "for the weakness of some" segregation would be the best and scripturally sound solution to whites' discomfort with black worshippers participating in DRC services. The decision spawned the establishment of the Dutch Reformed Mission Church (DRMC) in 1881 to tend to the so-called "colored" community, a term that referred to the predominantly Afrikaans speaking population group of mixed Asian, African and European heritage. Meanwhile separate "black" synods were formed for the various indigenous African communities that would later merge into the Dutch Reformed Church in Africa (DRCA). Eventually, communities with Indian and Asian backgrounds also received their own services and established the "Indian" Reformed Church in Africa (RCA). These three churches became known as the black Reformed churches or "daughter" churches while the DRC proclaimed itself as their white "mother" church. With its division into colored, black, Indian and white churches, the Reformed

---

1 Rodney Davenport, "Settlement, Conquest and Theological Controversy: The Churches of Nineteenth-century European Immigrants," in Elphick, *Christianity in South Africa*, 66.

family hence constituted an early model of the apartheid categories that were formalized by the National Party regime after 1948.

Along with the unfolding segregation in the church family and the country at large, voices also arose for unification. Throughout the twentieth century, each of the four churches at different times urged closer collaboration or even full integration of the churches' organizational structures, with varying degrees of response from the others. Perhaps not surprisingly, the three non-white Reformed churches often favored unity more strongly than the DRC, and at least partially succeeded in this aim. In 1994 the DRMC and the DRCA merged into the Uniting Reformed Church of Southern Africa (URCSA). It was established as a new church within the family of Reformed churches that, while tracing its roots to the DRC, would exist as an independent entity. The term "uniting" indicated URCSA's larger vision to include the other family members when they would be ready to accept the invitation. So far, neither the RCA or the DRC has done so.

The terminology used to describe the family relationships reveals a great deal about the challenges facing the churches' enduring search for unity. The family names that evolved throughout the nineteenth and twentieth century exemplified the deeply paternalistic attitudes embedded among the four churches. Though officially autonomous, the "daughters" heavily relied on the "mother" church for financial aid, education and leadership. White missionaries usually headed their congregations, while the few non-white leaders were essentially bound by DRC decisions and risked severe financial repercussions in case of any dissent.

Notably, the DRC distinguished between the daughter churches on the one hand and two "sister" churches on the other. The latter referred to the Reformed churches that had split off from the DRC mid-nineteenth century, the *Nederduitsch Hervormde Kerk* and the *Gereformeerde Kerk in Suid-Afrika*. Rather than racial segregation, this split occurred for reasons of theological discord. Both churches maintained a white Afrikaans speaking membership just like the DRC. Apart from their common background and constituency, the DRC's relationship with the two sister churches tended to be one of minimal contact. Occasionally they reached out to each other to discuss possible collaboration or future unification, but so far little has come of such efforts. Despite the nominal contact, the sister church terminology suggested a sense of equality quite different from the DRC's relationship with the DRCA, DRMC and RCA. For the three black Reformed churches, the mother-daughter language implied an inherent white superiority that came to be deeply despised during the years of the anti-apartheid struggle. Nonetheless, the terms prevailed among all four Reformed churches up until recently.

This book refers to mother and daughter churches to indicate the relationships between the churches and their self-descriptions during the time periods discussed. In the post-apartheid era this includes the notion of mother church as it has remained a predominant way in which DRC members identify with their church. The three former daughter churches are generally referred to with the umbrella term of black Reformed churches. Black in this case does not so much refer to one specific racial category as in the apartheid days, but rather points at the three churches' roots in being established for non-white populations. It has for many of their members become a proud self-description that denotes their distinction from the still predominantly white DRC.

2.1.2   *Schism versus Unity in the DRC*

As the self-acclaimed mother church, the DRC up until today holds a central position in South Africa's family of Reformed churches. Besides being its largest and wealthiest church, the DRC long dominated the other family members and continues to be seen by many as the leading mother church. Much of this perception was formed through the earlier mentioned mission policy. Gideon van der Watt describes the mission policy as first and foremost a race based system in which the white church sought to evangelize what it perceived as South Africa's black "heathen" communities.[2] It followed the church's ideal of embedding the Dutch Reformed tradition in all of South Africa in addition to a profound fear of mixing the country's different races. From its inception in the 19th century, the DRC mission policy comprised a strong preference for racially segregated churches that not only separated black from white, but also black from colored, colored from Indian, and even distinguished between the various black indigenous communities. The policy was justified with what later became a notorious motto of the apartheid regime: separate but equal development. Organizing church membership by race, the DRC asserted, formed the most suitable arrangement for each of the four churches to thrive within and help grow their respective communities.

The arrangement involved extensive DRC support for its family members in the form of church buildings, staff salaries and other in-kind or financial resources. While reinforcing their dependency on the mother church, the DRC exercised a strong hold on every aspect of its daughter churches. It demanded veto power in the DRMC and DRCA decision making, owned their properties and controlled their ministry education at designated seminaries. The black

---

2 Gideon van der Watt., "Die sendingpraktyk van die Ned.Geref. Kerk: Enkele tendense vanaf 1952 tot met die eeuwenteling" [Mission practices in the Dutch Reformed Church: Some trends from 1952 until the turn of the century," *Verbum et Ecclesia* Volume 24 (1) (2003): 2.

Reformed churches had little say in their own curricula development, nor were they consulted about the DRC missionaries that headed their congregations as ministers and chairmen of their local church councils.[3] Good family relationships for the DRC thus primarily implied a one-way street in which the mother church both supported and controlled the other three churches.

Comfortable in this unilateral position, the Dutch Reformed Church for decades expressed little interest in seeking closer unity with its family members. It wished to contain the black Reformed churches, but not cooperate with them on equal terms. The DRC leadership refrained from and even obstructed measures towards formally integrating the family's church structures. Illustrative is the case of the Federal Council of Dutch Reformed Churches. The DRC established this Council in 1964 primarily in an effort to keep the family together as racial tensions in South Africa heightened after the Sharpville massacre. The Council involved representatives from each of the four churches and provided them a platform to discuss common concerns and offer advice to the church family at large. Throughout the 1970's the DRMC and DRCA sought to transform the council into a more substantive general synod that could speak as one voice and help move the churches away from their segregated status quo. The DRC rejected this proposal, leaving the council a toothless advisory body. The Council could critique the political situation in the country but remained moderate in its statements. Though appreciated as a platform to meet each other, the daughter churches grew increasingly frustrated with the Council's refusal to push for reform. After the DRMC left in 1990, the Council died a slow death until it was officially disbanded by the DRC in 2004.

In spite of persistent resistance, the DRC also harbored voices favoring structural church unification. Initial echoes of a call for change came as the movement against apartheid intensified in the eighties. Through an Open Letter in *Die Kerkbode* of June 9, 1982 a group of 123 ministers and theologians urged a visible expression of the family's unity in the spirit of what they viewed as Jesus Christ's central message of reconciliation among people and between humanity and God. Later that decade, this vision was reinforced through the *Church and Society* documents of 1986 and 1990 and the DRC General Synod of 1990. Church leaders openly claimed church unity as a vital element of the Reformed faith. The DRC committed itself to developing a *kerkverband* [church association] that would unite the four churches without compromising their diversity in language, culture and liturgy.[4] Diversity should not hamper church

---

3   Pauw, *Anti-apartheid Theology in the Dutch Reformed Family of Churches*, 93.
4   *DRC 1990*, General Synod, Par. 236.

unity according to the General Synod, and church membership was to be open to all and no longer defined by race.

Ironically, this move towards integration resulted in a deeply traumatizing separation. In 1987, one year after the first *Church and Society* document, around 8000 DRC members split off from their mother church and established the *Afrikaanse Protestantse Kerk* (APK), a new Dutch Reformed church for Afrikaners only. The APK strongly opposed the *Church and Society* declarations, particularly regarding open church membership, and they persisted in segregated church services on the basis of race and ethnicity. In numbers, the loss was barely worth mentioning. Psychologically however, the "church schism" as the APK split-off was called, would haunt the DRC for years to come. It undermined a central part of the church's identity as an institution of unity for the Afrikaners. To leave the mother church was perceived to be a breach of loyalty that not only hurt those who left, but also those who stayed. Illustrative were the words in *Die Kerkbode* of July 1987 of Johan Heyns, the DRC moderator at the time: "... who accepts the church as spiritual mother and has been loyally nurtured by her with the word and the sacraments, cannot but cry about what just happened."[5]

The profound distress following the APK's establishment signals two interconnected and still prevalent themes in DRC attitudes towards unification. One pertains to the internal divisions that have long characterized the church in spite of its emphasis on Afrikaner unity. These divisions run along theological lines as illustrated earlier by the formation of the two Reformed sister churches mid-nineteenth century. More problematic however have been the vast differences between the DRC's regional synods. The latter operated independently and with barely any general oversight up until 1962. In that year the DRC General Synod was formed as an umbrella structure for the seven regional synods that existed at the time, guiding and reinforcing church policies for the entire DRC. Though united, the regional synods today often pride themselves for their autonomy and emphasize their cultural distinctiveness. The greatest divide is generally perceived between the regional synods of the Free State and Transvaal on the one hand and the Western and Southern Cape [abbreviated to Western Cape] synod on the other. The latter is known for its relatively affluent and liberal-minded urban constituencies in contrast to the generally more impoverished conservative rural communities in the Free State and Transvaal.

---

5   J.A. Heyns in *Die Kerkbode*, 22 July 1987, 22. Quoted in J.M. Van der Merwe, "Kerk En Samelewing 25 Jaar Later: Was Die Kool Die Sous Werd?" [Church and Society 25 years later: was it worthwhile?] *Christelike Lektuurfonds in collaboration with Stellenbosch University* 22 (2012), 571. Accessed 12 April 2015, http://ngtt.journals.ac.za/pub/article/view/65>.

Forging a joint church policy across these divides without alienating one or the other has often required the General Synod to walk a tightrope. This significantly complicates contemporary unification debates. Whereas the Western Cape has throughout the years pushed the topic on the agenda, the Free State and Transvaal synods have thus far opposed any formal arrangement that would integrate the Reformed family. In their resistance, these two regional synods often claim to express a primary fear among their congregations that such integration could endanger the DRC's internal bonds. Many would rather leave the DRC than merge into a new church with the other family members.

The threat implied in this last point brings us to the second recurrent theme, or rather dilemma in the DRC's unification priorities and sense of belonging. Fostering unity in the broader Reformed family, the church risks angering its more conservative members who seek to maintain their church's Afrikaner identity. The church they associate themselves with cannot be anything else but Afrikaans. Persisting this identity for the sake of internal DRC unity however is likely to constrain the already tensed relationships with the black Reformed churches.

The General Synod has responded to these pressures with conflicting messages. Since 1994 it claims to endorse and strive for "a greater structural expression of the unity in the DRC family." It would be imperative to its [reconciliation], joint witness and a more effective service" in South Africa.[6] Simultaneously, the General Synod today emphasizes the term "church association," indicating a preference for a loose affiliation of churches rather than one formally integrated church. It has moreover raised a number of church bureaucratic impediments to the unification process, demanding a substantive two-thirds majority not only among the General Synod's immediate representatives but also among local DRC church councils in favor of church unity. The ambivalence on display here is not unique to the DRC and returns in the next paragraph's discussion about the black Reformed churches and their position in the RC family.

2.1.3   *Unity versus Independence among the Black Churches*

Like the DRC, the three black Reformed churches were never unambiguous about church unification. They alternated between demanding a closer and more structural arrangement with the DRC on the one hand, and seeking distance from the church and its association with the apartheid regime on the

---

6   *DRC 2002*, General Synod, 1.9.1 Bybelse begronding vir eenheid. [Biblical foundation for unity].

other. The churches sharply denounced the DRC's segregation policies and at the same time urged the process of unification with the DRC. When the latter appeared unlikely to happen, the two main black Reformed churches, the DRMC and DRCA, in 1994 settled for a bilateral unity and dissolved themselves into the Uniting Reformed Church of Southern Africa. What drove them in their search for unity, and what held them back?

The roots of the black Reformed churches as mission posts are crucial in understanding their position in the church family. With the purpose of evangelizing South Africa's non-white population groups, the DRCA, DRMC and RCA were initially set up as but indigenous versions of the Dutch Reformed Church. As they developed their own identities over time, the three mission churches increasingly came to see themselves as independent entities that, while closely tied to the DRC, comprised their own styles of worshipping, church organization and scriptural interpretations. They not only differed from the DRC, but also from each other. Based primarily in the Cape region, the DRMC early onwards became an anchor of its colored community, reflecting the latter's puritan values and pietism and providing services in its prevalent language, Afrikaans.[7] Still referred to as the mission church, the DRMC resembled the mother church in terms of language and puritanism, but developed a distinct identity based on the hybrid Asian, African and European culture characterizing the Cape colored community. A relatively strong and homogenous base furthermore enabled the DRMC to sustain some of its own churches, making it less reliant on DRC subsidies.

Quite different was the context in which the DRCA and RCA evolved. Rather than serving one particular community, the former had been set up to tend to the various indigenous population groups in their separate languages, such as isiXhosa, isiZulu, Sesotho or Setswana. Whilst each group built its own church culture based on local customs and traditions, the DRCA maintained close relations with the DRC. Kinghorn aptly describes the black African church as "always cast in the role of grateful beneficiaries of white benevolence."[8] The dependency of DRC support combined with their varied localities hampered DRCA congregations to formulate one overarching church culture. The RCA in contrast, developed perhaps the most distinct identity of all three churches. Starting out as its own church entity in 1968 with only four congregations, the small Indian Reformed church primarily focused on spreading the gospel

---

7 Kinghorn, "Modernization and Apartheid," 151.
8 Kinghorn, "Modernization and Apartheid," 151.

among South Africa's Indian and Muslim population.[9] It also heavily relied on DRC financial aid but managed to distinguish itself from the mother church through its strictly evangelical character and almost exclusive focus on communities with Indian or Asian backgrounds.

In their relation to the DRC, the three black Reformed churches shared an initially submissive position. Dominated by white missionaries and financially tied, they abided by the DRC's policies of racial segregation. The 1950 DRMC synod affirmed the notion of separate development as the best way to uplift the impoverished colored community even after it had decided not to take an official stand on apartheid. Likewise, the DRCA and RCA refrained from criticizing the system that discriminated against their own constituencies. Notable is the DRCA Synod of 1975. For the first time in its history, this synod officially denounced apartheid as unscriptural and called for an end to the segregated status quo of the Reformed Church family. Still, DRCA ministers remained largely dependent on the main proponent of this status quo. Few dared to openly critique apartheid, fearing that the white mother church would retaliate by cutting subsidies for the black ministers' salaries. Taking money from the DRC was perhaps not a popular thing do, yet indispensable. In Leepo Modise's words, "[subsidies] felt comfortable within the racially separated church and society."[10]

Nonetheless, the 1975 Synod of the DRCA signified a change in attitude towards the DRC. Its condemnation of apartheid was followed by the DRMC Synod of 1978, which also concluded that "the apartheid policy, as maintained by the government, is in contradiction with the Bible."[11] The two Synod meetings reflected an increasing influence of the churches' black leaders and their theological contributions to the Reformed church family. As the DRCA elected its first black moderator, Rev. E.T.S. Buti, the DRMC saw the rising star of Rev. Alan Boesak. The latter became one of the DRC's most severe critics in the 1980s and a key church actor in the anti-apartheid movement. He set forward a theology of black liberation, combining Reformed traditions with the Catholic liberation theologies of Latin America that urged church solidarity with the poor.

---

9   P.J.P. De Beer, "The Reformed Church in Africa's Laudium Declaration. a Gift to the Ecumenical Community," Faculty of Theology, Stellenbosch University, (2013): 112–113. Accessed at 13 November 2014. http://hdl.handle.net/2263/21578.

10   Leepo Modise, "The Dutch Reformed Church in Africa's bumpy road to the establishment of the Uniting Reformed Church in Southern Africa: from Tshilidzini to Pretoria, 1971–1991," in Mary-Anne Plaatjies and Robert Vosloo, *Reformed Churches in South Africa and the Struggle for Justice: Remembering 1960–1990* (Stellenbosch: SunMedia. 2013), 124.

11   *DRCA 1978*, Acta Sinodi, 495. Quoted in Nico Botha, "The voice of protest within the Dutch Reformed Mission Church," in Plaatjies and Vosloo. *Reformed Churches in South Africa,* 85.

Boesak's theology claimed Jesus Christ to be a liberating Lord who called his followers to actively oppose injustices against deprived population groups.[12] According to this perspective, apartheid and its detrimental implications for black South Africans constituted a profound form of oppression and was heretical in the eyes of God. This theological view of apartheid as heresy came to prevail among the three black churches with Alan Boesak as its most prominent spokesman.

The rising critique of the DRC and its apartheid practices culminated in the 1982 declaration of a *status confessionis* in South Africa. The World Alliance of Reformed Churches (WARC), where the DRC and other churches in the Reformed family came together with groups of Christians from every continent, issued this statement asserting that the gospel itself was at stake and calling on Christians, as a matter of faith, to confront the injustices caused by apartheid. Under the leadership of Alan Boesak, the WARC suspended the DRC's membership in the Alliance until the church would renounce its apartheid theology. The DRMC followed the Alliance's example with a similar statement later that year. Lashing out at the DRC, the mission church denounced any theological justification of apartheid as a "mockery to the Gospel of Jesus Christ."[13] It confronted the DRC with its complicity in a system of racism and discrimination.

Both the DRCA and the RCA supported the rationale behind the *status confessionis* but remained internally divided about the extent to which they should formally antagonize the institution many of their members still perceived as their mother church. This caused severe tensions especially within the RCA. Although most of its ministers rejected apartheid, some feared that an outspoken position on the country's political situation could distract the church from its main evangelical calling.[14] They also dreaded the financial implications of such a position and preferred to remain under the DRC's wings rather than oppose it.

Another key event shaping the relationships between the black Reformed churches and the DRC comprised the *Belhar Confession*. This 1982 document was written by a DRMC commission as a "cry from the

---

12   Klaaren, "Creation and Apartheid," 378.

13   Eugene Fortein, "Allan Boesak and the Dutch Reformed Mission Church between 1976–1990," Plaatjies and Vosloo, *Reformed Churches in South Africa and the Struggle for Justice*, 312.

14   With the *Laudium Declaration* of 1990, the RCA did express its commitment to unity across denominational barriers as long as it would not "stifle the evangelical witness of the Reformed Church in Africa." De Beer, "The Reformed Church in Africa's *Laudium Declaration*," 112–114.

heart,"[15] a statement of faith against the quickly deteriorating political situation in South Africa. It did not discuss apartheid explicitly but rather called churches worldwide to reject any doctrine of "sinful separation" and confess their faith in unity, justice and reconciliation. These three themes were at the center of *Belhar* and became the DRMC's leading guidelines after the church adopted it as a fourth confession in 1986. Despite the call for unity, the *Belhar Confession* would evolve into a source of intense division within the Reformed family. DRC members widely renounced it for being but another political attempt to vilify their mother church while black and colored communities came to perceive *Belhar* as the cornerstone of their church identity. The next section expounds these intricacies and their implication for the churches' unity process. At this stage it is most important to mention *Belhar* as a watershed moment in the history of the black Reformed churches. From this point onwards there was no way back. The black churches, spearheaded by the DRMC, had taken a clear stance against the apartheid system of their mother church, and against the segregated structures characterizing their church family relationships.

The black Reformed churches thus moved from condoning to opposing apartheid along a bumpy road. In the years prior to *Belhar*, they went back and forth between mounting ideological opposition to racial segregation on the one hand and de facto preservation of the system they despised on the other hand. Throughout the apartheid era the three churches sought to transform the paternalistic family relationships into a more equal arrangement. Rather than the toothless Federal Council of Reformed Churches, they for instance pushed for an overarching General Synod that not only expressed the bonds between the four churches but also signified their rejection of racial segregation through joint policies and declarations on the situation in the country. Both the DRCA and DRMC called for structural unity in their respective 1975 and 1978 Synod meetings. The RCA in 1980 furthermore described unity within the church family as "God-given" and urged its realization at all church levels, from congregation to presbytery to synod.[16] Despite the solemnity of these statements, little was done towards implementing them. To a great extent this can be attributed to the DRC's dominance of the black Reformed churches through its missionaries and financial leverage. Stressing the need for the separate development of each ethnic church, the DRC pushed black church leaders

---

15   Accompanying Letter, 1982. Quoted in Johan Botha and Piet Naudé, *Good News to Confess: The Belhar Confession and the Road of Acceptance* (Wellington, South Africa: Bible Media, 2011), 23–25.

16   Pauw. *Anti-apartheid Theology in the Dutch Reformed Family of Churches*. 95.

to accept the family's close but invisible bonds as sufficient and refrain from seeking a more manifest expression of unity.

The black Reformed churches meanwhile had their own reasons for initially persisting in separation. Since their establishment as mission churches their primary aim had been to achieve greater independence. Having control over their own decision making, minister appointment and theological education constituted one of the few ways through which the three churches could protest the DRC in the early apartheid decades. Other forms of resistance were quickly cut off. The DRC and its missionaries successfully restrained the black churches from issuing even the most moderate statements on apartheid, leaving the latter with little space to maneuver in a system that pervaded society. Only towards the 1980s did the DRC reduce its influence over the daughter churches, notably when it allowed the DRMC full control of its theological training in 1982. By that time though, the desire for independence had declined in favor of an increasing urge for visible church unity.

What ultimately pushed the black churches towards integration rather than segregation had much to do with the quickly deteriorating situation in the South Africa of the late seventies and early eighties. The countrywide protests and their often violent crackdowns signaled an intrinsic failure of the DRC's separate but equal development policy. Racial segregation had created a deeply unequal society that was now on the verge of collapse. Through statements like the *status confessionis* and the *Belhar Confession*, the churches indicated their coming to terms with this reality. They no longer followed the DRC and its apartheid theology. Instead they formulated their own theological framework based mainly on the premise that God desired reconciliation among people and that the church could fulfill this desire through displaying visible unity. Structurally integrating its institutions had now become a litmus test for the Reformed family to show its sincerity in abandoning a doctrine of separation.

Formally, the black Reformed churches strove to unite the entire church family. But as the anti-apartheid struggle intensified, the DRMC and DRCA shifted their focus towards bilateral unity talks, excluding the DRC. The escalating political situation combined with the harsh criticism from the black Reformed churches towards the DRC had severely strained their family relationships. Especially the *status confessionis* generated deep controversy. For DRC members, the statement implied the betrayal of the daughter churches and their surrender to international pressure. The black churches meanwhile felt supported now that the wider global church community had voiced such strong condemnation of the mother church's apartheid doctrine. In this tensed climate, the DRC stepped up its resistance to the structural unification of the church family. By 1988 it had withdrawn entirely from the unity talks. The RCA meanwhile chose not to join as it remained internally divided on its position towards the DRC and apartheid. The DRCA and DRMC ultimately decided to continue their efforts bilaterally.

In April 1994 the two black Reformed churches dissolved themselves to jointly form the Uniting Reformed Church of Southern Africa (URCSA). The new name indicated an open invitation for the other family churches to join URCSA. Having taken out the "Dutch" of Dutch Reformed, URCSA also expressed its independence from the white church in both ethnic identity and in theology.[17] While the DRC continued to resist *Belhar*, URCSA adopted the *Belhar Confession* and its emphasis on social justice as a center piece of the new church's confessional base. Its congregations would no longer be obedient daughters in the Reformed family, but rather autonomous churches that retained relations with the other World Reformed churches on their own terms and not on those of the DRC. In stressing this autonomy, the new church's leadership also recognized the internal diversity embedded within URCSA. Congregations were encouraged to maintain the worship language and style they had been accustomed to, even as hope was expressed that the long segregated black and colored communities would ultimately overcome these divisions and integrate their churches. At last independent from the DRC, the black Reformed churches through their new URCSA institution continued to look for unity with the old mother church. The structural unification of all four Reformed churches was still viewed as the ultimate proof that they had left behind their convoluted past. Twenty years since URCSA's establishment, however, the churches remain far removed from this ideal. At the center of their enduring division is the one document that was supposed to bring unity, the *Belhar Confession*.

2.2   Belhar: A Symbol of the Past as Basis for the Future

2.2.1   *A Torch of Unity*
It appears to be a contradiction in terms. The *Belhar Confession* that speaks so highly of unity and reconciliation has since its first draft in 1982 been pivotal to the church family's discord. For URCSA, *Belhar* symbolizes its roots in a church that challenged apartheid. It today demands the unconditional incorporation of the confession in any new unity structure of the Reformed Church family.

---

17   Rothney Tshaka and Peter M. Maruping, " 'The hastening that waits': A critical assessment of the tangebility of unity within the Uniting Reformed Church in Southern Africa,"*Verbum et Ecclesia* [Online], 31.1 (2010): 2. Accessed at 5 September 2014, http://www.ve.org .za/index.php/VE/article/view/426/467.

The DRC in contrast, refuses to adopt it, pointing at a large segment of its members that would object to *Belhar* because of the political context in which it was written. Meanwhile, the confession is gaining acceptance among churches abroad as well as liberal DRC sections in South Africa. Entire presbyteries, congregations and even seminaries have moved autonomously to accept it as a basis of faith for their local or regional church bodies. While the DRC debates and wavers, *Belhar* has evolved into perhaps the most divisive issue in its ongoing unification process with URCSA. The latter refuses to proceed before the DRC's national leadership includes the confession in its confessional foundation, whereas the old mother church seems unable to make up its mind.

To understand this contention, we need to go back to the original confession and its meaning for the church family. The draft was barely four pages long and structured along five paragraphs that each referred to a wide array of Bible passages supporting its message. A small group of authors commissioned by the DRMC had formulated the confession, including most notably Dirkie Smit and Alan Boesak.[18] Their stated aim was to offer an unambiguous condemnation of a doctrine that sought to separate people on the basis of their descent. It followed the earlier mentioned *status confessionis* in asserting that the gospel itself was at stake due to the situation in South Africa. By adopting *Belhar* as a full confession in 1986, the DRMC elevated its status as a document of faith to church doctrine. It was added to the other three confessions that had until then formed the religious foundation of Reformed churches worldwide, with the most recent one dating as far back as the sixteen hundreds. Making *Belhar* into a fourth confession thus presented a powerful symbolic move through which the mission church not only clarified its position towards its own church members, but also sent out a strong message to the broader community of Reformed churches.

Unity constituted a prominent theme in this message. It was stated as both a "gift and an obligation" that any church of Jesus Christ should actively pursue. This meant the unequivocal rejection of any "false doctrine" that endorsed segregation, be it racial, ethnic or on sexual grounds. In addition, the confession called on the Christian church community to make its own unity visible by worshipping together and practicing faith with one another. The second theme of reconciliation further elaborated this active role for the church in bringing people together and opposing ideologies that promoted hatred or alienation. Thirdly, *Belhar* stated its commitment to justice and urged church

---

18   Mary-Anne Plaatjies-Van Huffel, "Remembering reformed documents: Reading the *Belhar Confession* as a historical text," Plaatjies and Vosloo, *Reformed Churches in South Africa and the Struggle for Justice*, 339.

solidarity with "the destitute, the poor and the wronged."[19] At all times, Christian communities had to take a stand against injustices in the special way that God supported the downtrodden. The confession did not specify which injustices the church should oppose. In an Accompanying Letter, *Belhar's* authors did explicate their particular concern with the situation in South Africa and within the Reformed Church family. The letter pleaded the family to make a new beginning with this confession and asked it to join those who drafted and adopted *Belhar* on a path towards unity, justice and reconciliation.

The Accompanying Letter formed a crucial part of the *Belhar Confession*. Up to this day, it is offered alongside the confession as an explanatory note on the context in which it was drafted. Although the letter specifically addressed the DRC, it made a point of not accusing the church or any distinct community. The authors instead highlighted their appeal to all churches and communities to reject any ideology that forcefully separated people. The DRMC and its successor URCSA long persisted this line of argument. *Belhar* in their view contained a universal statement of faith that applied to churches and people facing situations of oppression worldwide.

For the DRC, the Accompanying Letter did convey a rather particular message. It demanded the church to change and join a united Reformed church family. For, only when the churches would literally merge their services and structures, would they answer God's call for visible unity and leave behind their sins of segregation. Underlying this message loomed a strongly dismissive judgment of the South African context. The Letter depicted the country's political regime as sinful in the eyes of God and a direct affront to the gospel. Without blaming the DRC directly for these sins, the authors left little doubt as to whom they considered responsible for the deplorable reality of segregation in the church and the country at large. Attributing this reality to what the authors called a "false doctrine" only barely disguised their sharp condemnation of the apartheid theology everyone at the time knew to be associated with the Dutch Reformed Church in South Africa.

Belhar thus comprised a conciliatory as well as antagonistic component. It almost gently appealed to the Christian principles of the DRC and simultaneously denounced the politics it had been involved in with an unprecedented sharp edge.[20] Through this dual standard, the DRMC balanced its commitment

---

19   Botha and Naudé, *Good News to Confess*, 19–22.

20   *Belhar's* pleading tone particularly stood out in contrast to the Kairos Document of 1985. Developed as an ecumenical declaration rather than a Reformed confession, Kairos presented a forceful theological critique on apartheid in which the churches were called upon to not merely condemn the system but actively engage in the anti-apartheid struggle. See also section 1.1.

to the Reformed Church family with its growing resistance to the belief system still at the heart of the family. With the confession, the mission church moreover pronounced a deep sense of guilt for having been part of this system. None of the Reformed churches would have done enough to contest apartheid's destructive policies. *Belhar* provided an opportunity to admit – or rather *confess* – this sin and offer a remedy in the form of advocating visible church unity. The idea of guilt has remained influential up until today among both supporters and opponents of such unity. As chapter three will show, *Belhar* symbolizes for both the struggle with the churches' past. Where supporters reiterate the confession's urge for unity as the only way to make amends, opponents claim it an abject politicization of church affairs. Their contention displays the deep divisions that have transpired over the supposed torch of unity.

2.2.2   *A Source of Division*

Remembering the history of *Belhar's* adoption during the violent Struggle years, it is not surprising that it should be seen differently by various parts of South Africa's Reformed Church family. The confession extended a hand towards the mother church, asking it to join on a journey of racial integration, but simultaneously accused it of heresy. Without spelling it out, the confession's authors made it quite clear that the DRC bore the blame for the "objectionable doctrine" that had jeopardized the gospel itself. This implicit message came to define much of the DRC's response. For many of its members *Belhar* comprised a personal attack and demonization of their church for the eyes of the world. How could a confession of unity and reconciliation trigger such enmity?

Answering this question firstly takes us back to the politicized context in which *Belhar* emerged. For the black Reformed churches the *Belhar Confession* responded to decades of suppression. It appeared the only tool powerful enough to express their despair. URCSA in particular came to deeply associate its identity with the Confession. *Belhar* reflected the church's ultimate goal of unifying the Reformed family and presented its definite break with apartheid. In Johan Botha's words, *Belhar* "became a catechism of the heart ... not merely a confessional document for URCSA; the church now in fact *is* the Confession."[21] In the course of the 1990s and early 2000s URCSA has sought to incorporate the confession's principles into its church liturgy, sermons, hymns and worship services. It has on multiple occasions stated *Belhar's* importance for future unification with the other three churches. In 1996 URCSA specifically demanded

---

21   Botha and Naudé, *Good News to Confess*, 88.

the DRC's adoption of the confession before it would continue any conversations about unity. This precondition would later be withdrawn, but the image remained of a confession one could barely touch without also touching the church in which it had originated. URCSA had become *Belhar*, and for URCSA, *Belhar's* acceptance had become the acid test to show that the church family was serious about unity and about rejecting its past.

The Dutch Reformed Church on the other hand related *Belhar's* first draft in 1982 to a threatening context in which anti-apartheid protests ruptured the country and the church itself faced allegations of heresy by an increasingly critical international community. This last point touched a raw nerve in the DRC's still deeply devout constituency. The allegations were understood to suggest not only the heretical nature of a certain doctrine, but also of its adherents. Being associated with sinfulness instigated strong resentment among DRC members that found an outlet in the *Belhar Confession*. Regardless of its plead for reconciliation, many DRC members considered *Belhar* a highly accusatory document written with the specific aim to disparage the mother church and its Afrikaner membership. It did not help that Alan Boesak had been on the confession's drafting committee. The DRMC minister was widely held responsible for the DRC's expulsion from the World Association of Reformed Churches and for the condemnation of its apartheid theology. His association with *Belhar* turned the latter into an even more controversial document for the DRC. It came to be seen as part of the political struggle against apartheid and hence bereft of theological value for the church.

Belhar's theological meaning constitutes a second important source of controversy. Supporters have long pointed at the confession's extensive Biblical references and its overlap with Christian values of reconciliation and inclusivity. Opponents often claim the un-Biblical nature of *Belhar*, building their arguments especially on the way it sided with the poor rather than with humanity at large. This last point is most contentious. It comprises the accusation that *Belhar* involved the contested thought of liberation theologies emerging from Latin America. According to these theologies, God would have a special preference for the poor and the oppressed and called upon the church to actively engage with their struggles in society. In the viewpoint of the more conservative neo-Calvinist sections of the DRC, this notion stood opposite to their belief in the omnipresence of God and Christ's salvation of everyone, rich and poor, powerful and vulnerable.

Piet Naudé amongst others points out the difficulty with this line of argumentation. "The accusation that the confession reflects liberation theology cannot be taken seriously, as *Belhar* nowhere uses the class struggle as basis for its social analysis, nor does it confess the preferential option for the poor as advocated by Latin American liberation theologians from their specific context."[22] Naudé furthermore argues that the negative association with liberation theology was used by opponents to tarnish *Belhar* on purpose and undermine its value as a statement of faith for the church.

Whether or not *Belhar* represented liberation theology, the perception that it did remains prevalent inside the DRC, and problematic. Russel Botman perceives a deeper theological conflict at play here. The confession in his view pronounced an alternative take on the gospel that significantly diverged from the DRC's dominant belief framework at the time.[23] *Belhar* represented a stream of thought among the Reformed churches that drew heavily on the theology of Karl Barth and the 1934 Barmen Declaration against the Nazi regime in Germany.[24] It emphasized social justice and reconciliation. Above all, *Belhar* claimed a God who desired visible unity and who perhaps not favored, but still sided with the oppressed. This offered a sharp contrast to the DRC's doctrine of segregation, as well as to its historic attitudes regarding the public role of the church. *Belhar* squarely situated the church in the social-political context of South Africa. It required a timely response to its political and social-economic injustices. The DRC instead maintained Abraham Kuyper's claim of divinely ordained pluriformity and sphere sovereignty. Each sector or group in society was supposed to function according to its own distinct structures and the church was not expected to intervene with God's order through social activism.

The DRC's interpretation of Kuyper might have involved numerous inconsistencies, not in the least regarding its own extensive meddling with state politics in South Africa and its obvious siding with one distinct group namely the Afrikaners. Kuyper's ideas nonetheless dominated the DRC well into the 1990s and left little space for the alternative viewpoints presented by the *Belhar Confession*. This collision of theological frameworks, between the so-called Barthians and Kuyperians formed according to Botman a central impediment to the acceptation of the *Belhar Confession* in the DRC.

If we turn to the contemporary situation in the Reformed family, the above theological debates appear rather absent. The DRC General Synod in 1998 officially acknowledged that *Belhar* does not entail liberation theology and that its content is consistent with the other Reformed statements of faith.[25] The

---

22   Naudé, *Neither Calendar nor Clock,* 142.

23   Russel Botman, "*Belhar* and the white Dutch Reformed Church: changes in the DRC 1974–1990," in Weisse, *Maintaining Apartheid or Promoting Change?* 123–134.

24   See also Naudé, *Neither Calendar nor Clock,* 77–79.

25   Botha and Naudé, *Good news to confess,* 108–111.

misappropriation of Kuyperian theology and its contribution to apartheid has also gained wide recognition in the DRC. Few today would openly endorse notions of pluriformity or even sphere sovereignty. Among the DRC's leadership and academic elites, *Belhar* has moreover been receiving ever more support for the religious language it would offer on reconciliation and the need for inclusivity in the church.

Nevertheless, little agreement has been reached on what to do with the *Belhar Confession*. In the two decades since the first draft in 1982, the Dutch Reformed Church persisted in its resistance, just as URCSA continued to press other churches to adopt the confession. Through ambiguous statements, the DRC General Synod claimed to accept *Belhar* as a valuable document but refused to adopt it as a full confession "on the basis of the commentary received from members and church councils."[26] A consultation with DRC congregations in 2007 found a majority of these members critical of the confession primarily due to its politicized nature. Critical DRC theologians as well as members meanwhile developed an extensive semi-religious line of argumentation on why *Belhar* should also be rejected.[27] The confession would have little to add to existing church doctrines and trigger difficult emotions about the vilification of the church towards the end of apartheid.

Inside URCSA *Belhar* has not remained without controversy either. The confession tends to be more closely associated with the so-called colored sections of the church who once came from the DRMC. Congregations with their roots in the black DRCA often feel less affinity with *Belhar*. Both sections of the church moreover remain de facto segregated along the old lines of the apartheid regime. The reality of black and colored still worshipping separately has undermined *Belhar's* message, raising doubts as to whether URCSA can practice the principles it preaches.

Recent years show some progress regarding *Belhar's* acceptance in the church family. Notably, the DRC General Synod of 2011 officially launched a orderly church process through which the confession should become part of its doctrinal base.[28] A substantive vote was conducted in 2015 in which a majority of regional synods ultimately decided against the proposal to create "space for

---

26   *DRC 1998*, General Synod, Par. 10.3. *Belydenis van Belhar* [*Confession of Belhar*], 422–425.

27   Piet Strauss, professor at the Free State University and former moderator of the DRC, has been particularly vocal about his critique on *Belhar*. See for instance: P.J. Strauss, "Belydenis, Kerkverband En *Belhar* [Confession, Church Association and *Belhar*]," *Dutch Reformed Theological Journal = Nederduitse Gereformeerde Teologiese Tydskrif* 46 (2005): 560–575.

28   *DRC 2011*, General Synod Agenda. Par. B.3. *Belhar*. 292.

Belhar."[29] The low turnout – just about 17 % of all confessing DRC members voted – significantly undermined the anticipated process. If and when *Belhar* will in one way or another be included in the DRC's confessional base remains to be seen.

Politics, whether in relation to the church family or the country at large, has thus largely overshadowed any conversation about the *Belhar Confession* in the church family. Still today, the DRC as much as URCSA refer to the Struggle years to explain the need to either endorse or dispute *Belhar*. It has come to embody divergent narratives of the past and the role of the church. For URCSA, *Belhar* tells a tale of victimhood of the black churches during apartheid, their resistance and ultimate victory over the white church, while DRC members associate the confession with their own victimization as a beleaguered Afrikaner minority, cast aside by the rest of the world as the bad guys in the transformation story of South Africa. Amidst these narratives, the original message of the *Belhar Confession* not only appears lost. It has rather become a symbol of the divisions of the past and as such a highly contentious basis on which to move into future unity.

2.3   Post-1994: Struggling to Join a New Era

2.3.1   *URCSA's Rocky Start*

The establishment of the Uniting Reformed Churches of Southern Africa in 1994 aptly coincided with South Africa's first open democratic elections later that same month. It marked a symbolic change for the country and the churches involved with URCSA as they began their journey towards racial integration. Even before its inception though, the union of the former black DRCA and colored DRCM drew heavy antagonism from among regional church leaders. The cause of church unification had perhaps formed a crucial element of their struggle against the apartheid regime, and against the domination of the white church. Implementing it soon proved to be a whole different ball game. On either side, church leaders feared the loss of the distinct cultural identities of their congregations as well as the hard fought decision making power in their own segregated institutions. The struggle that evolved here, turned out to be emblematic for the future of URCSA in which the old apartheid categories have until the present day continued to divide the uniting church between black and colored.

---

29   *DRC 2015*, General Synod Aanvullende Agenda [Additional Agenda], A.3. Artikel 1.

To understand contemporary relationships between black and colored Reformed churches requires some background. Tensions erupted in the process leading up to the establishment of URCSA in the early nineties. Among DRCA leaders, concerns had mounted that their church would rapidly be dissolved for the sake of unity. They feared they would lose influence in matters of theological education, church order and confession.[30] URCSA's adoption of the *Belhar Confession* in particular roused emotions among DRCA clergy in the Free State and Northern Cape regions. They perceived the confession as a DRMC project that heightened frictions inside the Reformed family rather than reconciling them. Ultimately, two regional DRCA synods of the Free State and Phororo in the Northern Cape withdrew from the process. Instead of joining URCSA, they rather continued as separate churches.

As such, the two synods undermined URCSA's central premise to integrate all of the long divided black and colored churches. URCSA's leadership felt compelled to take the two synods to court and initially won the case. The DRCA synods were ordered to follow the unity agreement and dissolve themselves. Two years later though, in 1998, an appeals court decided in favor of the dissenting synods and granted them, and any other congregation objecting to the unity agreement, the right to retain their legal status as DRCA churches with their own buildings and properties.[31] This last decision instigated deep fractions within the still precarious unification process. The DRCA's continued presence in the Free State and Northern Cape confronted congregations with a difficult choice. Should they remain with their former church or join the newly established URCSA? Unable to reach consent, several congregations split up, sometimes with only a handful of members leaving for one or the other church. Their relations further deteriorated when congregations began to dispute each other's properties. By 2011, at least 39 court cases had been filed by either URCSA or DRCA congregations. Many of them took years to be resolved if they were settled at all.

---

30   A.M. Hoffman, D.T. Keta and M.J. Ramolahlehi, *The Story of the NGKA and It's Decisions Concerning Unification.* Presented in abbreviated version at the Achterberg Meeting of the family of DRC churches, November 6–8, 2006, 3–8.

31   An extensive and valuable discussion on the legal aspects of these decisions can be found in: Mary Anne Plaatjies van Huffel and Johan M. van der Merwe, "Die reis met kerkeenwording tussen die Verenigende Gereformeerde Kerk in Suider-Afrika en die Nederduitse Gereformeerde Kerk in Afrika" [Journey towards church unification between the Uniting Reformed Chuch of Southern Africa and the Dutch Reformed Church in Africa,] *Verbum et Ecclesia* [Online] 33.1 (2012): 7 pages, Accessed at 5 September 2014, http://www.ve.org .za/index.php/VE/article/view/724.

A key recurring point of disagreement concerned the decision making process at the point of unification. From the DRCA side, questions would be raised as to whether the congregation in question and its members had been fully involved in the decision to merge into URCSA. Without sufficient evidence to prove such involvement, several courts gave DRCA communities the benefit of the doubt and ordered URCSA to move out of the disputed church buildings.[32] URCSA churches meanwhile claimed the right to occupy the buildings as part of the 1994 unity agreement. Today many cases remain undecided. They involve convoluted arrangements in which one church might be using the congregation's original building while the other has its members worshipping in a shack on the same premises or in a congregant's backyard.[33] The split often runs straight through communities and families. It has incited prolonged disputes in which both sides disrupted services and at times even violently attacked members of the opposing church.

Although the most vehement antagonism tends to be limited to the Free State and Northern Cape, its impact reaches far beyond the two regions. Stemming from either the DRMC or DRCA, URCSA congregations throughout the country preserve strong affiliations with their former churches and respective colored or black constituencies. Especially the latter have maintained a deep sense of loyalty to their old church. Many display resentment about what is perceived as the DRMC's domination of URCSA. The colored mission churches historically presided over more financial and educational resources than the poorer black churches. Emblematic of these historic divisions is the high number of colored as compared to black representatives in URCSA's leadership and seminaries. This also helps explain the DRCA's early resistance to join the unification process. The Free State and Phororo synods did not merely withdraw because of discontent with the church order or confession of the new church. They responded to deep suspicions towards colored elites that would be controlling much of the new church at the expense of black communities.[34] The ongoing court cases severely aggravated these suspicions.

Further confounding the conflict is the role of the DRC. Officially, the old mother church has presented itself as a neutral actor that would not choose sides for either URCSA or the DRCA.[35] DRC leaders on multiple occasions

---

32   For examples, see: DRC *Free State 2012*. Verslag oor Eiendomdispute tussen Nederduitse Gereformeerde Kerk in Afrika enVerenigende Gereformeerde Kerk in Suider Afrika [Report on Properties Disputes between the DRCA and URCSA], March 2012.

33   See for instance the case of Excelsior, *DRC Free State 2012*, Verslag oor Eiendomdispute, 15–16.

34   Tshaka, "The Hastening that Waits," 3.

35   *DRC Free State 2012*, Verslag oor Eiendomdispute, 7–8.

helped broker agreements between the two parties upon the invitation of both. But the reality on the ground appears rather more convoluted. Throughout the Free State and Northern Cape, local DRC congregations are found to financially support DRCA communities. Without the evidence to prove it, URCSA claims these contributions a major reason why the often poor black churches can afford their lawsuits.[36] It has consequently accused the DRC of intervening in the conflict on behalf of the DRCA. What makes this allegation especially delicate is that many DRC congregations withdrew their traditional support to black and colored churches once they joined URCSA in the nineties. This caused particular hardship for black communities. Those that joined URCSA have up until today been suffering the loss of their financial lifeline, while those that continued as DRCA appear to be faring relatively well in their close relations with the DRC.

Beyond causing deep frictions among black and colored Reformed communities, the conflict between the DRCA and URCSA undermines hopes for uniting the entire church family. The DRC's assumed partiality has led URCSA to withdraw from several rounds of unity talks, stating it cannot engage with the white church as long as it helps finance the court cases. Similarly, the DRCA refuses to talk about unification while its church properties remain contested.[37] On the side of the DRC, the conflict has installed deep anxieties for the potential consequences of a future merger with the other churches. Moving too quickly in this process without clear stipulations on matters of ownership and church law is feared to repeat the same mistakes that were made on the road to URCSA.

URCSA's in-house contention furthermore reveals underlying dynamics bound to return in the family's larger unification process. At the core is the still deeply embedded racial categorization of South Africa's church communities and their distorted relationships during apartheid. The DRCA's fear in the 1990s of the DRCM dominating the new church had everything to do with the racial hierarchy of the past that privileged colored communities over black

---

36   Although URCSA has not issued a formal complaint on this matter, its leaders expressed their suspicions especially during mediation talks with the WARC. See for instance: *URCSA 2009*, Minutes of a meeting held with WARC, 4–6 March 2009 and WARC Mediasie/Facilitering NG Kerk en VGKSA Verslag [Mediation/Facilitation DRC and URCSA Report], Carmelite Retreat Centre, 14-15 October 2009.

37   This opinion was for instance expressed in a letter from the DRCA Free State Moderature presented to URCSA and DRC at a meeting of the Joint Working Team on settling the properties dispute, dated January 22, 2009 as well as a letter by the DRCA Free State Moderature to the WARC Consultation and Moderatures of the DRC, RCA and URCSA, dated February 27, 2009.

South Africans. Colored communities also experienced harsh deprivation as a result of discriminatory apartheid laws. But they were allowed to build and own buildings where blacks could not. Or they could work certain jobs that indigenous groups were prohibited from obtaining. The income inequality this system generated, left deep traces in South Africa's Reformed church family. Its congregations today not only continue to be divided by race, ethnicity and language. They also and especially struggle with differences in social-economic status.[38]

Class status tends to coincide here with diverging worship styles, languages and liturgies. A black Xhosa speaking township church might employ no instruments but its congregants' voices. A relatively wealthy colored community in central Stellenbosch meanwhile sings in Afrikaans alongside a small orchestra of trumpets and violins. URCSA struggles tremendously to bridge such differences. The fact that resources are limited on all sides also does not help. Ministers lack the time and money to attend to their own congregation's needs, let alone to translate hymns or facilitate better relations between the different communities. These relations are further complicated through long standing patterns of mutual prejudice inside black and colored populations and the sometimes blunt racism among them.

Consequently, URCSA faces a reality of official unity while its congregations remain segregated along the racial lines of the two former daughter churches. It sounds a warning to broader family unity. When black and colored churches experience such difficulties, what are the chances for unification between them and the white churches that headed the apartheid system's racial hierarchy?

2.3.2   *Two Decades of Unity Talks*

It is not for lack of effort that the churches struggle with their integration. The past two decades have seen scores of meetings and initiatives to merge church structures at local, regional as well as national levels. In 2006, a significant range of gatherings took place among top leaders from URCSA, DRC, DRCA and the still existing though very small RCA. During these gatherings, the churches agreed on a trajectory that should take them towards one united church association. Although none of the proposed actions were implemented at the time, it is critical for today's unification process to understand what happened here and why these gatherings occurred in the first place.

---

38   Tshaka, "The Hastening that Waits," 3

Already in the early 1990s – before the establishment of URCSA – did the Reformed churches talk about merging into one association. It was a period of relative optimism within the church family. While the apartheid system was gradually being dismantled, the four churches began to express renewed interest in extending their collaboration. All hoped to join in the new direction towards which the country was heading. In an illustrative *Kerkbode* article, DRC leader Frits Gaum wrote that this was the time for the church family to "show one united front and speak from one mouth: we now have to jointly witness what the gospel of Jesus Christ has to say to the people of this fractured country."[39] Several meetings took place in which leaders met to discuss the possibilities of unification.

The hopeful atmosphere of this time could however not conceal the churches' intrinsic differences. Key among them was the disagreement between the DRC and the black Reformed churches over the model of their future cooperation. Where the former envisioned a rather loose federation, the black churches argued for an organic process through which the family members would ultimately dissolve into one new church. They staunchly rejected the federation model, claiming it implied a mere continuation of the apartheid system in which separate churches persisted under the umbrella of one dominant church, the DRC.[40] The enduring dispute over the *Belhar Confession* did little to alleviate these differences. As the DRMC and DRCA moved towards bilateral unification without the DRC, family relationships further deteriorated. By the end of 1994, unity talks between the newly formed URCSA and the DRC had stalled and would not restart for nearly a decade.

In spite of this official deadlock, the two churches continued to explore informal ways of cooperation. Most of these efforts took place in the Western Cape. DRC and URCSA presbyteries in for instance Stellenbosch and Wesland began to hold joint meetings for their respective areas while the two churches' regional charity organizations merged into a joint non-profit organization, Badisa, to tend to the needs of both their constituencies together. In 2000, URCSA's theological seminary moved in with the DRC's theology department

---

39   Dr. Frits Gaum, "Nader aan eenheid." [Closer to unity], *Die Kerkbode*, 28 August 1992, 4. Quoted in Gensicke, *Zwischen Beharrung Und Veränderung*, 176.

40   Mary-Anne Plaatjies-Van Huffel, *Die Doleansiekerkreg en die kerkreg en kerkregering van die Nederduitse Gereformeerde Sendingkerke en die Verenigende Gereformeerde Kerk in Suider-Afrika* [The Doleansie Church Polity and the Church Law and Church Order of the Dutch Reformed Mission Churces and the Uniting Reformed Church of Southern Africa,] (PhD Thesis, University of Pretoria. Pretoria, 2013), 458–460. Accessed at 8 September 2014, http://upetd.up.ac.za/thesis/available/etd-04022009-190218/.

at Stellenbosch University, launching a complex but crucial collaboration between the two churches' main education institutions.

One year later, the URCSA and DRC synods of the Western Cape took an important step with the joint organization of the Cape Convent. It comprised two gatherings, in 2001 and again in 2004, in which local leaders from both sides developed a set of parameters along which they believed a future united church could be established. Central among these parameters was the adoption of the *Belhar Confession*. The local leaders furthermore agreed that the new church should be coordinated by one overarching general synod while congregations, presbyteries and regional synods retained the freedom to find their own "spontaneous" path of integration without coercion from outside.[41] As such, the Convent recognized URCSA's desire for full unification on the basis of the *Belhar Confession*. It simultaneously provided a sense of space to DRC communities that sought to preserve their autonomy in the new structure. The Convent presented its conclusions to the churches' national leadership with the hope that it would offer a basis for future conversations on church unity. Mary-Anne Plaatjies-Van Huffel emphasizes that none of the Convent's proposals held any official value as they were developed outside the general synods of either church.[42] The Cape Convent nonetheless sparked similar initiatives in other regions and as such paved the way for the 2006 breakthrough.

The first of the 2006 talks took place in June at Esselenpark. An essential outcome of the historic two day gathering comprised a statement asserting the unanimous commitment of DRC and URCSA leaders to their unification process. Widely disseminated to congregations and church councils on either side, the statement signaled a new phase in the family's history. Both churches apologized for the pain they had caused each other in the past and stated their shared vision to start anew with a united reformed church "committed to the biblical demands of love, reconciliation, justice and peace."[43] This vision was to be implemented within a three years' time frame. Three more meetings followed Esselenpark over the course of several months. In August of the same year, the executive committees of all four churches gathered in Bloemfontein where they prepared for a larger meeting of 127 representatives at Achterberg in November 2006 and a subsequent Achterberg II meeting in February 2007.

---

41 *DRC 2004*. Notule van die tweede vergadering van die Konvent vir Eenheid [Minutes of the second meeting of the Convent for Unity], Brackenfell, Bellville, 22–24 June 2004.

42 Plaatjies-Van Huffel, *Die Doleansiekerkreg*, 453–455.

43 *Esselenpark Declaration*, Covenanting for the Reunification of the Family of DR Churches, Esselenpark, 20 June 2006.

At the outset, the fast sequence of meetings spawned high expectations. With all four churches present, URCSA hoped to complete the broken cycle through which the church had symbolized its partial unity and reconcile with the two remaining DRCA synods and with the DRC. A younger generation of DRC leaders meanwhile emphasized the importance of unity for recovering its position in the new South Africa. To foster their structural integration, the churches agreed on four central themes. These involved the new church's confessional base, its organizational model, joint ventures, and reconciliation between the family members, particularly the DRCA and URCSA. Regarding the confessional base, the new church would adopt *Belhar* with a special clause of exempt for individual ministers and members unwilling to accept it. The church model itself resembled the Cape Convent's recommendations for one general synod and an organic process of integration while presbyteries and congregations retained their autonomy. Consensus was also reached on the importance of bottom-up initiatives to encourage organizational collaboration across the four churches.

Less successful were the churches on the topic of reconciliation. The DRCA and URCSA failed to settle their long standing properties conflict. Moreover, cracks soon appeared in the other agreements the churches thought they had accomplished. Following ambivalent statements by the DRC leadership, URCSA accused the former of shifting the goal posts for unity. It found that the DRC once again rejected *Belhar* and proposed a church federation, even while knowing URCSA's strong opposition to such a model. The DRC had thus made "a disturbing departure from our understanding reached at Esselenpark and the "Points of Consensus" reached at the Achterberg consultations."[44] According to the DRC however, the meetings had only generated proposals that the churches would each take back to their membership base before moving forward with the implementation. When DRC members gave negative feedback to these proposals in a 2007 consultation,[45] the church leaders felt it justifiable to adjust them accordingly.

A series of events further undermined the precarious relationships between the family's churches. Key among them was an exchange between the moderators of the DRC and URCSA at the time, Piet Strauss and Thias Kgatla respectively. In a number of public speeches and articles, each leader accused

---

44   *URCSA 2008*, The Complete Decision of URCSA General Synod on the Process of Church Unity, Hammanskraal. 29 September – 5 October, 2008.

45   This is the earlier mentioned consultation in which a majority of DRC members claimed to oppose a full adoption of the *Belhar Confession*. Pieterse and Steyn, *Terugvoerverslag aan die Moderamen*, 17–18 March 2008.

the other of obstructing the process on purpose.[46] What had begun as a clash of personalities evolved into a traumatic episode of back and forth messages between the two churches on how to resolve the leaders' conflict and whether or not unity talks could continue under these circumstances.

Ultimately, in October 2008, URCSA's General Synod decided to completely cease its engagement with the DRC. "Until the DRC is seriously committed and ready for unity talks" it placed a moratorium on these talks and would not take any further step towards unification on the national level.[47] URCSA explicitly encouraged churches to proceed with collaboration efforts at local or regional level. Few churches however heeded this call. The 2008 moratorium had signaled the defeat of the unification process. Throughout the church family, communities chose to halt joint operations until further notice from their national leadership rather than continue on their own accord.

In the years following the moratorium, church leaders continued to seek ways to revive the process. Both URCSA and the DRC extended an invitation to the World Alliance of Reformed Churches to facilitate mediation among them with the possibility of involving the DRCA and RCA at a later stage.[48] Early in 2009 the first such mediation rounds took place under the leadership of WARC General Secretary Jerry Pillay. Since then, several signs of progress can be observed. Key among them was the mentioned decision by the DRC General Synod in 2011 to start the process of adopting *Belhar*.[49] Within a year after this decision, URCSA's General Synod lifted its moratorium. Formal unity talks recommenced and resulted in a road map that stipulated ten stages through which a Reunited Church should be constituted. In addition, the churches drew up a Memorandum of Understanding on the main agreements underlying this new institute. Progress was seriously undercut in 2015 when DRC members voted down the proposal to include *Belhar* in their church order as an optional confession. Yet, DRC and URCSA leaders again found a way to move forward. In the same year, they agreed on the so-called Tussenorde. This interim church order sets out a common set of rules for congregations, presbyteries and regional synods that seek to merge. It notably allows for local unification

---

46 See for instance Prof. S.T. Kgatla, "Where are we with Church Unity within the DRC family?" *URCSA News*, 11 December 2007, 9; and Piet Strauss, "Message from DRC to URCSA," Delivered at *URCSA General Synod*, 29 September – 5 October 2008.

47 *URCSA 2008*, General Synod. Decision 22, point 4a.

48 *WARC 2009*, A Statement by the Delegation from the World Alliance of Reformed Churches, 6 March 2009.

49 *DRC 2011*, General Synod, B.3 *Belhar*.

processes to advance even when church leaders fail to find consensus at the national level.

All in all, there appears to be a sense of breakthrough in the family's unification process today – at least among its leaders. Many still refer back to the developments of 2006. Esselenpark and subsequent gatherings provided crucial space for church leaders to meet each other, often for the first time, on relatively equal terms. They found consensus on key issues regarding a future unity. Even though this consensus broke down in 2008, it forms the foundation as well as a major source of inspiration for current interchurch conversations. The Esselenpark and the first Achterberg meetings are often remembered as unique gatherings in which participants found spiritual common ground in an effort to overcome their historic divisions.[50]

Moving from words to deeds has remained highly problematic nonetheless. More than a decade after Esselenpark there is still no structural agreement for unification. The lack of tangible progress undermines confidence among the churches' constituents of their potential to actually unite. Few members are keeping track of the national unity process or are even aware of the conversations taking place at the top. In DRC congregations, members rather tend to withdraw within their own communities, showing little interest in collaboration with other churches in the Reformed Church family. URCSA congregations are struggling with internal challenges as they seek to integrate their own communities. Where the family stands exactly is hence hard to say these days. It has taken significant steps towards unity, but at what costs?

2.4 Conclusion

Looking back at the recent history of the Reformed Church family, a deeply conflicted attitude towards unity emerges. The DRC has claimed it as the rightful return to the family's joint past and an imperative to strengthening its voice in society. When it comes to actual implementation, the church however tends to raise all sorts of bureaucratic barriers. URCSA meanwhile speaks passionately of unification as the litmus test to overcome their apartheid divisions, but makes it almost impossible to pass this test by setting stern conditions to the other family members. It makes one wonder about the churches' commitment

---

50   Ben du Toit shared such memories in two messages disseminated among DRC Congregations: *Muur van skeiding ... oopgeskuif!* [Wall of separation ... opened!] 21 June 2006; and *Indrukke uit Achterbergh: Die Here gaan voor ons uit!* [Impressions from Achterberg: The Lord leads us the way!] 8 November 2006.

to unity. Does the DRC refuse to adopt *Belhar* because of the confession's presumed politicization, or rather because it is not ready for the unification that could follow such adoption? And how prepared is URCSA for a unity that does not answer to all its demands, especially considering that church's persistent internal struggles?

Four key factors still hinder unity processes at the national level. They relate to the particular South African context of the Reformed churches, yet also reveal a broader story of religious institutions seeking to reframe their identity and adjust their normative frameworks accordingly. A first factor concerns the immense difficulty of determining what this new identity is supposed to entail. What does this identity reshaping mean for the deep sense of belonging still felt by the communities in which the churches are rooted? It is a question that surfaces in the DRC's hesitance to make decisions that could upset its traditional membership base of white Afrikaans speakers. As a majority of them is thought to oppose the adoption of the *Belhar Confession* and structural church unification, DRC leaders have been cautious to advance these issues. Fearing another church schism, they seek to build broad consensus by first consulting congregations before making any final decisions. This has resulted in significant delays. It also signals unwillingness on the part of DRC leaders to risk internal unity for the sake of the broader church family.

On the part of URCSA we see similar trends. Resolving internal struggles or the dispute with the DRCA often receives priority over greater family unity. URCSA leaders have refused to participate in unity talks before finding an accord with their DRCA counterparts. Black and colored congregations meanwhile have been sustaining their specific community cultures rather than integrate. After decades of suppression, few are willing to relinquish the autonomy they gained since 1994. Deciding on their own liturgy and language symbolizes this independence, but also impedes the development of a joint URCSA identity, not to speak of a common Reformed family identity.

The churches' conflicting narratives of history form a second significant obstruction to unity. It shows the dual challenge of coming to terms with one's own wrongdoing in the past and finding common ground on how to present this past. Both URCSA and the DRC tend to agree on the destructive effects of the apartheid policies. The DRC has on multiple occasions expressed regrets for its involvement in the former regime. URCSA meanwhile apologized for its predecessors' long lack of resistance. This exchange of apologies still does not alter the widely divergent perspectives with which the churches view their history. The DRC wavers between recognizing its faults and displaying solidarity with a white constituency increasingly fed up with the perceived vilification of their mother church. Its leadership has been careful to address the difficulties of white South Africans and the so-called "crises of faith" they experienced after the apartheid doctrine collapsed.[51] For URCSA however, the DRC's guilt is beyond doubt. URCSA demands that the old motherchurch renews over and again its commitment to justice and reconciliation. Deriving part of its identity from the black churches' struggle against the white DRC, URCSA has been reluctant to lift its demand. The requirement to adopt *Belhar* epitomizes this narrative. For the DRC on the other hand, *Belhar* remains part of an account of isolation, symbolizing a traumatic time in which the church came to be associated with heresy.

Intertwined with the churches' stories of the past is a third factor of contrasting visions about the future. These visions display notable incoherencies regarding the liturgical and theological practices that return to their divergent roots as either mother or daughter in an unequal family situation. Where the DRC sees a close united faith basis among the four churches ever since the 17th century, URCSA doubts there ever was such unity. Any prospect of unification for URCSA requires a tangible process through which the various churches will ultimately merge their structures. It has to be manifested first and foremost in terms of liturgy, with shared songs, prayers, rituals and sermons. The DRC is generally content to strengthen the existing family's spiritual bonds and cooperative efforts. It stresses the theological necessity of such bonds to prove adherence to the gospel's message of inclusivity. The church however sees less urgency in visibly translating them towards joint worshipping. What shape a future church association should take remains, therefore, deeply contested. Throughout the unity talks, leaders from both sides have avoided the topic. Instead of discussing their vision for unity, focus is given to immediate matters such as the development of a new church order and the integration of the churches' charity divisions.

This leads us to a fourth factor regarding the process itself. Here we encounter typical challenges of institutional change. High-minded ambitions falter on authority crises, transfixed organizational structures and intransigent personalities. The churches' unity talks have been fraught with misunderstandings and clashing leadership styles on top of practical difficulties and lack of capacity or willingness to commit available resources. Especially the issue of finances forms a major stumbling block. As the DRC presides over a larger budget than the other three churches, it has been providing most of the funding for the joint meetings and rounds of mediation. This puts the white church

---

51   *DRC 2013*, General Synod Agenda, A.12.11.3 Die NG Kerk en Apartheid [The DRC and Apartheid].

in a powerful position reminiscent of its past paternalism. Memories of this past in combination with the inherent organizational differences between the churches engender intense frustration on the part of the black Reformed churches, as expressed for instance through URCSA's 2008 moratorium. The DRC with its strong focus on congregational autonomy perceived it a logical step after Achterberg II to consult members on the agreement and make the necessary adaptations. Inside URCSA, which is known for a more hierarchal leadership structure, the agreement had been interpreted as an actual decision ready for implementation. It found the new proposals deeply disrespectful and indicative of the DRC's hidden agenda to reshape the process along its own terms.

It should be clear that these factors are neither exclusive nor complete. They broadly indicate the key points of contention on which national unity talks have continued to falter over the last two decades. At every turn, one question encapsulates the differences: What should be the role of the *Belhar Confession*? The DRC and URCSA each link *Belhar* to their identities. These would be either compromised by adopting the confession or harmed by rejecting it. *Belhar* also significantly emerges in the churches' narratives of their past and present relationships as it symbolizes their struggles with the family's segregation. Finally, the *Belhar Confession* has evolved into an almost insurmountable obstacle during the churches' joint meetings and unity talks. Leaders on both sides go back and forth on whether or not its adoption should be a condition for unification and if so, how this should be phrased. They fluctuate between including *Belhar* as a full-fledged confession or an optional one that exempts individuals who prefer not to accept it. As long as the churches fail to agree on this matter, it is unlikely for them to make progress on other elements of the unity process.

Still, the current impasse cannot be attributed to *Belhar* entirely. It is a symbol more than a cause. As we move towards a deeper assessment of the church family in the next chapters, it will be crucial to see how these dynamics are being played out on the ground. How important is *Belhar* for local congregations and church organizations seeking to integrate? What role do they play in the larger unification process and how does this intersect with the churches' discourse on unity?

PART 2

United in Christ Alone

∴

Talking Unity, Living Apart

Throughout South Africa's recent history, the family of Reformed churches has employed religious discourse to shape its communities' social identities. Building up to and during the apartheid regime, the Dutch Reformed Church helped consolidate distinct racial and ethnic group categories through its Christian-nationalist ideology. In the early nineties, the black Reformed churches along with other denominations undermined these categories by reframing segregation in terms of sin and heresy. Today, the Reformed Church family as a whole touts a discourse of racial integration and of disentanglement of the churches' entrenched religious-nationalist and ethnic affiliations. At the center of this discourse is notion of "unity in diversity" as Biblical imperative. Envisioning one unified Reformed church with room and respect for local distinctions, the DRC and URCSA pronounce an inclusive Christian identity that is engaged with all South Africans, while remaining close to specific community values and traditions.

The following pages investigate how the Reformed family has been seeking to reframe its identity in post-apartheid South Africa through a discourse of unity. What, first of all, does this discourse entail, and to what extent does it comprise a break with former discourses of racial and ethnic exclusivism? Secondly, this chapter asks the question of how effective the talk of unification is in facilitating reconciliation between the long divided churches. After a concise discussion on discourse analysis, we will turn to the official party line of the two main Reformed churches, assess the key tenets of their retrospection and major constraints at the leadership level. A next section further analyzes these arguments through the perspective of popular and academic church debates. Since the 2006 breakthrough in unification talks, these debates show both progress and deep contention. Where some perceive the establishment of a Reunited Reformed Church as the logical next step, others refuse to have anything to with it. We will look at both supporters and a growing number of skeptics in the Reformed family. This last group represents a significant backlash to the churches' unity discourse. It claims the ideal of integration as unhelpful if not detrimental to dealing with the vast inequalities congregations face in contemporary South Africa. In this polarized setting, the church family confronts the challenge to not only transcend the divides of the old regime, but also those of the new nation.

© KONINKLIJKE BRILL NV, LEIDEN, 2019 | DOI:10.1163/9789004385016_005

3.1 Analyzing Identity Discourse

To analyze the churches' intricate unity discourse, this chapter incorporates some of the religious-nationalism debates addressed in the initial theoretical framework of this book. Especially significant are Anthony Smith's and Claire Mitchell's contributions regarding the role of religion in bolstering national and ethnic identities.[1] Smith refers to the Afrikaner Christian-nationalist ideology of the previous century as a classic example of the covenant myth he finds among "chosen peoples" around the world, from Armenia to Israel. Its main tenets involve the belief in ethnic election, sacred territory and sacrifice. A group of people presents itself as a distinct nation, divinely chosen to live on a certain land, for which its members are willing to give their lives. Above all, it claims to live under a special covenant with the deity that implies mutual obligations to fulfill the deity's wishes on earth with the expectation of certain divine benefits in return.[2] The covenant language Smith detects among global religious-nationalist movements returns in rather unexpected ways when Reformed Church leaders use it to affirm their commitment to unity. We will look at the extent to which this commitment departs not only from the old doctrine of ethnic election, but also from the underlying premise of an ethnic "volkskerk" [people's church], that exclusively serves one community.

Mitchell indicates in her analysis of Northern Ireland the "thick fabric" religion provides to communities' sense of national or ethnic belonging. It is not merely a boundary marker that in her case distinguishes Catholic from Protestant contestants. Religion gives actual content to their identities. It supplies certain values and lifestyles, a physical space to gather in, and a common cause, the preservation of the faith community, to gather around. Crucially, religion often offers historic narratives as well as rituals through which this cause is being passed on to future generations. In South Africa, churches have for decades served as sanctuaries for particular identity groups, the only place relatively safe from the regime. Religious, ethnic and racial identities are profoundly intertwined here, presenting severe challenges for a church family that seeks to build one church upon these group divisions.

Contributors to the unity debates do not cease to reiterate the hope of breaking down their communal distinctions. Highlighting the Reformed faith as primary motivation for doing so, they appear to follow the trend Brewer, Higgens and Teeney discern among faith-based organizations that seek to play a role

---

1 Smith, *Chosen Peoples*, 2003; Mitchell, *Religion, Identity and Politics in Northern Ireland*, 2006.
2 Anthony Smith, "The Sacred Dimension of Nationalism," *Millennium. Journal of International Studies,* Vol. 29, no. 3 (2000): 803–810.

in peacemaking. Such organizations according to the authors, tend to "stake a claim to expertise in dealing with issues like restorative justice, forgiveness and 'truth' through their spiritual texts and traditions." They employ religious language to help their communities develop alternative visions for societies torn by conflict and in the process claim a special moral status.[3] The authors also point at South African churches as example, this time of developing a discourse of reconciliation instead of nationalist exclusivism. Under leadership of Archbishop Desmond Tutu, a number of churches helped initiate and implement the Truth and Reconciliation Commission in the nineties. Christian values of forgiveness and loving one's neighbor were often called upon during the Commission to help steer South Africans away from violence.

With their unity discourse, the DRC and URCSA are offering their own vision of a cohesive South Africa that figures the churches at the forefront of racial reconciliation. The realization of this ideal has however been a source of sharp disagreement. It involves intense discussions on how to be reformed on the African continent today. What does it mean for a church to be both Christian and South African, conservative and liberal, black and white, Afrikaans and Suthu speaking, poor, middle class and wealthy?

Paul Lichterman's discussion of civic identity has particular relevance here.[4] In comparing two groups inside the same church alliance in a mid-sized American city, Lichterman looks at how religion helped both to frame their roles in society, but in largely conflicting and situation-specific ways. Christian terminology was used by one group towards a broad vision of community engagement meant to bridge racial and economic differences, where the other group preferred a more specific secular language of anti-racism to strengthen their collaboration across denominational differences. Both struggled to define what their group stood for and how to relate to others. And in each case, Lichterman finds religious rationale at the center of the contention. Depending on their context, members selected different aspects of their faith to defend their proclaimed cause, thus allowing for what the author calls diverging styles of identity mapping. It helps explain a remarkable trend we also see in the Reformed churches' polemical unity discourse. Religion plays a key role here but seldom in the principled ways in which church actors like to present their faith. Instead, religious language tends to be employed pragmatically to justify different responses to a given socio-political reality. It is constantly intertwined

---

3   John Brewer, Gareth Higgins, and Francis Teeney, "Religion and Peacemaking: a Conceptualization," *Sociology* 44.6 (2010): 1024–1026.

4   Paul Lichterman, "Religion and the Construction of Civic Identity," *American Sociological Review* 73.1 (2008): pp. 83–104.

with secular arguments on either the benefits or dangers of integration. Unity supporters and skeptics may even refer to the same Bible passages, only to bolster opposite strategies of social outreach versus inward group protection as the presumed best approach to adapt to South Africa's current conditions.

Analyzing debates about religious and social identity among the Reformed churches, it is hard not to encounter lingering group biases, if not blatant racism. This chapter is not aimed at uncovering the various layers of prejudice inside the churches' discourse. It will be necessary to indicate their presence though and the way they help shape arguments for and against integration. Critical discourse analysts Wodak and Van Dijk have conducted extensive studies on how discourse, especially that of elites, reinforces ethnic or racial group boundaries.[5] Van Dijk particularly describes the euphemisms and linguistic hyperboles leaders often use to present their own constituency as victims and the perceived outsiders as potential threats to "our" culture and security. Internal solidarity is highlighted, while members of other communities, "they," tend to be described in negative terms as unreliable, opportunistic and violent. Such us-versus-them language long characterized the official discourse of the Dutch Reformed Church during the apartheid years. To what extent have Reformed church leaders and ordinary members been able to change this language? Can it now support the inclusive identities to which they claim to aspire today?

3.2   The Party Line

The official motive for unification is straightforward in the family of Reformed churches. "… because He is the One who made the church one, we want to obey Him."[6] "… so that the world may believe that separation, enmity and hatred between people and groups is sin which Christ has already conquered."[7] Both DRC and URCSA say that God wants their churches to be united and that they are obliged to follow God's wishes. One does not need to dig deep though to find a more convoluted message that undermines the inclusivity to which the churches claim to aspire. The DRC General Synod hardly conceals its interest in unification for the sake of restoring the DRC's voice in society. URCSA's General Synod Committee has made the unity question inextricably linked to

---

5   Wodak and Dijk, *Racism at the Top*.

6   *DRC 2007*, Konsultasie oor Kerkhereniging [DRC Consultation about Church Reunification], 30 July 2007.

7   *DRMC 1986*, The *Belhar Confession* and Accompanying Letter, Point 2. Accessed at 27 January 2015, http://www.vgksa.org.za/documents/The%20Belhar%20Confession.pdf.

its own agenda of ensuring the adoption of the *Belhar Confession* in the entire church family. Meanwhile, the leaderships of both institutions question the probability of their actual integration. They express, through countless reports and meeting documents, doubts about the benefits unity could have for ordinary members. Above all, they warn about its potential to endanger local culture and language.

The debates among the two churches show a complex struggle of reshaping their identities, still largely based on communalism, to fit with an ideal of interracial and interethnic partnership. Desperate to preserve their communal base within either white or black and colored population groups, DRC and URCSA leaders often appear to reinforce antagonistic stereotypes of each other. How do they balance a discourse of racial reconciliation with mutually accusatory narratives of the past, on top of deep concerns for internal polarization?

3.2.1 *Love the DRC, and Please Do Not Leave It*

In the early nineties, the Dutch Reformed Church leadership began to undertake efforts to renew its identity from a church deeply associated with apartheid and the Afrikaner community to a more inclusive institution equally engaged with all of South Africa's populations. Early onwards, these efforts became intertwined with debates about unifying the Reformed Church family. A milestone in this respect constituted the General Synod of 1994, also known as the "Synod of Reconciliation." It involved a remarkable visit of the newly elected President Mandela, who called the church that once supported his long imprisonment to now join the country on its journey away from apartheid. The DRC for its part apologized to several of its former ministers, including most notably Beyers Naudé, for rejecting their opposition to the National Party regime. It also urged its members to cooperate in deconstructing the negative attitudes of the past and in reconciling the nation.[8] In the following years, the DRC General Synod would often reiterate this position and relate it to the goal the church had set itself: to foster unity within the larger Reformed Church family. Close and structural collaboration across the color line were according to the DRC inevitable if the churches wished to help rebuild a post-apartheid South Africa. It constituted a significant departure from the DRC's long held position as stronghold for white Afrikaners. How to implement the professed aims however soon turned into a source of great contention.

Considering first the official discourse of the DRC as expressed through its General Synod from 1994 until today, we discern a relatively consistent support

---

8 *DRC 1994*, General Synod Besluite [Decisions], 20, 36.

for reunifying the church family for the sake of national and church reconcili-ation.[9] Ten years after the Synod of Reconciliation, the DRC leadership stated it "is afraid to say this, but we are of the opinion that a failure in this respect [reunification] will not only mean we failed the Lord, but also the South Afri-can society."[10]

Proposals for what such unity entails have changed only slightly over time. At its core remains a structural arrangement through which the DRC, URCSA, DRCA and RCA form a new reunited church association ["kerkverband"]. In more recent statements, leaders have specified that they envision one joint general synod and a gradual and completely voluntary integration of regional synods and local congregations. The latter will remain autonomous legal enti-ties in the new church association. Central to the DRC's official vision for unity is furthermore some level of support for the *Belhar Confession* as one of the churches' main guiding documents. As we saw earlier, the General Synod is still working towards the adoption of *Belhar* as a confession of the DRC, with considerable difficulties. Finally, the General Synod has emphasized the im-portance of joint projects ["gesamentlijke projekte"] through which all four churches collaborate at local and regional level, for instance to build a neigh-borhood youth center or help renovate church buildings. Such projects should in the DRC's view take place outside the official unification process. They allow for a more grassroots approach that does not require formal commitments or approval from the churches' national leaderships.[11]

To justify the need for reunification to its constituency, the DRC formally tends to point out four key motivations.[12] Essential is first of all its claim on the Bible's endorsement of unity among all Christian churches and their members. The General Synod of 2007 specifically quoted the Gospel of John in the New Testament with the phrase: "I pray that they will be one, so that the world can believe."[13] The New Testament, DRC leaders claimed, emphasizes the sense of

---

9   Unlike URCSA, the DRC is consistent in using the term reunification ["hereniging"] when it speaks of the merger of the four churches in the Reformed family. It encompasses a direct reference to the notion that the churches used to be one in the past before the consolidation of apartheid practices.

10   *DRC 2004*, Besluite Kerkhereniging 1966–2004 [Decisions Church Reunification 1966–2004], 9.

11   *DRC 2008*, Besluite van die uitgebreide moderamen oor kerkhereniging [Decisions from the extended moderamen about church reunification], 11–12 June 2008.

12   See for instance: Pieterse and Steyn. *Terugvoerverslag*.

13   The Gospel according to St. John, chapter 17. Quoted in *DRC 2007*, General Synod Aan-vullende Agenda [Supplemental Agenda] 1.2.2. Posisie tov kerkeenheid/kerkhereniging [Position towards church unity / church reunification], 26–27.

communion among the followers of Jesus Christ regardless of their different backgrounds. A second related argument pertains to the churches' unique calling. God sent Reformed churches on a joint mission to bring the gospel to Southern Africa. To fulfill this mission, it is of paramount importance that they overcome their former divides. For how could the churches convey the gospel's message of reconciliation and love in South Africa as long as they remain embroiled over the past?

Thirdly, the DRC alludes to the family's history. It promotes the fact that the Reformed churches used to be one during the first two centuries of their existence. The segregation at the time of apartheid was unbiblical. It should not result in the church family's permanent division along racial lines. In this respect, the DRC has often praised URCSA for its crucial efforts to help eliminate the sins of apartheid by reunifying part of the family in the early nineties. This exemplified the reunion DRC leaders pursue for the entire family. Such a reunion should not only bring the churches back together in one alliance, but also highlight their compatibility. In an elaborate introduction to the 2007 Consultation on *Belhar* and church unification, the DRC underlined this fourth motive, stating that "we have become increasingly aware that there lies a richness in our diversity and that our differences are a miraculous gift of the Lord with which we have to serve each other."[14]

The rationale for unity is emblematic of how the DRC has been presenting itself in recent years. Above all, it claims the church should look outward towards the world and live up to what the General Synod has been calling its "missional identity." This involves a commitment to not only spread the word of God, but also to reach out to people in need and, significantly, engage across social divides. Missional according to the DRC implies a celebration of diversity "in yourself, your marriage, your relationships, the broader community, our beautiful rainbow country, globally, and in the whole creation."[15] Congregations are encouraged to look beyond their immediate local concerns and collaborate with people with different backgrounds and beliefs than themselves. Through their variety in worship style, liturgy and traditions, the DRC argues, the communities of the Reformed family can build a better understanding of the entirety of God's grace and love.[16] It is within this diversity, that they can be one with God and with each other. To fortify this argument, church leaders

---

14   *DRC 2007*, Konsultasieboek Kerkhereniging [Consultation Book Church Reunification], 10.

15   *DRC 2013*, General Synod Agenda. 12.7 Raamwerkdokument oor die Missionale Aard en Roeping van die Kerk [Framework document on the Missional Character and Calling of the Church], 204.

16   *DRC 2008*, "Die kerk wat ons wil wees ..." [The church we want to be ...], 11–12 June 2008.

increasingly refer to the content of the disputed *Belhar Confession*.[17] It is said to offer the church a spiritual vocabulary of reconciliation imperative for fostering social cohesion in church and nation. The confession that originated in the black Reformed churches is considered a "truth that can help churches in South Africa with their witness."[18] In rejecting the oppression of the past, it would provide an essential platform from which they can jointly address the inequities of today.

DRC leaders thus urge members to be open-minded and prepare for a reunion with their black and colored brothers and sisters. They however run into heated debates amongst themselves about what such a union should imply for the future of the mother church. Inside the General Synod, fights have evolved over the meaning of diversity in general, the model through which the churches should be integrated, *Belhar* of course, and the reliability of the main partner at stake, URCSA. Tensions run so high at times that DRC leaders fear for a repetition of the bewailed schism in the 1980s when a group of dissidents left to form the pro-apartheid APK.

The debates over diversity are interesting first of all because of the way racial differences among the churches and in society at large have been approached here, or rather avoided. Accepting diversity as a welcome reality has since the early 2000s formed a central tenet of the DRC's unity discourse. It also ties in with the mentioned missional identity and the idea of being an outwardly focused church that engages with the many different backgrounds and worldviews present in South African society. Opinions widely diverge though about the actual inclusion of people with diverging backgrounds in church organizational structures, generating sharp controversies between the so-called morally conservative and more liberal segments in the church. Notably, these controversies revolve around issues of gender and sexuality rather than racial divides.

Illustrative is the Diversity Committee the DRC General Synod installed in 2004. At its inception, the Committee indicated that it was to be above all a platform for raising awareness about the position of women and people with different sexual preferences within the church. In subsequent years, it also came to address racial and cultural differences in the larger church family, but

---

17   Neels Jackson, "NG Kerk wil *Belhar* ter wille van homself insluit" [DRC wants to include *Belhar* for the sake of itself]. *Die Kerkbode*, 2 October 2014. Accessed at 24 November 2014, http://kerkbode.bybelmedia.org.za/2014/10/ng-kerk-wil-belhar-ter-wille-van-homself-insluit/.

18   *WCRC 2012*. Letter from DRC and URCSA management teams and Dr. Jerry Pillay after conversations on 25–27 Februari 2012.

only nominally. Of an eleven-page report from the Committee to the General Synod of 2011, less than one page is devoted to race related questions among the different Reformed churches or in society at large.[19] The other ten pages focus on divides within the DRC regarding gender, homosexuality and interpretation of the Scriptures. They mention staunch antagonism between proponents of a strict Bible interpretation that leaves little room for female or gay clergy, and supporters of a more liberal approach in which the church adapts to ever changing circumstances.

In both groups, racial diversity appears a sideline discussion. It forms but one of the many differences the church needs to deal with. The debate on diversity has been problematized itself, with several key actors lamenting its limited definition.[20] "The only "diversity" that has been noteworthy in the past three years," the late Charles Malan and former moderator of the Diversity Committee stated, "was hence the difference between "us" and women."[21] Even after confessing guilt over apartheid, the DRC according to Malan had done little to put matters of race and racism on the table.

Besides contentious language over whom to include or exclude, the DRC leadership has been scrambling to preserve consistency on how to present the organizational format through which its unity ideal should take shape and the place of *Belhar* within this format. Few agree with the official stance the church adopted years ago to work towards a church alliance including the four Reformed churches with *Belhar* as foundational document. For some, the envisioned alliance appears too vague, where others think even the loosest arrangement between the DRC and the black Reformed churches would impose too much structure on local congregations.

The divisions about the ultimate implementation of church unity present a chief concern for the DRC leadership. Its discourse shows a great deal of fear about members leaving the church entirely once the DRC decides to unite with URCSA, especially while the latter continues to demand the adoption of *Belhar* as precondition. Arguing that such "schism has to be avoided at all cost," the

---

19   *DRC 2011*, General Synod Agenda. Attachment 4. Diversiteitsbestuur [Diversity Committee].

20   See for instance: Cobus van Wyngaard, "The language of diversity in reconstructing whiteness in the Dutch Reformed Church," in R. Drew Smith, William Ackah and Anthony G. Reddie, *Churches, Blackness and Contested Multiculturalism* (New York NY, 2014), 157–170.

21   Charles Malan, "Die NG Kerk se hantering van diversiteit – 'n kritiese bestekopname" [The DRC's approach to diversity – a critical assessment," Internal DRC discussion document, Pretoria, 2010.

General Synod of 2004 adopted the "Ruim Huis" [open house] principle.[22] In general, it pleaded for an attitude of tolerance towards different points of view inside the DRC and in the broader church family. More specifically, the open house principle served to bolster a proposal made at the same Synod to make the *Belhar Confession* optional. This implied the possibility for ministers and members to refuse its acceptance on an individual basis. In a similar trend, the DRC has issued compromising language on an actual merger between the four Reformed churches, prioritizing spontaneous collaborations, or the previously mentioned "joint projects," over formal commitment and suggesting an additional synod with limited powers to be added to the existing ones instead of one integrated general synod at the head of a future reunited church.[23]

Part of the contention here is, as numerous church leadership sources display, the insecurity regarding DRC members' readiness for a future unity. This emerges in unofficial discussions, during meetings of the Moderamen, the church management team, interviews with leaders, and mediation sessions with the World Council of Reformed Churches (WCRC).[24] Throughout these rather informal conversations, DRC leaders stress the importance of finding internal consensus first in order to avoid an exodus of members at the time of an actual church fusion. Regular references are made to the 2007 Consultation[25] that showed severe resistance among church members to the idea of one united church with *Belhar* in its confessional base. In response to the Consultation, DRC leaders have proposed offering multiple alternatives for members to choose from so as to take away their concerns that unity is imposed from the top.[26] These include amongst others more time for a decision on *Belhar* and a looser alliance, at least to begin with. The DRC has asked both the World Council and URCSA to be considerate of the political sensitivities surrounding Belhar.[27] It would be associated with an era most members do not want to be reminded of. Rather than finding a way to adopt the confession directly, the DRC has called on the black Reformed churches for help in guiding its members towards a better appreciation of *Belhar's* content. The church has often stressed its "sentimental value" for URCSA, but with the immediate caveat that

---

22   *DRC 2004*, General Synod Decisions, 2–3.

23   See especially *DRC 2008*, Besluite van die uitgebreide moderamen oor kerkhereniging.

24   The mediation commenced in 2009 after negotiations with URCSA broke down and have continued up until today. They involve talks with the WCRC (or WARC prior to 2010) alone and together with URCSA about the challenges as well as possibilities for a joint future.

25   See section 2.2.

26   *DRC 2008*, Moderamenvergadering. [Meeting of the Moderamen], 17–18 March 2008.

27   See for instance: *WARC 2009*, Notas van die gesprek tussen die NG Kerk, WARC en die VGK-SA [Minutes of the conversation between the DRC, WARC and the URCSA], 6 March 2009.

DRC members bear equally sentimental anxieties about *Belhar* due to the political context in which it was written.

Finally, leaders inside the DRC have been raising doubts in their internal communication about the main family member it wishes to include in a new church association. Behind closed doors, URCSA is often referred to as a capricious partner, unprepared for an actual integration process and coercive in its effort to get other churches to adopt *Belhar*. The sense of coercion is especially delicate. The former moderator of the DRC General Synod, Piet Strauss, emphasized the voluntary nature of confessions and accuses URCSA of undermining this principle by making *Belhar* a condition for further negotiations.[28] With such a harsh condition, URCSA would moreover make it very difficult to come to an agreement. This has made DRC leaders like Strauss wonder how committed their partner really is to turn the talks into a success. The persistent conflict between URCSA and the DRCA and the ensuing tensions among the former's black and colored congregations have stirred questions about how serious a "uniting" church can be about the unification process when it fails to reconcile its own communities.

Deep frustrations in this respect also emerge towards procedural aspects of the two churches' unity trajectory. During internal debates, DRC leaders quarrel about the misinterpretation of its proposal for an optional *Belhar Confession* during unity talks. This was never meant to be a final resolution as URCSA claimed it to be. Much of the conflict that followed URCSA's 2008 Moratorium, DRC leaders attribute to the churches' divergent leadership styles. In the black churches' hierarchical culture, statements during joint meetings are said to be taken far more seriously than in the consensus approach characterizing the white church. The latter tends to move proposals back and forth multiple times between national leaders, regional synods and local councils before they are finalized, where URCSA leaders would be used to enforce their decisions from the top down. Not everyone appreciates the DRC's consensus style. Coenie Burger, also a former moderator of the General Synod, signaled the difficulty it causes in terms of efficiency and clarity towards members as well as the other churches in the family.[29] Until this approach changes however, Burger along with many of his colleagues expect continued disputes with their peers at URCSA about how to advance the churches' fragile unity agreements.

Despite the many reservations, church unity remains a vital element of the DRC leaderships' outward and internal discourse to revamp its identity from

---

28   Interview, Piet Strauss, 11 April 2014.

29   Interview, Coenie Burger, 12 March and 18 February 2014.

an Afrikaner bastion to an inclusive institution at the heart of society. Merging with the black Reformed churches constitutes the perhaps most tangible expression of this identity. Significantly, it is supposed to help the DRC fulfill the divine task it has set itself of spreading the gospel on the African continent. Church leaders have been reiterating these arguments for over two decades now, typically without much reference to the apartheid past or Afrikaner nationalism they seek to dispose of. Instead, focus tends to be given to a broad spiritual rationale involving Jesus Christ's message of reconciliation. Equally important appears the church's responsibility to help foster cohesion among different people by actively bringing them together in worship. As such, the vision of unity in diversity has triggered reflections that were long considered impossible, about what it really means to be an open church in contemporary South Africa.

Much of the debate inside the church leadership however, centers on internal cohesion and displays what Van Dijk calls a strong level of in-group favoritism.[30] Ultimately, the church gives priority to the interests of its own white Afrikaans-speaking constituency. It tries everything to maintain this membership basis and convince diverging voices within the church to accept each other's presence. As part of the "open house" principle, DRC supporters of *Belhar* are asked to give space to opponents to refuse the confession as individuals. Those favoring a more conservative approach towards homosexuality in the church are asked to be tolerant and engage with "the other" in their families.

Values of inclusiveness and tolerance are hence primarily called for to ward off frictions inside the DRC and far less to interact with different racial communities, let alone integrate with URCSA. The latter is often presented in stereotypical terms as an autocratic and difficult partner. Instead of furthering an agreement between the two churches, DRC leaders have made their talks subordinate to membership consensus. On every step of the way, members need to be involved in the decision-making. This has allowed for an impasse in which DRC leaders might employ ambitious language about the need for a united and diverse church, but put the brakes on its implementation as they wait for their constituents to come along. For all its high minded discourse and Scriptural references, the DRC's practical concerns about internal polarization retain precedence over family unity, inhibiting the church from translating its Biblical imperative into concrete action.

---

30   Teun van Dijk, "The reality of racism." *Festschrift für die Wirklichkeit* VS Verlag für Sozialwissenschaften, (2000): 211–225; Wodak and Dijk, *Racism at the Top*, 213.

3.2.2   *URCSA between Devotion and Distrust*

Building up to the formation of URCSA in 1994, the two merging churches had a clear common cause: to prove their break with the existing apartheid system by establishing one church that united communities across racial boundaries. As Nelson Mandela's South Africa took shape, URCSA was poised to find itself a new cause to identify with. The former DRCA and DRMC congregations turned out to have little in common though, besides the old fight against apartheid, as illustrated by the court cases that soon followed. During the former regime, both had struggled to form their own church cultures independent from the DRC and both had remained closely tied to the mother church. URCSA would have to show its autonomy from the DRC as well as bridge the different traditions the black Reformed churches had built for themselves. The *Belhar Confession* emerged in this context as the cornerstone of URCSA's identity in a post-apartheid South Africa. Above all, URCSA emphasized *Belhar's* message of unity among the Reformed churches. How this should be accomplished however remains a matter of controversy. Inside the uniting church, heated debates take place about how to proceed with the DRC. To what extent does URCSA's understanding of the unification process differ from that of the DRC and which constraints has it encountered?

Compared to the DRC, URCSA's formal discourse on unity is less elaborate. Agendas and reports by URCSA's General Synod Committee, the equivalent of the DRC's General Synod, include abundant mentioning of the general value of church unity, but in an almost taken for granted way. If further explanation is offered, it is usually through the *Belhar Confession*. URCSA's Strategic Plan for 2010–2016 includes a lengthy quotation from the confession to describe how it understands unity in the church's core vision.[31] Elsewhere, URCSA leaders merely reference *Belhar* and its three major themes of unity, reconciliation and justice. Their language reveals a strongly faith-based rationale. Reiterating *Belhar's* claim that separation of people is sinful, URCSA emphasizes that God wants the churches to be visibly united and that Christ has already shown the way in bringing people together and fostering reconciliation. On the point of family unification, the General Synod Committee states, "our own integrity and faithfulness are at stake."[32] URCSA is called specifically to live up to God's standard of unity.[33]

---

31   *URCSA 2012*, Sixth General Synod Acta. Strategic Plan 2010–2016, 9–10.

32   URCSA General Synod Committee 2005. Resolutions Church Unity, in *URCSA 2012*, Compilation of Documents on Church Reunification: Process Between URCSA and DRC 2004–2012. Edition July 2012, 7.

33   *URCSA 2004*, Decision on DRC General Synod 2004.

The sense of calling is important. As we saw earlier in the DRC, URCSA also puts itself in a special position towards Southern Africa. It is here that the church has a mission to bring the gospel and act as an example of Jesus Christ's message of love and healing. The past plays a central role in this argument. Recognizing the DRC's support for the atrocities of the previous regime and the relative silence from the black Reformed churches during much of the apartheid era, URCSA leaders state it is their responsibility to now become a model of integration that will help overcome South Africa's divisions.[34] They used to be one before the sin of segregation took hold of the Reformed churches. Now they have to be together again to display their belief in Christ who broke down the walls between people and between people and God.[35] Once more, the *Belhar Confession* returns here as reinforcement. URCSA communities owe it to God and their country to implement the confession they adopted and should do so in concrete ways. Rejecting an unjust ideology of the past is not enough. The churches have to work actively to overcome social and political injustices today. To do so with credibility demands unity of the entire Reformed church family. "The church is inherently inclusive or would otherwise come to annul its calling."[36]

URCSA thus presents in its discourse the structural unification of the family of Reformed churches as the only way through which the church can answer God's call. At the core is an organic unity arrangement that includes all four churches deriving from the Dutch Reformed tradition and that is based on Presbyterian principles. It entails a united church with one general synod and locally distinct congregations that actively work towards their ultimate racial integration. URCSA starkly contrasts this organic structure to DRC proposals for a loose federation of individual churches with each their own leadership bodies. Such an arrangement would not merely reaffirm the racial divisions still present among the Reformed churches. It signals, in URCSA's view, the DRC's historic reluctance to partner with the black Reformed churches on equal terms. As such, the DRC's proposal would fundamentally imply a return to apartheid practices.

---

34   Mary-Anne Plaatjies van Huffel, "Twenty years of unity talks. The journey towards the merger of the Dutch Reformed Family." Article submitted for publication in *URCSA News*, March 2014.

35   *URCSA 2006*, Moderator's Address to Joint DRC Family General Synodical Commissions, 6–8 November 2006.

36   Pieter Grove, *Groeteboodskap aan NGK Wes en Suidkaap Sinode* [Greeting message to DRC West and Southern Cape Synod], 7 May 2015.

While emphasizing this visible and organic unity, URCSA does make a point of creating space for different expressions inside the church. Congregations are encouraged to seek integration but simultaneously assured that they can preserve their own traditions when it comes to for instance singing, worship language or costume. This appears reminiscent of the DRC's focus on internal diversity. Still, where the DRC stresses the need to listen to such differences by allowing ample congregational autonomy and members' consent, URCSA rather highlights the need for firmly established core teachings and principles that are the same for everyone. The basis for organic unity is a "home with enough space, with freedom for people to be different from one another, provided everyone eats from the same pot in the kitchen."[37]

Eating from the same pot or not, URCSA is no stranger to vast internal conflict. Recent years have seen increasing support for family unification within the church's national management team. But further down the hierarchy, regional synod leaders and representatives from local church councils have been challenging this position as they put large question marks over the trustworthiness of the DRC as unity partner. These disagreements become apparent in URCSA's General Synod Committee documents and official statements towards its church base. They repeat the firm belief in unity and inform members about positive developments in the contact between the two churches.[38] Such statements are quickly followed though by a host of concerns about the DRC. Key among them is the sense that the DRC lacks dedication to the process and that it willfully seeks to obstruct integration. The 2008 moratorium decision, which was disseminated broadly among URCSA congregations, referred to the DRC's wavering on *Belhar* and its suggestion for a federal rather than an organic model as clear indication that the old mother church was not yet ready for unity.[39] A church that took "unity so lightly" was, as URCSA's moderator of that moment, Thias Kgatla described it in *URCSA News*, "not ready to obey God."[40]

Above all, URCSA's internal divisions play out in debates around *Belhar*. The question on whether or not the Confession forms a prerequisite for unity has been a source of contention throughout the past two decades. Since URCSA made this demand and almost immediately withdrew it in the mid-nineties, its

---

37   *URCSA 2008*, General Synod Committee Decisions. Decision 24.

38   See for instance: *URCSA 2011*, Pastoral letter to URCSA congregations on the decision of the Dutch Reformed Church General Synod's Acceptance of the *Belhar Confession*, 20 October 2011.

39   *URCSA General Synod 2008*, Recommendation.

40   Thias Kgatla, "Where are we with church unity within the DRC family? *URCSA News*, 11 December 2007.

leadership has repeatedly and officially assured the DRC that it does not expect anyone to accept *Belhar*. Its adoption cannot be coerced and should always be a matter of free will. In an internal discussion the General Synod Committee observed that "... we could make too much of *Belhar*, making it into an imposition on the members of sister churches. That would be in conflict with the nature of a confession as a voluntary, Spirit-induced stand that a person takes in the midst of a community of faith."[41] URCSA has therefore asked its family members to find a way to include the confession in their doctrinal base without necessarily adopting it.[42] While the church does not explicate what such inclusion then should entail, it emphasizes this request as non-negotiable for the continuation of unity talks. The result has been great confusion. By referring to *Belhar* in terms of non-negotiability, URCSA creates the impression that coercion is after all applied to the unification process. Of little help are its haphazard and often contradictory statements on the matter. After the DRC requested a joint study of the confession at a 2009 mediation session for instance, URCSA responded with its own request that the DRC should still work towards a full acceptance of *Belhar* and not merely "assess the possibility."[43] Beyond confusion, such statements have stirred deep indignation across the church family about a unification process that is already complex and that should not be made dependable on a contested confession.

Underneath URCSA's mixed messages regarding *Belhar*, lingers profound suspicion of the DRC as a conversation partner. This emerged particularly in the church's early mediation sessions with the World Council of Reformed Churches.[44] In these sessions, URCSA leaders asserted that the DRC was never really interested in structural collaboration and had been intentionally delaying the talks. They perceived a pattern throughout the church's history of seeking to substitute halfhearted arrangements like the Federal Council for true unity. Still allowing the churches to maintain their separate leadership bodies, the Council enhanced rather than changed the segregated status quo. Also the DRC's emphasis on joint interracial projects has according to URCSA formed a mere technique to frustrate unification rather than expand it. It would divert attention away from the official process and towards low-impact

---

41　　URCSA *General Synod 2008*, Executive Report. Point 7.d.

42　　DRCA 2009, General Synod Attachment 1:The discussion between the DRCA and URCSA concerning *Belhar Confession*.

43　　URCSA 2009, Minutes of a meeting held with WARC, 4- 6 March 2009.

44　　See for instance URCSA 2009, Minutes of a meeting held with WARC; and WARC 2009, WARC Fasilitering/Mediasie NG Kerk en VGKSA [WARC Facilitation/Mediation DRC and URCSA], 14–15 October 2009.

and paternalistic exchanges. Presenting the joint projects as interracial cooperation would moreover enable the DRC to claim it has overcome racial prejudice without making any actual commitment. The refusal to accept *Belhar* constitutes for URCSA the ultimate proof that the DRC does not want to unite with people of color. After all, *Belhar* requests churches to put into practice its principles of unity, justice and reconciliation. Central to URCSA's language about the DRC here is the notion that the old mother church should first replace its apartheid mindset with *Belhar's* principles in word and deed before either church moves ahead with unification. As Thias Kgatla conveyed in a speech in front of the WARC: "The DRC needs space to think about its racist attitude but never rushed into unity prematurely."[45]

Running through the discourse of URCSA leaders are, besides concerns about the DRC, qualms over their own communities' preparedness for unity. Two recent moderators, Thias Kgatla and Marie-Anne Plaatjies Van Huffel, have both addressed the problem of racism among URCSA members. Congregations still struggle, according to Kgatla, to cross the color line. Rather than building relationships across former DRCA-DRMC divides, they have been wedged in parochial attitudes with an inward focus on their own racial or ethnic community.[46] Plaatjies Van Huffel quoted one of the authors of the *Belhar Confession* in saying that "[r]acism is lurking in all of our hearts" and stresses that all, not merely the DRC, should work to deconstruct it.[47]

URCSA's leadership appears aware that its membership base is hardly more enthusiastic about unity than that of the DRC. The conflict with the DRCA and ensuing court cases have sapped energy from congregations and caused deep cleavages inside the church. The 2010–2016 Strategic Plan mentions inadequate internal unity as the number one threat the church is facing today and warns of further polarization. It also indicates URCSA's overall dearth of resources in this respect. Congregations that can hardly afford to pay their minister, if they even have one, are considered unlikely to engage in projects with other churches, in or outside the Reformed family.[48]

For all the hostility towards the DRC, URCSA's leadership discourse shows some striking parallels with that of the former mother church. Both involve ambitious language about the significance of unity for church and society. Both refer to their faith as primary source of inspiration and perceive a calling from

---

45   URCSA 2009, Minutes of a meeting held with WARC.
46   URCSA 2012, Sixth General Synod Acta. Addendum 1. Outgoing Moderator's Opening Address by Thias Kgatla, 136–144.
47   Plaatjies van Huffel, "Twenty years of unity talks," 6.
48   URCSA 2012, Strategic Plan 2010–2016, 4–5.

God to help heal South Africa's divisions as one integrated church. Similar to the DRC, URCSA struggles with internal critique not so much on this vision but rather on how it should be executed. It is equally concerned about the danger of further polarization inside the church and the threat this implies to its very existence. Contrary to the DRC though, URCSA does not seek to placate these differences. Nor does it put the traditions and viewpoints of local members on a pedestal, as is often the case inside the DRC. Instead, URCSA issues strong statements and expects its members to comply.

In an apparent paradox, URSCA at the same time ensures congregations the protection of their local cultural expressions against domination from any church authority. The combination of a top-down hierarchy with strong congregational autonomy however primarily appears an expression of pragmatic necessity. URCSA does not have a building for its General Synod Secretariat and has hardly been able to raise money for the hundreds of representatives traveling to the next General Synod Committee meeting. The lack of resources significantly impedes communication between national leaders and local church actors, making it harder to inform the latter about the unity talks, let alone involve them in the decision making process. Conversely, national leaders can barely spare time or resources to supervise what is happening within congregations. They have little choice but to allow the preservation of still largely segregated communal church cultures.

URCSA's internal divides are hence less about particular issues on which members disagree and more about its larger identity. This counts for another key contrast with the DRC. While the latter has been going through an intensive rebranding process, it can still fall back on a long-standing and recognizable church identity rooted in a relatively homogeneous white Afrikaans speaking community. URCSA on the other hand wrestles with a constituency as heterogeneous as the South African society at large. It serves communities in eleven languages across the various population groups. URCSA is thus, more than the DRC, familiar with negotiating multiple affiliations under one umbrella organization. The church constantly has to balance between the specific identities these groups seek to reenact mostly through religious ritual, and ensuring their shared connection with the larger URCSA institution. Vast ethnic and cultural differences make this almost impossible, but not entirely. The discourse on church unity has enabled URCSA to consolidate a common sense of belonging to a church that links its communities through past and present concerns. It places *Belhar*, the struggle against apartheid and current injustices deriving from this era above differences in worship, socio-cultural values and liturgy. The church was established with the belief in integration, and the fulfillment of this belief forms the chief mission for everyone.

Whereas the notion of unity is reiterated over and again, relatively little is said about why the church should partner with the DRC specifically. Here lies a crucial inconsistency in URCSA's unity discourse. It speaks of the need to integrate black and colored communities in the church and of the significance of a formal arrangement with the white church. The idea of URCSA's black and colored congregations merging with DRC ones is however barely encouraged in practice. Apart from some broad references to the churches' family ties and the need for grassroots unity initiatives, URCSA's discourse on the DRC tends to be disparaging and intransigent. It comprises a perception of the white church as the bully of the past with little eye for any changes it might have made in recent years.

Notable in this respect is that the church barely speaks of "re-unification." In a 2006 address to the other three churches, URCSA presented its desire to reunite so as to return to the situation before 1857 when the family was one.[49] But most other documents talk about "unification," or perhaps alternate between the two terms. It signals the sense of inequality through which URCSA perceives its relationship with the DRC from the very beginning. It also flags the gap between URCSA's spiritually induced ideals and its historic skepticism of the DRC. Leaders pride their record of uniting the Reformed churches. But when it comes to actual integration, many struggle to muster enough devotion to overcome their deep distrust of the white church in everyday life. The ambivalence at play here ultimately returns in the disparate measures URCSA uses when it weighs relationships among its own black and colored members against those with the DRC. For the former, integration has top priority and race is dismissed as a factor of importance. For the white church however, integration is conditional and racial divisions underscored as an unfortunate but highly present reality that makes the cause of family unity all but impossible.

3.2.3　Two Churches Inching towards Unity

The mutual suspicions discussed above have not prevented church leaders from jointly demonstrating their fervent resolve to merge into one new institution. Since talks recommenced in 2006, a steady flow of official statements has been disseminated among URCSA and DRC members. They are signed by leaders from both sides and outline spirited motives for a new Reformed Church identity in unity. These statements display a gradual transition over the past decade from an almost entirely faith-based rationale towards an increasingly pragmatic framework of the required steps to be taken. What they

---

49　URCSA 2006, Moderator's Address to Joint DRC Family, 5

barely show are the tough preceding discussions. Pivotal in this respect are the WARC/WCRC mediation sessions and a number of letter exchanges through which the churches have been debating their convoluted relationship. What narratives emerge here and how do they shape the unity conversation?

The previous section already indicated several common fundamentals on which the two churches have built their vision for a united future. Primary among them are the shared belief in God's wish for unity and the sense of a divine calling to carry out this wish on the African continent. As the churches re-launched their unity talks in 2006, they jointly bolstered these fundamentals with an even more powerful religious language than they had been employing individually. The first time leaders from both churches met at Esselenpark, they declared that the churches were not merely trying to integrate their organizations to adhere to Christian values of unity and reconciliation. They claimed they entered a deeply spiritual covenant together. It is a covenant for the reunification of the church family, "not from our own will or under pressure from social and political processes, but because we believe that the Lord ... requires this of us."[50]

Likening this covenant to the one between God and the people of Israel, URCSA in a separate statement stressed the mutual obligations it implied for both parties, which the church intends to "honor at all costs."[51] For the DRC, the covenant language signaled to its membership a break with the political context that long overshadowed unity attempts. The church was not coerced into this process by external forces that sought proof of the DRC's departure from apartheid, but pursued unity voluntarily and on the sole basis of faith. Rather than lingering in the past, the covenant language displayed a sense of urgency. The churches both emphasized that their unity was meant to make a difference in Africa today. Setting out a timespan of three years, they committed themselves to a new reunited church in which the various communities would work together to resolve their problems, rather than each by themselves.[52] Within two years however, the covenant had broken down dramatically. After the 2008 moratorium it took the churches another four years to pick up the thread. By the time URCSA lifted its ban on national unity talks in 2012, the churches had replaced much of their religious language with a highly practical discussion on the what and how of a future merger.

---

50   *Esselenpark Declaration*, 2006.

51   *URCSA 2006*, Moderator's Address to Joint DRC Family, 3.

52   *Achterberg Declaration*, Signed by delagates from the DRC, URCSA, DRCA and RCA, 6–8 November 2006.

What drove the churches towards this pragmatic approach becomes clear when we take a closer look at the conversations taking place between the DRC and URCSA since Esselenpark. Key here is first of all the contradictions emerging in the ambitious covenant language. Even as the churches were alleging their conviction in God's calling to unite, they already stressed the pertinence of protecting each community's individual identity. At the meeting at Achterberg, both URCSA and the DRC vowed to protect their communities' distinct cultural riches in whatever church structure they would end up with by allowing them to maintain their own language, customs and traditions.[53] Ensuing agreements have continued to describe the congregation as the ultimate expression of the church in a local context.[54] Unity could not be imposed on congregations but should engage them in an inclusive bottom-up process. How the churches intended to balance their communities' diversity with the desired integration into one organic unity model was rarely elaborated.

This brings us to a second and perhaps most significant problem in the churches' joint unity discourses. Beneath the spirited talk of reconciliation in the name of Christ one discerns a thorough skepticism on both sides regarding the feasibility of an actual merger. It builds on antagonistic narratives of the churches' approach to past and present racial divisions. Behind closed doors, in discussions with the World Council of Reformed Churches and through abrasive letter exchanges, URCSA and the DRC have each in their own way stated apartheid as a persistent barrier to accomplishing the future partnership their faith calls them to. One question appears particularly tenacious here. Has the DRC truly moved beyond its segregation doctrine? URCSA tends to doubt this. In mediation sessions with the World Council of Reformed Churches it has on multiple occasions presented its everyday confrontation with racism in the white church. As an URCSA representative exclaimed during one of the sessions: "[they] think we are beggars ... No more!"[55] The few non-whites that have come to attend DRC congregations in recent years would according to URCSA involve mostly domestic workers of wealthier white church members. They still worship at separate times than their white employers, during services specially set up for them in their own language. Rarely are these black and colored churchgoers seen to rise to leadership positions in local DRC councils, let alone in regional or national synods. All this is considered to be indicative of the underlying resistance in the DRC to perceiving all believers, across different races and ethnicities, as equal.

---

53   *Achterberg Declaration*, 2006.

54   *Memorandum of Understanding Between URCSA and DRC*, 2013.

55   *WARC 2009*, WARC Fasilitering/Mediasie NG Kerk en VGKSA, 2.

A 2008 exchange about membership to the All African Church Council (AACC) further underscored the above argument. The DRC had asked URCSA to formally recommend it to join the Council. In two scourging letters URCSA explained its reluctance to do so. It is a "painful exercise," the church management wrote, "to describe the DRC's continued defense of apartheid ... even in the democratic South Africa."[56] A church so obsessed with the interests of its white constituency, URCSA asserted, would be unfit for membership in an all-African church council. The DRC was said to consistently hamper the possibility of integrating with its black and colored partners by opposing *Belhar* or awaiting the full approval of constituents who will likely refuse this. Also DRC efforts to include the other two black Reformed churches in the unity talks were mentioned in this respect. Considering the ongoing court cases with the DRCA, URCSA stated that the DRC could have known how disruptive it would be to try to include this church in the unity talks at this time. Significantly, the letters stated that the DRC was not ready to join an interracial alliance because it never fulfilled the requirements the World Alliance of Reformed Churches[57] made for re-admitting the church in the nineties after it had withdrawn DRC membership due to its involvement in the apartheid regime. The requirements encompassed church unification and the inclusion of *Belhar* in its doctrinal base, both as litmus tests for the DRC's departure from the old doctrine of racial inequality. The lack of any tangible accomplishment in either proved to URCSA that the DRC remained stuck in a past it never completely acknowledged. At the time of the letter exchange URCSA however left out of the equation that the DRC was in fact readmitted to the Alliance.

The DRC's response to these charges shows a quite different narrative. It reacted to the letters exchange with disappointment, if not indignation. How could URCSA claim the DRC still defended apartheid when the WARC it referred to fully vindicated the church over ten years ago?[58] The DRC was allowed back into the Alliance in 1998 because it had demonstrated serious engagement with the unity process. The Alliance never required the acceptance of the *Belhar Confession*, but rather an affirmation of the *status confessionis* and a sound rejection of apartheid ideology, to which the DRC obliged. Beyond

---

56   *URCSA 2008*, Letter to DRC on Application for Membership of the AACC and Related Matters; *DRC 2008*, Letter to URCSA on Application Membership AACC, 4 August 2008.

57   The World Alliance of Reformed Churches merged in 2006 into the World Communion of Reformed Churches, the same institute that has been facilitating mediation sessions between the DRC and URCSA on the unification process. Early mediation documents still refer to the Commission's old name and abbreviation, the WARC.

58   *DRC 2008*, Letter to URCSA on Application Membership AACC.

these technicalities, the DRC disagreed with the portrait URCSA had painted of an exclusively white church. This ignored the changes the DRC said it made over the years to become a more diverse place and the actual presence of "persons of color (if we still need to talk about color)" in its church offices and congregations.[59] Particularly congregations in the Free State and Western Transvaal regions were mentioned in the DRC's response to URCSA as serving between 40 to 50% non-white worshippers. Elsewhere, the DRC described this change in more personal terms. It perceived "wonderful energy and positive relationships" between the different churches, as expressed through collaborative social works and other forms of cooperation.[60] "We experience how race barriers disintegrate."

While trying to point out positive developments, DRC leaders have throughout their unity talks with URCSA also indicated distress over the constant referrals to its history, whether by URCSA or others. The association between the church and atrocities of the apartheid regime is often said to be painful for its communities that seek to move on in the new South Africa.[61] Reminiscing about the past not merely inhibits the pursuit of a joint future according to the DRC. It distracts from the challenges facing churches in the present. Rather than racism, congregations should struggle with secularism. It is not a matter of welcoming different people in the sanctuary, but of welcoming anybody at all.

Over the past two decades the DRC has seen a steady decline in numbers. Just in 2012 the church was estimated to have lost over 20,000 members.[62] Those who remain are conflicted about the extent to which they should adapt to a rapidly changing society in which youth want band music where there used to be only organ playing, or women request influence in traditionally male dominated church councils. They confront a difficult social reality of unemployment, crime and deteriorating public services. Families are split up as children emigrate to find work elsewhere. Once flourishing rural congregations can no longer afford their own minister as congregants are leaving for the cities or losing interest in church life in general. Notably, the DRC does recognize in its conversations with URCSA that many of today's problems are connected with the former regime. Against this acknowledgement it however puts forward the

---

59   *DRC 2008*, Letter to URCSA on Application Membership AACC.

60   *DRC 2009*, Submission by the Dutch Reformed Church to the Plenary of October 14–15, 2009 Meeting Between Task Teams of the DRC and URCSA, 8.

61   *DRC 2009*, Minutes of the conversation between the DRC, WARC and the URCSA.

62   J. De Villiers,"NGK-lidmate 20.000 minder in een jaar" [DRC members 20,000 less in a year], *Rapport*. 18 February 2012.

victimhood endured by the DRC's own Afrikaner constituency before 1948. In a 2012 mediation session DRC participants explained how the Anglo-Boer wars and the poverty that followed caused great pain and "determined their [the Afrikaner people] way of doing over the past decades."[63] Ironically, the DRC thus urges everyone to focus on current affairs rather than the past, except when it concerns Afrikaner history and suffering at the hand of the British.

As the churches fail to align their diverging identities and narratives, their unity debates have come to display increasing realism. If the countless meetings and conversations since the first Esselenpark meeting reveal anything, it is the improbability that the churches will anytime soon find consensus on matters of principle. This consensus pretty much stops at the joint belief in a God of unity. It breaks down as soon as the churches enter any conversation about *Belhar* or the proper acknowledgement of the churches' apartheid past and its enduring impact. Recent years hence show a shift in focus towards the more pragmatic aspects of a future church merger. These involve concrete proposals for collaboration, mostly to help elevate South Africa's poor, and secondly, to change the churches' organizational structures and allow for tangible integration.

Regarding the first, it is interesting to note the mounting attention the two churches pay to issues of social justice. Removed from the immediate context of the congregation, this appears a principled matter on which the DRC and URCSA have been able to find relatively neutral common ground. Both agree that their country is plagued by socio-economic inequity, partly as a result of the previous regime's oppression, and partly due to the current government's ineptitude to distribute the country's wealth equally. They also agree these days on the understanding of justice as a restorative process to ensure all South Africans fair treatment in different aspects of life, from work and politics to personal and church relations. URCSA introduced this conception during a WARC mediation session in 2009 after which it has gradually been incorporated into the churches' official unity agenda, culminating in the 2012 Memorandum of Agreement. The Agreement presents restorative justice as a Scriptural duty that the churches should embrace not as a goal in itself, but as a means towards their ultimate goal of reconciliation. It recognizes the persistence of racism and classism in South Africa and finds major reasons for today's injustices in bad leadership, past and present ideologies and power imbalances in society.[64] Above all, the Agreement calls for practical measures to help restore

---

63   Minutes of a Meeting Between the Moderamena of the DRC and URCSA, 23–25 February 2012; *URCSA 2012*, Compilation of Documents on Church Reunification, 52.

64   *Memorandum of Understanding Between URCSA and DRC*, DRC General Synod Agenda 2013, 162–165.

communities. The most tangible proposal here constitutes a church property audit that could enable black and colored congregations to obtain rightful ownership to the buildings that are often still registered under the DRC's name.

The plea for concrete measures then returns in the churches' initiatives for a step-by-step plan to merge their separate structures. A 2013 joint statement tells URCSA and DRC members not to expect any "quick fixes."[65] With all of God's will and authority, the churches no longer believe church unification can happen as swiftly as they thought in 2006. Rather than speaking of covenants, the churches now call for visible actions to show society they are serious about reconciliation. For the DRC, such actions are essential to prove its transparency towards members and its seriousness towards URCSA. With the entrenched distrust of the DRC and few achievements so far to take back to their constituency, URSCA leaders have been equally eager to stress the need for hard results rather than broad spiritual promises. With a detailed Road Map, also in 2013, the two churches outlined their next moves, such as the development of a joint church order or the moment when the first joint general synod will be convened. Finding a solution on *Belhar* also constitutes part of the Road Map. Here the churches however remain stuck. Their practical approach enabled URCSA and the DRC to book some successes in drawing the specifics of a future unity and reaching consensus on the social focus of their collaboration. Thus far however, it has failed to move them beyond their mutual suspicions and conflicting stories of victimhood, of which *Belhar* remains a pivotal symbol.

With the past hovering over the unity talks, the churches' leaderships struggle to build trust. Their discussions tend to be painted in black and white, literally and figuratively. No adoption of *Belhar* means no break with apartheid and hence no church merger. Commitment to unification is measured by the number of black worshippers in white churches and vice versa. Both churches seem to employ narratives of the past to fortify their own group identities and interests, at the cost of a more inclusive sense of belonging. Hammering on apartheid's continuing legacy, URCSA has portrayed itself as the primary and much needed force of resistance to the lingering white supremacy inside the Reformed Church family. The harsh conditions it has set for the unification process help advance this image. URCSA continues the fight for justice and will not let the DRC get away with the past by boasting about integration with a black church. Unity must come at a price, which URCSA has set at the adoption of *Belhar* and concrete restorative justice programs. Until it meets these terms, the DRC retains the image of the old white mother church that

---

65   *Statement by the executives of URCSA and DRC*, 9–10 April 2013.

requires remorse for its past mistakes, rather than of a viable colleague with whom URCSA can build a new church. The DRC challenges this imagery with its own narrative of the past and present. It displays a more complicated history in which apartheid's persecutors used to be victims themselves, who today once more face threats to their identity as a white Afrikaans speaking minority. Church unity in this narrative is not merely about breaking with the past, but about restoring a community and recognizing its constructive role in society. It depicts URCSA as an indispensable yet largely impeding factor towards this goal.

The joint unity discourse hence exhibits critical discrepancies between official statements stressing partnership on the road to a common destiny, and underlying narratives that pit the churches against each other in an enduring battle over the past. Still, the surfacing of such inconsistencies through mediation sessions and letter exchanges seems to have brought the unification process to a more manageable level. Church leaders today are careful about promising a quick resolve and prefer pragmatism to the deeply spiritual but barely feasible ambitions they began with.

3.2.4   *Our Cultural Homes*

The above paragraphs display a leadership discourse fraught with high ambitions as well as deep inconsistencies on the matter of unity. Both URCSA and the DRC go to great lengths to emphasize their belief in the visible integration of their institutions and present this as a cornerstone of their post-apartheid identity. The religious language with which the church family tries to depart from the past however is reminiscent of how the DRC used to justify segregation. Most striking is the "covenant" terminology of the initial unity declarations URCSA and the DRC made in 2006 and 2007. In stating their joint commitment to church unification, neither makes any mention of how this term used to be at the center of the DRC's apartheid theology. Back then, the church claimed there to be a covenant between God and the white Afrikaner nation. Today, it includes black Reformed churches that actively join in the same divine calling the DRC once professed for itself: to bring the gospel to the different peoples of Southern Africa. The churches might no longer be sacralizing a sense of nationhood, nor do they claim the ethnic election myth Smith attributed to the Afrikaner religious-nationalist movement of the early 20th century.[66] Through their unity talks, the DRC as well as URCSA do seem to persist in a profound entanglement between their faith and the specific territory

---

66   Smith, *Chosen Peoples,* 77–85

of South Africa, and between the institutions and the ethnic or racial communities they serve. These affiliations are continuously reaffirmed. It is through their specific religious rituals, texts and music, that the churches assert an essential role in supporting their distinct constituencies, perhaps underneath a spiritual mantle of unity, but still in separate realities.

The general lack of references to the old ideology is remarkable here, especially considering URCSA's sharp critique of the churches' history as segregated ethnic bulwarks. For all their concerns about the lingering racism or ethnic divisions inside the church family, URCSA leaders are surprisingly silent about the religious-nationalist beliefs that used to inform such practices. Together with a small number of critical voices in the DRC, they state every now and then the danger of too close an affiliation with a single group of people. Far more common however is the stipulation that communal identities deserve utmost protection. Both churches throughout the unity process prioritize local culture over a broader sense of belonging. They do so in a way that, intentionally or not, reproduces the racial stereotypes they claim so eager to break with. Both celebrate their own history, as heroes or victims, while dismissing the other as domineering and obtrusive. In doing so, both employ stylistic euphemisms like "local," "culture" and "language" to substitute for the more loaded notions of race or ethnicity. URCSA may discuss internally its problems with crossing the color line between former DRCA and DRMC congregations, just as the DRC has recognized in closed management meetings the overwhelmingly white composition of its members and their general lack of sensitivity towards black neighbors. Neither will explicate this in their public communication though. Rather, leaders seek to reassure constituents their church will always remain their cultural home and will not be pushed to adopt someone else's traditions.

In much of the discourse, diversity is thus prioritized over unity, even though the churches pronounce the compatibility of these terms. Both claim to celebrate difference while striving for integration, but neither broadens this ambition beyond their immediate constituencies. Focus is given to soothing internal differences rather than bridging divides in the larger church family. These divides are being maintained through contrasting narratives in which each portrays the other as opponent rather than equal partner. Through the narratives church leaders on both sides reinforce a rather profane "us versus them" line of thinking that undermines their own spiritual vision of unity. Even so, their repeated call for one new church should not be taken lightly. It returns in conversations across the family and forms the basis from which local church actors have been seeking to forge closer connections between long segregated communities. Significantly, it has stirred debates among church members and theologians moving well beyond their leaders' careful statements and onto the controversial issues the latter seek to avoid.

3.3   Into the Debates

The centrality of the congregation is perhaps one of the few things that most inside the Reformed Church family agree on. General Synod leaders can reform the national church order, coordinate minister education or provide recommendations on how to interpret the main doctrines. But the congregation is an autonomous body that decides about what happens at local level and how their leaders' guidelines will be implemented on the ground. This opens up a broad space for debate. Through an array of social and academic church media, from blogs, Facebook pages and magazines such as *Die Kerkbode* and *URCSA News* to theological journals and seminars, congregants vent their opinions about what occurs at leadership level and beyond. Ministers challenge national efforts to curb their pensions. Meanwhile, theologians offer alternative interpretations of the Reformed confessions vis-à-vis homosexuality and members lament the use of instruments during Sunday service.

At stake here are convoluted perceptions of church and social identity. Debates on music, liturgy or morality often end up with questions, and strong statements, about what the Reformed churches should stand for, to what extent they have adapted to the new South Africa or whether and how they should do more to reconcile its communities. Church unification reoccurs, almost always in association with the *Belhar Confession*, throughout these debates as a central dividing issue. On one side, stand the critics who do not believe that unity between URCSA and the DRC can do much good. The church for them primarily comprises a space in which certain groups can find peace from the rest of society. On the other side, we find fervent supporters of unification and of the idea that the church should engage with the larger society and its diversity.

This section investigates the discourses of these two seemingly opposite camps: the skeptics and the supporters of unity. It assesses their argumentation in formal and informal media outlets as well as in conversations with Reformed theologians, theology students and church leaders.[67] Key to the analysis is to see what has made the stakes of a unified church identity so high

---

67   These informal conversations were conducted during my field research in South Africa in 2012 and 2014. They involved (emerging) church elites speaking about their personal opinions regarding unification and not in the name of the particular church body, e.g. General Synod or theology faculty, they represented. Their conversations and contributions are

inside the Reformed family and what this tells us about the intersections between religion and identity. Why do some perceive unification as a panacea for a broken family and nation, where others fear it could mean the end of their church?

3.3.1   *A Church for the Locals*

"Although we might be part of one family, adult children cannot all stay once again with their families under the same roof."[68] This statement was made by a respondent in the Eastern Cape region to the DRC Consultation in 2007 on unification and *Belhar*. It is emblematic of a sentiment felt strongly across the Reformed churches that they are meant to live separate lives. Support for some form of segregation never fully disappeared in the church family and appears to have grown in recent years as counter reaction to the national unity debates. In this perspective, a merger between URCSA and the DRC is not merely considered unfeasible. It would be disadvantageous to either church, and notably, beyond God's desire for Christians to live together only in spiritual unison. As we saw earlier, church leaders regularly point to their members' skepticism to account for the failing unification process. But who are these members and what motivates their position?

Opposition to unity generally reaches beyond the churches' historic divisions by race, class, region or theology. Critics are found in both black and white congregations, rural and urban, poor and wealthy. They emerge in conservative and liberal church media, in the Free State as well as the Western Cape regions. But background and situation do influence the intensity with which members express their critique and how they form their own and others' identities around it. The most antagonistic voices inside the DRC tend to be white and based in struggling rural areas in the Free State or Transvaal. They describe themselves as bearers of the original DRC identity that is Reformed, socially conservative and white Afrikaans speaking. Their contributions appear in Afrikaans media such as *Die Kerkbode* or *Die Volksblad,* on blogs like *Hier Sta Ek* [Here I stand] or in online discussions on the DRC's official Diversity Forum.[69] Relevant sources also include regional synod meetings and

---

hence analyzed here as part of the popular discourse rather than in relation to the official leadership discourse.

68   Pieterse and Steyn, *Terugvoerverslag*, 20.

69   The Diversity Forum was an online discussion forum started at the official DRC website in 2010. It was deactivated after little more than a year due to personal attacks and removed from the website. Some of the discussion is still available at the conservative website *Glo die Bybel* [Believe the Bible]: http://glodiebybel.co.za/index.php/ngk-diversiteitsforum-m.html. Visited at 4 December 2015.

consultations, especially in the Free State, and Reformed theology articles or books. These often present a broader critique on current directions inside the DRC – whether in terms of church unity, *Belhar*, or interpretation of the Scriptures – that are perceived to undermine its core traditions.[70]

On the other end of the spectrum among black and colored URCSA communities, a quite different profile appears. The most vocal opposition to unity here has long been expressed through the church magazine *URCSA News*.[71] Published and read by only a small number of URCSA members primarily in the Western Cape, the magazine is hardly representative. Yet, its often controversial statements on unity return in informal conversations with URCSA leaders and theologians across the country. That these opinions are rarely written down apart from *URCSA News* publications is an interesting feat in itself. While the lack of established media outlets and resources certainly play a role here, it also signals URCSA's strong identification with the idea of unity. Challenging this idea happens mainly in off-the record discussions or while emphasizing the DRC as the major problem, not unity itself.

This last point is key to almost all critique. Rarely do members question the principle value of unity for their church and for their personal beliefs. In an article posted on the *Hier Sta Ek* blog, a DRC affiliated author begins his attack on URCSA and *Belhar* with the statement that "I am absolutely in favor of church unity."[72] Throughout *URCSA News,* contributors proclaim unification as the ultimate goal that should never be compromised.[73] They employ the same broad religious terminology that emerged in the churches' leadership discourse, including references to a God of unity and Christ's message of reconciliation of all people regardless of color or class. Remarkably though, such notions appear in this context as reasons not to pursue actual integration of the four Reformed churches. Unity in spirit is considered, especially among DRC critics, sufficient

---

70   This position emerges with vehemence in the book *Die Trojaanse Perd in die NG Kerk: Die Kanker van Evolusie en Liberalisme* [The Trojan Horse in the DRC: The Cancer of Evolution and Liberalism. The book was published privately in 2010 by a group of authors, most notably Henrietta Klaassing and Hennie Mouton, and has been heavily debated inside the DRC for its rigid opposition towards evolution theory and homosexuality in the church.

71   Throughout my visit to South Africa in May 2014, URCSA leaders indicated that *URCSA News* was about to be reorganized and that they expected a change in the paper's leadership to result in a more supportive position towards unity. In 2015 it was still unclear how this reorganization would proceed.

72   Piet Theron, "Nooit weer synode toe" [Never return to the synod], *Hier Sta Ek Blog* [Here I stand Blog], 25 June 2013, http://hierstaanek.com/2013/06/30/belhar-instrument-van-eenheid-of-kerkskeuring/.

73   See for instance: "Samewerking" [cooperation] is not unity, says Dr. Daniel Maluleke," *URCSA News*, 21 July 2008, 10.

to obey God's wishes. The Bible makes no mention of the need for a visible unification of all churches that exist in the world, but rather embraces their diversity. It is within this diversity that they are united through their shared belief in Jesus Christ. As followers of the son of God and with their common basis in the Reformed tradition, Piet Strauss argued in *Pilgrimage to Unity*, the DRC and URCSA are already one.[74] The former General Synod leader and professor in theology at the University of the Free State thus expressed a sense of redundancy prevalent among both churches. Many DRC members wonder what an official merger would add to the churches' existing bond as family members and fellow Christians. They do not oppose contact between black and white congregants per se. On the contrary, interracial interaction is strongly encouraged. But it should occur as a result of spontaneous actions from within the community and not because church leaders say so.

The notion of "joint projects" returns here. DRC critics of unification often prioritize small-scale pulpit exchanges or a joint church bazaar[75] over national structures. They claim that the former allow the various church communities to engage with each other while maintaining their distinct identities. Inside URCSA, few mention such joint projects due to the term's negative connotation. It is broadly considered a code for the DRC to resist any formalized alignment with the black Reformed churches while upholding the appearance of interracial collaboration. Nonetheless, URCSA members also doubt the added value of a formal merger. They caution against its legal ramifications and fear a repeat of their church's destructive property conflicts with the DRCA.[76] Again, the overall value of unity remains unquestioned. It should have occurred long ago, immediately after apartheid ended. But when considering the present deadlock, URCSA critics similar to their peers at the DRC, prefer a gradual process that starts at community level. A white and black congregation might pray together in a special joint Pentecost service during the week, but then return to their respective church buildings on Sunday to worship God in the language and style they feel most comfortable with. It is through such grassroots initiatives that the churches express their unity as fellow instruments of God's will

---

74   Reggie Nel and Howard Du Toit (eds.), *Ons Pelgrimstog Na Eenheid / Our Pilgramage to Unity. Conversations on Healing and Reconciliation Within the Dutch Reformed Church Family* (University of Pretoria, 2007), 93–94.

75   A pulpit exchange in this context involves an URCSA and DRC congregation that exchange ministers or join each other's worship services for a number of Sundays. A church bazaar involves a fair usually organized on church property at which members sell small home items or baked goods, often for the benefit of a common public cause.

76   "Re-unification: Judges show the legal way," *URCSA News*, 11 December 2007, 5.

on earth, much more so than through infinite meetings on how to integrate presbyteries and synods.

Resentment towards structural unification furthermore feeds on members' pervasive distrust of their leaderships and what is widely viewed as excessive church bureaucracy. "It is the red-tape that keeps us divided," said a DRC affiliated theology student Stellenbosch University in reference to the unification process.[77] In both the DRC and URCSA, members are increasingly frustrated with the enduring impasse this process appears to be in. The difficulties are partly attributed to clashing personalities and the fixation with church rules and regulations. Above all, however, outrage is directed towards leaders' inability to reach an agreement on the *Belhar Confession*. The constant back and forth on its adoption in a new united church has triggered deep contempt among the churches' constituencies. DRC members wonder why so much energy and money is spent on a doctrine nobody reads or needs. In an extensive discussion on the topic at the church's official Facebook page, a contributor noted: "I think the DRC misses the point - ministers can better visit members than spend so much time on confessions."[78] Others referred to the *Belhar* debates as mere church politics, a way for liberal leaders in wealthy suburbs to divert attention from the real problems rural communities are facing as their churches empty and their traditions fade.[79]

Meanwhile inside URCSA, many complain that leaders fail to understand what is truly needed. The churches should be talking about the meaning of Belhar, not about the form in which it will one day be included in a church order few members are even aware of. According to the Dean of Stellenbosch' Faculty of Theology, Nico Koopman, the confession pertains to URCSA's identity as an autonomous institution with its own dignity.[80] The urge for *Belhar's* adoption relates to a much deeper yearning for recognition of this identity, as well as an ingrained fear of domination by the DRC. *Belhar* also addresses, in Koopman's view, the inequalities that still linger between the churches and their communities. The vast disparities in wealth, education and living circumstances should be the main concern of both churches' leaderships today, whether or not they are working towards official unification.

---

77   Conversation, DRC student Stellenbosch Theology Faculty, 26 March 2014.

78   *NG Kerk [DRC] Facebook Page*, 16 September 2013. https://www.facebook.com/NGKerk/posts/10153427805885001.

79   See for instance: Johannes De Koning, "Om te *Belhar* of nie," *Woord-Skatte Gemyn op Tsumeb Blog* [Mining Word Treasures in Tsumeb Blog], 21 October 2013, http://skattegemynuitgodsewoordintsumeb.blogspot.com/2013/10/om-te-belhar-of-nie.html

80   Conversation, Nico Koopman, 17 February 2014.

The critique that debates about unification and *Belhar* deflect the churches from problems inside and among their communities is pertinent. It emerges in relation to DRC congregations situated in poor rural areas or deteriorating city centers. For them, the church's focus should be on local challenges of crime, unemployment and care for the elderly. We also find it among struggling URCSA communities that rather want their leaders to help pay for ministers and church buildings than travel across the country for unity talks with the DRC. A letter to *URCSA News* utters a member's vexation with the resources spent on such talks, urging the church to "leave the DRC (and church family)" and concentrate on the "neediness and poverty within our congregations."[81]

Inside both churches, emphasis is put on resolving one's own problems before reaching outward. Where property disputes paralyzed URCSA, the DRC has been stuck in debates about social and moral questions. Unification has long been far from a priority. On either side, critics argue that efforts to merge two churches that can barely retain their own members will likely exacerbate internal tensions. Collaborations with the DRC have in the past caused frictions between black and colored URCSA communities when the former would favor certain congregations and for instance provide a black church with more financial support than a neighboring colored one. DRC members in turn expect that engagement with URCSA could result in the departure of entire congregations and even regional synods that do not agree with the latter's demand to include *Belhar* in a future unity agreement. Many also fear that such an agreement will compel them to partner with ailing URCSA communities, generating conflicts in and among both churches about how to evenly distribute the few resources available. In this perspective, an official church merger is not only redundant or a distraction. Unification, ironically, has become associated with potentially lethal polarization. It constitutes a severe threat to the internal solidarity communities say they need to survive in South Africa's hostile environment.

Beyond material loss, church members dread the ultimate demise of their identity. In a united church, DRC participants in a Western Cape Consultation wondered, "will we still hear Afrikaans," or "will the new General Synod force us to sing Xhosa-songs?"[82] Identity tends to be described firstly in terms of language, culture or social values. But contributors to the unity debates do not shy from discussing racial dimensions. On the DRC side, regular references surface

---

81   Zack Mokgoebo, "Los die NG Kerk (familie) uit" [Leave the DRC (family)], *URCSA News*, 12
      December 2008, 10.

82   DRC Western and Southern Cape, *Opsommend Verslag: Konsultasie-vraelyste oor
      Kerkhereniging* [Summarizing Report: Consultation Questions about Church Reunification], 2007.

to the white Afrikaans character of the church. It should be maintained to prevent even the last "Afrikaner-Bastion" from falling.[83]

The unity discourse obtains a politicized quality here. It triggers negative connotations with South Africa's post-apartheid transition and the chaos and insecurity the black majority government would have generated. In *Die Kerkbode* Coenie Burger, a DRC leader generally in favor of unity, recognized that his constituents are fed up with change. "We are all a little bit transformation-tired."[84] Unification presents yet another transition for a community that for the past two decades has experienced a deep sense of bereavement. In the words of Burger: "We have not only had to surrender power (not a bad thing actually!), but we also had to see how many of the things we love and care about were taken away."[85] From this perspective of loss, URCSA tends to be equated with the ANC: another black majority threatening to outnumber and culturally diminish the white minority. URCSA members meanwhile fear having to relinquish their traditions for the sake of racial integration. Many carry with them a deep apprehension of white power, internalized through decades of oppression.[86] The DRC is still considered a strong and wealthy institution that could easily dominate needy black and colored congregations. With little hope of the DRC adapting to their customs, they are concerned about potentially painful concessions they would have to make in the practical implementation of unity. In future integrated structures, URCSA members wonder, would there still be space for key aspects of their church's identity? From the traditionally extensive singing and clapping in black congregations to, evidently, explicit support for the *Belhar Confession*?

The surfacing of racial identities in the above line of unity critique is confusing. Beyond entrenched patterns of prejudice, it conveys the comprehension that church unification touches upon chief concerns regarding the future of South Africa. It is not merely about two churches joining hands, but about the larger process of reconciling the nation's historic divisions. This realization however appears a source of exasperation rather than inspiration. Considering church relations in the context of racial integration, DRC critics argue, puts the church in a volatile position, alongside national leaders who employ the "race

---

83   Pieterse and Steyn, *Terugvoerverslag*, 32

84   C. Burger, "Wat is aan die gebeur met ons? [What is happening with us?], *Die Kerkbode*, 10
       November 2006, 9.

85   Burger, "Wat is aan die gebeur met ons?" 9.

86   The sense of an internalized suspicion of white power comes up in many conversations
       with URCSA theologians and leaders, for instance with Pieter Grove, 5 March 2014; and
       Marie-Anne Plaatjies Van Huffel, 20 February 2014.

card" towards their own political interests.[87] They lament the pressure put on their congregations to unify, and adopt *Belhar* along the way, in order to prove the departure from apartheid. It would capitalize on feelings of guilt, rather than the message of the Bible. It also brings back a past most church members seek to forget. "The DRC is now open for all races - is that not enough?"[88] Its members ask why URCSA wants their church to once again deal with matters of race after it closed this chapter in the 1990's. Racial bias is no longer the issue. Churchgoers say they simply prefer to worship in familiar settings, involving people with similar backgrounds, whether in terms of race, language, upbringing or social-economic position. Blaming today's divisions on racism is beside the point as well as an easy excuse to discard a far more complex reality.

Inside URCSA, we come across another argument towards a similar dejection. Its leaders emphasize the need to look beyond race especially when considering an emerging trend of URCSA members leaving to join DRC churches. These members tend to be coming from middle class, higher educated, Afrikaans speaking colored communities.[89] They gradually blend into suburban white churches that worship in Afrikaans and better match their lifestyles with shorter services and more casual dress than is common in URCSA churches. Racial boundaries might be crossed here, but this is not the kind of integration URCSA envisions. It signifies once again the lingering threat of the former mother church taking control of black and colored communities. Color plays a part, but should always be discussed alongside issues of power and inequality.[90]

The sense of threat reoccurs throughout the Reformed church debates and seems intrinsically linked with how the communities view their past and present position in society. The domination of one group by the other remains a raw nerve. For black and colored communities, apartheid never completely ended, whereas white communities claim increasing discrimination at the hands of the current regime. In either case, the church emerges as a prime site of group protection. It is often romanticized among critics of unification as the one space in an ever changing and confusing society, where they can find continuity and familiarity. In this ideal, the church figures first and foremost as a social body vested in the community it serves. Its main priorities involve

---

87   "Teenstanders van *Belhar* word afgedreig met die rassisme kaart" [Opponents of *Belhar* are threatened with racism card], *Hier Sta Ek Blog,* 23 August 2013, http://hierstaanek. com/2013/08/23/teenstanders-van-belhar-word-afgedreig-met-die-rassisme-kaart/.

88   Pieterse and Steyn, *Terugvoerverslag,* 30.

89   For more on this topic, see sections 4.2 and 4.3.

90   Interviews, Marie-Anne Plaatjies van Huffel, 20 February 2014 and 6 March 2014.

the spiritual, and quite often also physical care of the people in its immediate environment along with the preservation of social order. It is an order mostly conceived of in local context. The church answers to the needs of a particular region, town or neighborhood and reinforces the social bonds and identity of its community. Davies has described the focus on local solidarity as a historical trend among Afrikaners and key to their survival strategy as a group.[91] It also appears in URCSA's discourse. Internal cohesion is valued over engagement with the rest of society. The Biblical imperative of unity is employed here not towards embracing differences, but rather to avoid them.

Beyond this imperative it is remarkable how little religious language occurs among opponents of church unification. They mostly rely on secular rationales to claim boundaries around culture, race, ethnicity and language. These four categories are used interchangeably without any one of them being singled out as major identity marker. If anything, the churches themselves tend to be recognized as the primary indicator of group boundaries. It happens often in combination with another category like race or language, as a way to differentiate for instance between a black Xhosa and an Afrikaans speaking URCSA community. This brings us back to Mitchell's discussion on the "thick fabric" religion provides to an otherwise thin ethnic affiliation. Following the unification critique, this appears the case in both churches as they reiterate the importance of buttressing their communal identities through specific faith traditions, texts and rituals, instead of merging them into one united church. Conversely however, race is mentioned repeatedly as the defining characteristic of the different churches. It is the church identity that remains thin without the distinct customs of the racial communities that attend them. In this narrative, the DRC would no longer be the DRC without the solemn Afrikaans preaching style its white constituency prefers, while URCSA could just as well dissolve into the DRC if it no longer provides a home to the lively songs and healing prayers of its black and colored congregants.

Whereas the above discussion exposes mostly parallels between DRC and URCSA critics of church unification, it should be said that the two groups rarely agree with one another in public. Both present the other as major impediment to the kind of spiritual grassroots unity to which they claim to aspire. Above all, the two sides attribute the strained relationships inside the church family to the other's attitude towards *Belhar*. "If it was not for *Belhar*, we would have long been united," Piet Strauss is known to proclaim.[92]

---

91   Davies, *Afrikaners in the new South Africa*, 99–129.
92   Interview, Piet Strauss, 17 April 2014.

But even without the controversies surrounding the Confession, Strauss expects DRC constituencies to find reasons for keeping unity at bay. A similar sentiment is found among his colleagues at URCSA who, while strongly committed to the basic premises of unification, see few immediate prospects for the project.[93] Even when *Belhar* would be accepted, they are unsure if it would be enough to bring the deeply divided churches closer together. Important to note here is that the various camps represent perhaps crucial but by far not the only dividing lines in the church family. Church actors often dither between multiple views on unity, borrowing from both supportive and critical perspectives to help make sense of their vastly diverging realities.

What nonetheless stands out in this section is the almost unanimous agreement that unity skeptics should not be cast aside as segregationists or proponents of apartheid. Only a very small minority claims to desire a return to the old regime. Most others vouch support for at least the idea of unity, but with strong reservations regarding its implementation through a structural merger of the DRC and URCSA. Their arguments exhibit the profound entwining of religious and theological power with social identity, political and racial power. Opposing unity has become a way through which church members express their position towards post-apartheid South Africa. It presents a deep commitment to the local community as a way to survive amidst enduring insecurity and engrained distrust of national authorities. The churches' search for unity, including a solution for the *Belhar* question, has been made synonymous here with South Africa's problematic transition towards full democracy.

The Confession and its convoluted role in the anti-apartheid struggle provides a discursive instrument through which unity opponents inside the DRC make their case that the churches should not engage themselves in thorny political conflicts and instead focus on members' immediate concerns. URCSA critics also employ the confession as rhetoric weapon, but rather to bolster their claim that seeking unity with a church that refuses to accept the black churches' core confession is a waste of scarce resources and time. All relate the churches' plan to realize a visible union at national level with the country's handling of diversity. Forced integration, whether at school or at work, has for black, white and colored come at the cost of social cohesion within the various population groups without offering a working alternative to ensure safety and trust in society. Until such safety is felt, the churches remain more than ever havens in which communities withdraw from anything associated with

---

93   Conversation, John Letsie, 4 April 2014.

the complex world outside, which at this moment comprises both unification and *Belhar*.

3.3.2 *A Church for the World*

"[I]nstitutional unity is a prerequisite for restoring the legitimacy of the public witness of the churches of the DR family … Practice what you preach!"[94] With his elaborate defense of church unification, Etienne Dawid de Villiers represents a circle of South African Reformed theologians who believe in the absolute necessity of structural unity for the church family's future. Only together, can the Reformed churches sustain their presence and adhere to the gospel's call to foster love and forgiveness on the African continent. The academics are not alone in this belief. They find support in popular church magazines, among ministers and members of middle class churches in the suburbs of the Western Cape, and notably, among a younger DRC and URCSA generation. The profile of unity supporters thus tends to be higher educated, younger, urban and relatively well-off in comparison to the above discussed critics. They also send letters to *Die Kerkbode*, write on blogs such as *Die Ander Kant* [The Other Side], and contribute to Facebook and online discussion forums like *Kerk in Konteks* [Church in Context]. They appear to be a small group, with the same names reoccurring across the various media outlets. Yet, they often belong to existing or future elites and have been central to reinforcing and disseminating the churches' official unity message. Once again, URCSA is conspicuous by its absence in these debates. Its only active media outlet, *URCSA News*, might publish every now and then a leadership essay supporting church unification, but has otherwise remained largely on the opposing side. The informal conversations I conducted with theologians and students as well as local leaders will therefore be of particular importance to obtain a better understanding of the pro-unity rationale inside URCSA.

In both churches, this rationale builds to a large extent on what De Villiers calls the "Reformed approach of transformation."[95] It involves the conviction that God not only creates, but also transforms the world and that he calls the faithful to be instruments in his transformation work. This implies for

---

94   D.E. De Villiers, "The interdependence of public witness and institutional unity in the Dutch Reformed family of churches," *Verbum et Ecclesia* 29 (3) (2008): 741.

95   De Villiers, "The interdependence of public witness," 729–730. De Villiers contrasts the transformation approach with the two-kingdom and sectarian approaches that the author claims are gaining prevalence among DRC members. These two approaches generally stand for a separation between the Biblical realm of ethics and morality, and a public realm of politics, culture and economics, where the transformation approach calls for their integration.

Christian churches and individual Christians a critical responsibility to bear witness to public issues and actively engage with their societies. They should embody their faith by helping achieve God's desire for a just and unified community of believers throughout the world. According to Dirkie Smit, such embodiment entails, in the context of South Africa, living unity, real reconciliation and compassionate justice. To act as public witnesses of God on earth, the churches need to join hands in concrete actions towards diminishing violence, prejudice and oppression. On the theme of unity, Smit bolsters his vision by referring to John Calvin's discussion of baptism and the Lord 's Supper. "How can those who have together been baptized in Christ through the one Spirit live without mutual love and unity? (...) How can we rush forward (like swine, says Calvin) to receive the bread and wine, yet not receive one another..?"[96] His reference to the three central themes of the *Belhar Confession* is no coincidence. Theological reflections in support of unity among the Reformed churches often employ *Belhar* as means of endorsement. Even those resisting the confession's full adoption in the DRC, emphasize its value for the churches' unification process.[97] By outlining concrete ways in which the church can further social cohesion, *Belhar* would offer crucial language for congregations to translate their belief in being tools of God towards practical engagement across social divides. It ties the unification of the Reformed churches to their duty to help heal the nation and take care of its most vulnerable populations. To fulfill this duty, the churches need to be integrated, not just in spirit, but visibly before the eyes of the world. Separately, they lack the resources and above all the credibility to alleviate South Africa's enduring inequalities.

The concern about credibility also surfaces as a distinct argument for unity in non-academic debates. A DRC minister writing in the popular and rather conservative Christian magazine *Juig!* [Praise!] lamented the great animosities between South African communities despite the fact that the vast majority is Christian. "That clearly does not rhyme with expressions in the Bible!"[98] The author urged unity among the churches to prove to themselves and society that they take seriously the gospel's message of justice and peace. As illustration he told the story of two regional DRC and URCSA synods that jointly helped mitigate a labor dispute in the Western Cape. There is more at

---

96   Dirkie Smit, "What does it mean to live in South Africa and to be Reformed?" In Dirkie
      Smit and Robert Vosloo, *Essays on Being Reformed: Collected Essays 3* (Stellenbosch: SUN
      Press, 2009), 253.
97   De Beer, "Die Missionêre Waarde Van Die *Belhar*," 61–63.
98   Johan Kriel, "Waar Vrede Heers" [Where Peace Rules], *Juig!* December 2012, Accessed at 14
      May 2013, http://www.juig.co.za/article.php?id=235.

stake here than the defense of Christian values. For many supporters of unity, enhancing the credibility of the church is a matter of sheer survival. It relates to the growing perception that the status quo of the Reformed church family has become untenable. For twenty consecutive years, the DRC has been losing members. The family as a whole can barely compete with South Africa's wide array of denominations, particularly with the ever expanding charismatic church movement.

Unification hence emerges as a key strategy to prevent the churches from falling into complete obsolescence. It presents a powerful symbolic move towards a closure of the past, and an opportunity to improve the churches' standing in society from a last source of segregation to a model of reconciliation. Beyond symbolism, pro-unity voices highlight the practical benefits of family integration for the communities involved.[99] As one single institution, the two churches will be better equipped to respond to the country's many social ills. Both refer proudly to a 2013 statement DRC and URCSA leaders made with regard to hydraulic fracturing for the exploration of natural gas.[100] It pressured government officials to prohibit this practice by expounding the churches' shared faith-based concern for the environmental risks involved as well as the immediate damage it could inflict on their communities. Unfortunately for this side of the discourse, such initiatives remain rare. The lack of progress after two decades of unity talks has instigated quite some soul searching among the Reformed churches. *Die Kerkbode* and to a lesser extent *URCSA News* offer a relentless flow of articles and letters by members for whom their segregation has become a source of utter embarrassment. "As separate churches," the late Reverend Nico Smit writes in *Die Kerkbode*, "the family of Reformed churches will retain the stigma of an apartheid church."[101] This is especially painful in light of the extensive deliberations the churches have conducted in recent years about their calling to spread Christ's message of reconciliation in South Africa. Other sections of society, from schools to sport clubs, seem to be moving further ahead with this message than the very institutions that claim it intrinsic to their conviction. "If we as believers, the carriers of faith, hope and love, cannot agree with each other, how can we expect non-church people to

---

99   Interview, Frederick Marais, 28 February 2014.

100   *Statement on The Proposed Regulator Framework for Hydrolic Fracturing*. Signed by Dawid Kuyler (URCSA), Kobus Gerber (DRC), Ben du Toit (DRC), Victor Pillay (RCA), 7 November 2013.

101   Nico Smit, "Die kerk wat ons moes wees" [The church that we must be], *Die Kerkbode*, 18 July 2008, 8.

take us seriously?"[102] The churches are not merely losing their credibility. They are losing South Africa's struggle to defeat the past.

For many unity supporters, overcoming the past is equally if not more important than their churches' survival. Unification constitutes an absolute necessity to make amends for the damage the DRC in particular caused the country by legitimating a racist system as the will of God. "Confessions of guilt," URCSA theologian Jaap Durand argues, are but the "symptoms of a disease" if they don't include visible change in the form of one new church association.[103] Years of futile joint projects and ineffective exchanges at local level have turned institutional integration into the only viable path forward. It should happen sooner rather than later, without expecting full consensus. Unity supporters lament their leaders' hesitance and flawed attempts to appease everyone inside the family. Yet, they also wrestle with the thought of unity exacerbating division. On the opinion pages of the Afrikaans newspaper *Beeld*, concerned DRC members debate how to respond to the intensifying animosities between pro- and anti-*Belhar* voices, those for and against unification, liberal and conservative or in the eyes of some, fundamentalist. Should the latter receive special guidance to come to terms with the inevitability of church unity?[104] Or should everyone learn to be more tolerant of differences, regardless of color, politics or income?[105] To what extent is unity about diversity, and what will be the costs of a merger for the various cultures inside each of the Reformed churches?

Especially this last question torments church members in favor of a fusion between the DRC and URCSA. Realizing the bitterness among the churches, many doubt its probability and call for restraint. Their rationale in favor of unity is rarely expressed without stipulations that, ironically, mirror many of the arguments critics have been making against it. One major stipulation pertains to the need to be considerate of church communities' cultural and ethnic

---

102   Nico Jacobs, "Hereniging: kerk verloor geloofwaardigheid" [Reunification: church lost credibility], *Die Kerkbode*, 21 March 2008, 15.

103   Jaap Durand, *Ontluisterde Wereld: Die Afrikaner En Sy Kerk in 'n Veranderende Suid-Afrika* [Degraded World: The Afrikaner and His Church in a Changing South Africa], (Wellington. South Africa: Lux Verbi. 2002), 66.

104   Mynhardt Kok, "Begelei lidmate wat teen hereniging is" [Guide members who resist reunification], *Beeld*, 18 October 2013. Accessed at 20 October 2013, http://www.beeld.com/opinie/2013-10-18-brief-begelei-lidmate-wat-teen-hereniging-is; Daan Cloete, "New people for a new nation! ... And the church?" *URCSA News*, 13 December 2013, 12.

105   Jan Venter, "Skep ruimte vir ander se standpunt" [Create space for other person's point of view], *Beeld*, 3 October 13. Accessed at 20 October 2013, http://www.beeld.com/opinie/2013-10-03-brief-skep-ruimte-vir-ander-se-standpunt.

affiliations, particularly when it comes to language. Illustrative is a 2009 DRC document to encourage intercultural congregations. It showed concern with what is broadly considered the growing sentiment to reinforce Afrikaans as the main, if not sole, language of worship. The church, according to the document, epitomizes for many of its members a final stronghold of the language that once dominated the country, to the extent that some "bluntly refuse to speak any other language."[106] The author urged congregations to be more open-minded but simultaneously stressed the need to be mindful of this sentiment. We find similar emotions inside URCSA. In a public church meeting for Afrikaans speaking URCSA congregations in the Free State, members vehemently defended the right to be served in the mother tongue of their colored community.[107] Barely able to sustain their church buildings or minister salaries, many claimed to fear the Suthu speaking majority in their regional synod taking over their minority churches. Speakers at the meeting expressed careful support for collaboration with Afrikaans speaking DRC communities instead, but under strict conditions that this would not compromise their distinct style of worshipping or decision-making power.

Language is rarely the real issue here. It nonetheless emerges throughout the unity discourse as a well-recognized problem that should be addressed before proceeding with unification. Language here symbolizes, and is continuously related to, other insecurities regarding the perceived debilitation of minority cultures by an increasingly dominant English media, political and education landscape. In the DRC, language debates tend to be entangled above all with discussions about its past and present identity as "volkskerk" for the Afrikaner people. It is an identity that is both recognized and denounced. "We are an Afrikaner church. We cry over this. We confess guilt because of this. We work very hard (at least I hope we do) so that this no longer needs to be true."[108] Cobus van Wyngaard, a young DRC theologian, repeatedly acknowledges on his blog *Die Ander Kant* the "volks" disposition of his church simply due to the fact that the vast majority of its members remain Afrikaans speaking and white. But he refuses to identify with this character and rather perceives himself as member of a broader ecumenical voice in South Africa.

---

106   Andries N.E. Louw, *The management of cultural differences between congregations who are working together,* DRC Synodical Witness Forum, August 2009.

107   Conversation between the URCSA Moderature and representatives of Afrikaans speaking URCSA Congregations in the Free State, Heidedaal South, 1 May 2014.

108   "Die NG Kerk praat saam Afrikaner organisasies?" [The DRC speaks along with Afrikaner organizations?] *Die Ander Kant Blog* [The Other Side Blog], 10 May 2012. http://anderkant. wordpress.com/2012/05/10/die-ng-kerk-praat-saam-afrikaner-organisasies/.

Wyngaard's views find echoes among younger generations across the Reformed family. They feel less Afrikaans or Suthu or Xhosa than their parents and are comfortable speaking English, in and outside the church. Still, they are highly aware that their churches' strong communal and language affiliations will not soon be broken down. Unity for them is on the one hand taken for granted as the future of the church family. In the words of a DRC student at Stellenbosch: "[I]ntegration is the reality of South Africa ... today and tomorrow."[109] With little confidence in the churches' ability to change however, few expect them to merge even in their lifetime. URCSA students I spoke with expressed their strong endorsement of integration at the level of the Stellenbosch Theology Faculty. But they doubted the advantages of such inter-racial and inter-church collaboration for their own congregations. "My priority," one student asserted, "is to make the black church grow, to make it more involved in the broader community ... and involve them in being part of the church."[110]

Pro-unity voices, young and old, often reference congregations' persistent communalism to account for the lack of progress in their cause. The persistent "apartheid state-of-mind" they discern among fellow churchgoers, emerges as another key argument for constraint. Theologian Piet Naudé admonished the DRC General Synod of 2013 during his opening sermon, claiming that "[t]he biggest danger is to think small about God. To put God away in your tradition, your history, your language, your customs, *or for that matter*, your church order."[111] Naudé in the same sermon stressed his vision for a united South African Reformed church "in ten years." Many of his colleagues though, refer to members' supposed narrow-mindedness to advise against setting any deadline on the unification process. DRC as well as URCSA leaders and theologians warn for undercurrents of racism that are impeding unification processes and that they fear will worsen if integration happens too rapidly.

The perceived constraints of language, communalism and resistance to overall change have hence led unity supports to step down their ambitions. Many end up drawing the same conclusion as unity critics: that if any form of unity is desirable, it is best to start small. Instead of great new church structures, unity proponents increasingly lean towards local initiatives with congregations already willing to cooperate on concrete matters. Alternatively, they prefer the intermediate level of the churches' social service programs through which DRC and URCSA members can jointly organize a soup kitchen without necessarily integrating their worship services. Both strategies are

---

109   Interview, DRC student at Stellenbosch Theology Faculty, 2 April 2014.
110   Interview, URCSA student at Stellenbosch Theology Faculty, 3 April 2014.
111   Piet Naudé, *Opening Sermon at the DRC General Synod Meeting 2013*, 6 October 2013.

pointed out for their clear focus on community development in contrast to the general obscurity surrounding national unity talks. The talks are said to be alienating communities, whereas bottom-up collaborations offer an accessible path towards integration bereft of church politics. This message shows up prominently in *Die Kerkbode* and academic or semi-academic publications on the benefits of church unity.[112] They involve examples of a DRC congregation helping out an URCSA community that has been unable to afford a minister, or of joint fundraising festivities or even dialogue sessions about the apartheid past.[113] Different kinds of "good news stories" appear in *URCSA News*. Instead of cooperation, signs of autonomy are celebrated here, such as the congregation of Polokwane that raised its own money for a new church building, or a Western Cape URCSA church taking the initiative to integrate Afrikaans and Xhosa speaking services.[114]

Amidst these diverging stories, DRC and URCSA actors make their support for unity conditional to its implications for communities on the ground. However high the stakes, church unification should not cause further membership decline or aggravate dependency patterns. Although some have called on church leaders to be more forceful in the process, most agree that unity cannot be coerced. The reluctance to deal with social, racial and cultural differences in worship is considered a major reason for people to leave churches that are trying to change their ways.[115] Given the volatile circumstances of Reformed communities across the country, unification might bring more diversity than congregants can handle at the moment.

In an effort to avoid further polarization, unity proponents have in recent years begun to align their agenda with their general synods' broader focus on missional identity. This entails, as we saw in chapter two, the calling to spread the gospel and its message of love and reconciliation in South Africa. It appears a reversal of the initial pro-unity argument that the churches' ability to bear public witness is contingent on their structural unification. Instead, DRC and

---

112   See for instance Nel and Du Toit, *Ons Pelgrimstog Na Eenheid / Our Pilgramage to Unity.* Deel IV. Vandag: Verhale van Eenheid [Part IV. Today: Stories of Unity], 116–147.

113   "NGK en VGK hou saam 'kerkjol' op Groot-Brak" [DRC and URCSA organize church fair together at Groot-Brak], *Die Kerkbode*, 7 November 2008, 3; Attie Nel, "NGK en VGK vat hande" [DRC and URCSA join hands], *Die Kerkbode*, 7 March 2008, 3.

114   "URCSA Polokwane celebrates God' grace," *URCSA News,* 11 December 2007, 2; "Scottsdene shows the way to a truly United Church," *URCSA News*, 28 March 2008, 12.

115   Braam Hanekom, "Moontlike Redes Hoekom Mense die Kerk Verlaat" [Possible Reasons for Why People Leave the Church] *Nuusperspektief Blog* [News Perspective Blog], 17 January 2014. http://www.nuusperspektief.co.za/?p=871. This article refers to research by a DRC General Synod committee on Congregational Development.

URCSA communities should first expand their scope and actively engage with the larger society so that they will be better prepared for an interracial alliance in the future. They should support people in need wherever and whoever they are. Outreach might take place through official church programs or in the form of small group initiatives. It is through such social works, students, ministers and academics from the Western Cape to the Free State hope, that congregants will be exposed to the difficulties of their fellow South Africans and gradually overcome their prejudice. In this view, unification of the Reformed family is considered helpful, but scarcely a purpose in itself.

The mentioned restrictions and their implications exhibit once again the incongruity of the Reformed churches' pro-unification rationale. In popular and academic debates, unity supporters mirror in the churches' leadership discourse. They waver between on the one hand fervent beliefs in its practical and principled necessity, and on the other hand concern for deepening internal divisions as result of a future church merger. Unity supporters seem determined to distance themselves from the skeptics, however, by offering an alternative vision for the church, and the country at large. It is a vision in which the church's primary goal is to serve the world and all its various inhabitants, not just the immediate congregation. Racial and ethnic differences are to be welcomed, not evaded. The vision is carried by an extensive theology based on the Reformed tradition of public witness and transformation. And also here, the *Belhar Confession* serves as a key discursive device, be it this time to boost the notion of visible integration as the only way forward for the Reformed family. In presenting this vision, DRC as well as URCSA unity supporters claim for themselves a moral high ground based on religious belief. Similar to Brewer, Higgins and Teeny's discussion of Bishop Tutu and the TRC, they reiterate the special position of the church as a bearer of truth and justice. From this position it has a social obligation to foster racial integration in the heart of South Africa's communities, for "who else but the church has to give moral guidance?"[116]

Yet, unity supporters simultaneously and perhaps unintentionally, reaffirm major arguments with which skeptics question the attainability of such moral high ground. Especially notable is the reiteration of congregations' supposedly innate communalism. Both camps seem to take their members' attachment to a single racial or ethnic identity for granted and employ it as rationale against an official fusion at this time. Unity supporters will not go as far as the skeptics in warning of the endangerment of distinct community identities. They do

---

116   Malan, "Die NG Kerk se hantering van diversiteit – 'n kritiese bestekopname."

however urge the acknowledgment of so-called identity crises among church members. It is remarkable how frequent terms like Afrikaner, Afrikaans, "volkskerk" and communalism surface in this discourse, often with negative connotations, but with the constant recognition that these remain significant traits of the Reformed church family, above all the DRC. The terms emerge in defense of not pursuing structural unification momentarily. "We are not ready now," is said, without detailing what time and conditions would signal the churches' readiness.

It would do the pro-unity camp injustice to be cast aside as merely inconsistent. They might not have worked out the details. But through a constant deeply devout unity discourse, its supporters have helped create an intellectual climate, at least inside their own churches, that ties Christian credibility to interracial collaboration. This moves beyond the reconciliation paradigm of the 1990s. It calls for not just forgiveness, but brings into the living rooms of ordinary church members a concrete responsibility to cooperate across social divides. While faith is claimed as a major motivator here, it is certainly not the only one. In the end, unity supporters, again just as their critics, are primarily concerned for their churches to survive amidst the stiff competition from other religious and non-religious worldviews. They believe that a fusion of the Reformed family into one multiracial institution will help strengthen its position in South Africa's intricate political and religious landscape. As such, adhering to God's will for unity is as much a means to an end, as it is an end in itself.

3.3.3   *Divided Identities*

The above debates offer an intriguing perspective on the entanglement of religious and social identities within the Reformed churches. The persistent contention over unity and *Belhar* has become a way for members across the church family, and to an extent across racial divides, to draw boundaries between themselves and others, between so-called conservatives and liberals, impoverished farmers and plush academia, those stuck in apartheid and those who moved on. Faith appears at the center, with both critics and supporters claiming the gospel and their Reformed tradition as the basis on which their arguments are built. Paradoxically, the two camps employ almost identical Bible references to argue for quite a different take on the position of the church in society. Both claim their faith in the spiritual unity of the Christian church and in its moral duty to build bridges between people of different backgrounds. Both also pursue roughly the same goal of a continued presence and significance of the Reformed churches in South Africa. For the anti-camp this implies the rejection of any structural arrangement to enforce integration, whereas unity proponents perceive a clear message in favor of such an arrangement.

To understand what then causes this antagonism, it is helpful to return to Lichterman's discussion of religion and civic identity. As in his study of divisions inside a local church alliance in the United States, the clashing discourse on unification in the Reformed family has little to do with diverging principles or interpretations of faith. It appears chiefly about context and identity. Unification supporters often speak from a position of relative comfort and homogeneity in terms of social-economic class. As academics or based at middle-class urban or suburban church communities, many seem eager to fit in the new South Africa and portray themselves as open-minded citizens who have overcome the prejudices of the past. Church unification helps them map this identity. It offers a story of racial integration on their own premises, beyond the country's polemical political landscape. Emphasizing faith as major motive is crucial to avoid association with contentious government initiatives of restorative action or black empowerment. It is also the faith-based identity those on the more liberal spectrum of the Reformed family seek to put forward as part of the change they have made since the end of apartheid towards an inclusive church for everyone.

Conversely, critics of unification tend to view themselves and the church communities on whose behalf they write, in an enduring battle against the direction in which South Africa is heading. They do not want to conform to a rainbow ideal that for many failed to bring the welfare and equality it promised, but rather generated insecurity and chaos. In rallying against a church merger, critics find a way to manifest such sentiments and reinforce their groups' boundaries. They present materially and culturally endangered minorities that need the church as a source of protection and stability rather than a platform for change. It is an identity that is primarily framed in worldly arguments of custom, language and, not seldom, race. If religious rationale is employed, it is to boost internal unity and solidarity through particular church rituals, along with a socially conservative interpretation of the Reformed faith.

Critics and supporters of unity hence not only use different styles to map their identities depending on the contexts from which they discuss a potential fusion between URCSA and the DRC. They also end up with widely diverging perceptions on what these identities imply in everyday life, from one that seeks to relate to the broader society, to a more inwardly focused sense of belonging. Both perceptions, and many in between, have long been present in the church family. They cannot be understood independently from the discussions tearing the churches apart towards the end of the former regime. Questions about the potential benefits or disadvantages of the separation of church communities by group identity are as relevant today as they were in the 1980s and 1990s. The main difference is that all sides generally agree these days on the detrimental effect of the way segregation was enforced during apartheid. Whether separation practices are inherently bad remains for many undecided. A climate of political correctness inhibits contributors to the popular and academic debates to express what many across the Reformed family, and across both camps, will quietly admit in conversations: that in their daily realities, they still prefer to worship in separate churches.

## 3.4	Conclusion

Following the above unity discourse, one wonders whether it comprises a mere cloak for the same old segregated church, or a truly new vision of a transforming institution. It would not be the first time that the Dutch Reformed Church employed an official vocabulary of inclusiveness while inwardly sustaining its position as the Afrikaner "volkskerk." During much of the apartheid period, the church said it aspired to unity with the black Reformed churches, at least spiritually. From the moment it opened its doors to non-white members in the late eighties, the DRC reaffirmed its mission to be a welcoming place for all South Africans. But most of its in-door debates continue to reveal a church highly protective of its white Afrikaans-speaking character and suspicious of outside influences. It emerges implicitly when leaders stress the importance of consensus to avoid a schism in the church's traditional membership base, and explicitly among members urging the preservation of their "Afrikaner bastion." URCSA is problematic in different ways. Unity is intrinsic to its identity, but has been compromised ever since the church's establishment. Discourse by its leadership abounds with hostility towards the other churches URCSA claims to pursue a merger with, chiefly the DRC. Leaders and members often justify the reality of segregation among their own congregations as a consequence of local differences. Meanwhile the church lacks a coherent policy to tend to the many different languages of these local communities, providing documents in either English or Afrikaans if a choice is given at all.

Nevertheless, both churches have for two decades now persisted in a certain ideal of church unification. This in itself presents a significant departure from Smith's discussion of the DRC's religious-nationalist past. Emphasizing the increased effectiveness of a joint interracial institution to act as instruments of God on earth, the unity vision breaks with the long prevalent notion that the Bible urges the separation of different racial communities and their churches. It also undermines the basic premise that the church serves to enhance these communal identities. The church might still be a space where local culture is expressed, but should in the vision of unity proponents, always seek to engage with the broader society. As such, unification not merely comprises an ideal for the future. It evinces a particular understanding of the position of the church and its members in society today as public witnesses of God's wish for justice for all of humanity.

Notable here is furthermore what is not mentioned. No references are made to a chosen nation or the idea of sacrifice for a sacred territory, whether in official, popular or academic debates. What used to uphold the DRC's myth of ethnic election appears to be forgotten or willfully ignored. When one of its pillars, the covenant between Afrikaners and God, does reemerge, it is rephrased towards an almost diametrically opposite goal of forging a joint agreement across different communities, rather than one single people.

Compared to the old apartheid doctrines, today's unity discourse hence seems to present an actual innovation. A key intricacy remains the ongoing discussion within the church family about its practical implementation. Here we find not only a gap between words and deeds, but also between faith and reality, religious rationale and secular interests. Spiritual terms have crucially helped the DRC and URCSA to map the common fundamentals on which to base their future united church. The main document employed here, the *Belhar Confession*, has however evolved into a rhetorical object symbolizing the improbability of unity rather than its potential to resolve the churches' embedded divisions.

This is emblematic for the larger unification discourse. Leaders have despite their increasing pragmatism on this matter continued to use a mostly religious and moral line of argumentation to convince their constituencies of the need, or rather the Biblical imperative, of unity. It pays little attention to the political, racial and social-economic tensions congregations face in their struggle to survive. Highly sensitive to any form of change and lacking details on how this change could benefit them, communities have been turning against unification proposals. Similar to *Belhar*, church unity now epitomizes church polarization. Contributors to popular debates ask what unification, even when done in the name of God, will do about the deterioration of rural and inner-city communities. Especially when the mere idea of unity generates so much friction. How will it prevent a further decline of membership, compensate for the loss of ethnic dignity or language, or help congregations compete with other denominations?

When church leaders do respond to such questions, they often fall back on a largely secular default discourse of community preservation. They emphasize over and again that unity will not undermine the very unique traditions of each individual church and its local congregations. Leaders talk about culture where members allude to racial and ethnic distinctions. Either way, they reaffirm the profound attachments their churches have long claimed to exclusive identity groups. This is often accompanied with mutually stereotypical language. DRC members find the loose style of black and colored congregations incompatible with their own. URCSA warns of the domineering character of the white church. For neither church has the spiritually induced unity discourse been sufficient to disentangle the profound religious-ethnic and racial affiliations at play here. Perversely one could say, it has spawned further divisions within and between the churches.

The intertwining Claire Mitchell and others denote between religious, ethnic and racial identities thus remains a significant element of how South Africa's Reformed churches present themselves, inwardly and outwardly, in favor of, or opposed to unification. Across the board though, the churches agree this does not necessarily impede a sense of belonging that transcends social divisions. The shared belief in Christ along with a deep-seated commitment to the land of South Africa continues to tie the various groups together, whether they like it or not. Significantly, the churches' past appears a source of bonding as much as division. The fact that they have not visibly overcome the legacy of apartheid is painful for everyone. Throughout formal and informal church debates, this reality has instigated intense self-reflection, if not outright self-flagellation. DRC and URCSA communities may vastly disagree about what happened during and after apartheid. They seem to find each other in a discourse of frustration with the status quo, and in the awareness that they can only change it together

Joining in Prayer, but Not in the Pews

Over the past two decades, the Reformed churches have concentrated on moving their institutional discourse and practice away from segregation. The separate reality of most congregations forms a thorn in the side of unity proponents and evidence for many in and outside the Reformed family that it remains unable to put its apartheid past behind. What tends to be overlooked here are the gradual changes happening within church communities on the ground, not necessarily in conjunction with national processes of unification or reconciliation, but rather in response to constantly altering social-economic circumstances as well as broader dynamics of religious change. Church members may resist formal efforts to integrate their home institution, but perceive little problem, or even inspiration, in engaging with other communities in a local soup kitchen or drugs prevention project. At this small scale, interracial contact appears easier than in the churches' general synods. People find common ground in addressing local concerns and in a broad religious language of helping each other in the name of Jesus Christ. As with the churches' changing discourse, problems however arise with such practical unity efforts. Often they rather end up deepening divides if they generate any sustainable change at all.

This chapter analyzes the implementation of the hoped for changes in the Reformed family, and the lack thereof, in the Western Cape, the Free State and through the churches' social works programs in both regions. The provinces were selected since they account for two important and rather opposite developments inside the church family. In the relatively wealthy Western Cape, the DRC and URCSA have been expanding local leadership alliances but with strikingly little involvement of congregations on the ground. The Free State rather represents a survival struggle that has forced church communities on either side of the old color line to consolidate their resources, whether they like it or not. The social works programs finally display a rare example of cross-community partnerships directed towards poverty relief.

In both regions as well as the social works programs, increasing emphasis is put on the need for a grassroots approach to racial integration in the church family. Communities are invited to contribute to the national unification process by furthering contact between different churches and racial or ethnic communities at their own local level. Only very few do so, and even less succeed. The intricacies at play here will be studied on the basis of field studies in five communities, urban and rural, and four social programs. They display stories of intentional transformation and accidental change, strategies and challenges in overcoming entrenched racial, ethnic and social-economic divisions. It is important to note the predominant focus of these stories on white and colored communities. Black Reformed communities have generally remained more secluded and less involved in the churches' transformation process. The fact that there are barely any cases of black and white or even black and colored unity initiatives indicates a crucial void in this process that to this date has received little recognition among the Reformed churches at large.

Overview Congregations and Church Organizations

This table presents an overview of the congregations discussed in this chapter and whether or not integration has taken place on the level of church organization, leadership, worship, exchanges or social works. Included are also the four Reformed church organizations addressed in the section on social programs. The table indicates if any integration takes place (Yes); if there is no significant integration to speak of (No); or if a certain type of integration is not applicable (N/A).

City/town and region	Congregation or organization	Integration in organization/ leadership	Integration in church worship	Pulpit exchanges	Joint social works
Stellenbosch, Western Cape	URCSA Rynse	Yes	No	Yes	Yes
	URCSA Ida's Valley	Yes	No	Yes	Yes
	URCSA Cloetesville	Yes	No	Yes	Yes
	DRC Welgelegen	Yes	No	Yes	Yes
	DRC Moedergemeente	Yes	No	Yes	Yes
Cape Town, Western Cape	URCSA Wynberg[a]	Yes	Yes	Yes	Yes
	DRC Wynberg[a]	Yes	Yes	Yes	Yes

City/town and region	Congregation or organization	Integration in organization/ leadership	Integration in church worship	Pulpit exchanges	Joint social works
Bloemfontein, Free State	URCSA Heatherdale	No	Yes	No	Yes
	DRC De Bloem	No	Yes	No	No
Ladybrand, Free State	DRC Ladybrand Moedergemeente	No	Yes	No	No
Philippolis, Free State	URCSA Bergmanshoogte	Yes	No	No	Yes
	DRC Philippolis	Yes	No	No	Yes
Western Cape	Commission for Witness (CFW)	Yes	N/A	N/A	Yes
	Badisa	Yes	N/A	N/A	Yes
Free State	Partners in Witness	No	N/A	N/A	Yes
	Towers of Hope	No	Yes	No	Yes

ᵃ Situation prior to breakdown in unification process

4.1 Religion, Race and Integration: A Critical Debate

What does it take for faith communities to leave their comfort zones and engage across the social divides their places of worship so often cultivate? And what to make of the interracial or interethnic contact that evolves in such situations? These two questions returned throughout my field research in South Africa in 2012 and 2014. They emerged within DRC and URCSA communities that actively pursued interracial partnerships and among congregations that were forced into collaborations after they could no longer pay the bills independently. Most sought to explain their diverging trajectories through the specific settings in which they had occurred. It was this particular minister or the new demographics of that neighborhood that compelled the churches to alter their ways, or inhibited them to do so.

Many of these stories relate to the changing position of religion we see in societies across the world. The transition from institutional to individual religious experience, and from a single taken for granted truth to a pluralist landscape of religious and secular belief systems has not bypassed South Africa's Reformed churches. On the contrary one could say. The churches appear primary examples of how this transition is affecting the ways in which faith communities are reshaping their religious identities, and subsequently, their social identities.

A critical challenge the DRC and URCSA face is what Hervieu-Léger and Bruce amongst others denote as the weakening of religious authorities in modern society.[1] Churchgoers prefer to develop their own individual relationship with God to observing ancient traditions based on doctrines that bear little affinity with today's fast-paced lives. They tend to focus more than ever on the immediate concerns of their congregation rather than the collective rulings of national church leaders and general synods. Above all, DRC as much as URCSA members have over the past decades been following the trend scholars such as Berger and Casanova call the awareness of choice and change in contemporary religious experience.[2] People who have been born into these churches increasingly recognize the availability of other religious options that are potentially more fitting to their personal needs. They try out different denominations, spiritual workshops or no religion at all. Moreover, they mix and match their experiences into a changing patchwork of worldviews. Many do return to their Reformed tradition, an interesting feat in itself, but with new expectations. They demand vibrant services with English gospel songs, modern Bible classes for children or space for meditation and spiritual reflection. The churches confront the dilemma of adapting to such new demands and lose those members who prefer a more conservative approach, or maintaining the status quo and miss out on new growth opportunities.

This dilemma also affects the churches' approach to questions of racial integration. With their dwindling membership numbers and the devaluation of church authority, DRC and URCSA congregations can no longer afford the exclusive approach to membership they long sustained. Once homogeneously white Afrikaner, black or colored communities are falling apart as the original members leave for other churches or become absent members with little involvement in the community. Partnerships with other churches, including

---

1 Bruce, "Cathedrals to cults," 23; Hervieu-Léger, *Religion As a Chain of Memory*, 167–8.
2 Peter L. Berger and Anton C. Zijderveld, *In Praise of Doubt: How to Have Convictions Without Becoming a Fanatic* (New York: HarperOne/HarperCollins Publishers, 2009); Casanova, "Rethinking Secularization: A Global Comparative Perspective."

those that tend to different racial and ethnic population groups, are deemed necessary to help congregations survive amidst the steep competition of South Africa's pluralist religious landscape. Still, congregations continue to resist such partnerships as they fear the loss of their particular church identities. They dread a takeover by the other party of the communal safe haven their church has always offered. As we will see in the following pages, churches across the Reformed family have been exploring different responses to deal with such dilemmas, from the full merger of congregations with a newly formed multiracial identity to a merely pragmatic agreement to share a minister position with the preservation of each church's own and largely segregated services.

The interactions that emerge through these divergent responses to diversity take us to another line of debate about the changing position of religion in today's increasingly pluralist societies. To what extent should faith communities actively bring together people with different ethnic, racial and national backgrounds, or even with different worldviews or sexual preferences? In the United States, heated debates have emerged in recent years regarding the rise of so-called multiracial or multicultural Christian congregations. They involve congregations in which "no one racial group is 80% or more of the people."[3] These debates are extensive and cannot be done justice within the parameters of this research. Noteworthy however for the South African context are the questions emerging here about the potential of racially diverse congregations to foster social cohesion. Proponents of church unification in the Reformed churches often perceive this potential as a given. While acknowledging the many challenges, DRC and URCSA unity supporters generally assume that the mere increase of interracial contact through the church will help improve relationships between their respective communities in as well as outside of the sanctuary.

Studies of racial diversity in American church life indeed highlight its advantages. Central to the conclusions of for instance De Young, Emerson, Yancey and Chia is the idea that separate churches for the country's various population groups reinforce racial segregation and stratification in society whereas more diverse congregations can help overcome communal tensions.[4] Stephen Warner famously speaks about "the capacity religion has to bridge

---

3   Korie L. Edwards, Brad Christerson and Michael O. Emerson, "Race, Religious Organizations, and Integration," *Annual Review of Sociology* 39, (2013): 213.

4   Curtiss P. DeYoung, Michael O. Emerson, George A. Yancey, and Karen H. K. Chia, *United by Faith: The Multiracial Congregation As an Answer to the Problem of Race* (Oxford: Oxford University Press, 2003).

boundaries, both between communities and individuals" through embodied ritual.[5] Physically sharing meals and music in church would allow people from different backgrounds to bond and build religious solidarity. Scholars such as Yancey and Kim have additionally found that multiracial congregations tend to involve a greater diversity in terms of income and help foster more social-economic solidarity than in homogenous congregations.[6]

Besides these apparent benefits, scholars in the United States have been pointing out significant drawbacks of church integration. Well-known among them is Peter Wagner's argument that diversity can harm the growth of strong internally harmonious congregations.[7] Other scholars emphasize that only very few congregations manage to build and maintain a diverse membership and that their impact remains limited to the individual level. Becker finds in her study of a liberal and conservative multiracial congregation in the United States the tendency to perceive race as primarily an interpersonal problem that can be resolved through more contact and spiritual self-reflection about one's own racist attitudes.[8] Also Emerson and Smith indicate a trend among American Evangelicals to evade difficult discussions about institutionalized discrimination and rather focus on racial reconciliation between individuals. Tranby, Hartman and Edwards take this critique a step further.

Not only are structural forms of racism dismissed in multiracial church-es, they tend to be reinforced through the persistence of a dominant white culture and leadership at the cost of minority groups. According to Edwards, racial integration in the church usually does not move beyond symbolism. African-American or Hispanic churchgoers might be represented through certain emblems in a once chiefly white church, or through special holidays or services in their language. But rarely are they involved in the "more core congregational characteristics, such as the theological orientation, worship service structure, sermonic presentation, and leadership structure."[9] Even when white people comprise a minority in a multiracial church, their styles

---

5   Stephen Warner, "Religion, Boundaries and Bridges," *Sociology of Religion* 58:3, (1997): 217–218

6   George Yancey and Ye Yung Kim, "Racial Diversity, Gender Equality, and SES Diversity in Christian Congregations: Exploring the Connections of Racism, Sexism, and Classism in Multiracial and Nonmultiracial Churches," *Journal for the Scientific Study of Religion* Vol. 47, No. 1 (Mar., 2008): 103–111.

7   C.P. Wagner, *Our Kind of People: The Ethical Dimensions of Church Growth in America* (Atlanta: J. Knox Press, 1979), 150.

8   Penny E. Becker, "Making Inclusive Communities: Congregations and the "problem" of Race," *Social Problems* 45.4 (1998): 470.

9   Korie L. Edwards, "Bring Race to the Center: the Importance of Race in Racially Diverse Religious Organizations," *Journal for the Scientific Study of Religion* 47.1 (2008): 5.

of worship, music and other religious traditions often prevail over those of non-white communities. For Tranby and Hartman, the white predominance in multiracial congregations demands a more critical deliberation of whiteness theories. Especially important in view of these authors is the recognition that American society is still largely organized along the norms of white Anglo-American culture in which whiteness is considered "mainstream" and everything else a deviation from the norm.[10] When in a church setting, groups from non-white backgrounds mix with whites, the former are expected to adapt to the latter rather than the other way round.[11] Church integration in these cases not merely conforms to the existing situation of white dominance in the country according to Tranby, Hartman and Edwards. It runs the risk of fortifying racial hierarchies and deepening divides between different population groups.

The above criticisms on multiracial churches in the United States are rare in the context of South Africa's Reformed churches, but not completely absent. Research about the topic is limited to isolated case studies with little consideration of broader church unity or racial reconciliation processes. During my conversations however, Reformed leaders and theologians regularly noted the importance of incorporating critical race theories as well as their frustration with the lack of a more structural approach to the integration of the church family. One young DRC theologian, Cobus van Wyngaard, has been particularly active in "reconstructing whiteness in the Dutch Reformed Church."[12] In his assessment of the DRC's diversity discourse, Wyngaard laments the lack of critical self-reflection. The church has in his view concentrated its pursuit of greater inclusivity on overcoming divides between black and white without contemplating persistent power dynamics or how these identity categories have been constructed and kept in place.

---

10   Eric Tranby and Douglass Hartman, "Critical Whiteness Theories and the Evangelical "race Problem": Extending Emerson and Smith's *Divided by Faith*," *Journal for the Scientific Study of Religion* 47.3 (2008): 346–349.

11   Cobbs, Perry and Dougherty for instance found that in multiracial congregations in the US, explanations for racial inequality shift among black congregants from structural towards the individual causes more commonly mentioned among white congregants. See: R. J. Cobb, S. L. Perry, and K. D. Dougherty, "United by Faith? Race/ethnicity, Congregational Diversity, and Explanations of Racial Inequality," *Sociology of Religion* 76.2 (2015): 177–198.

12   Cobus van Wyngaard, "The language of "diversity" in reconstructing whiteness in the Dutch Reformed Church," in R. Drew Smith, William Ackah and Anthony G. Reddie, *Churches, Blackness and Contested Multiculturalism* (New York NY, 2014): 157–170.

Problematic in both American and South African debates about racial integration in the church is the reiteration of race as an identity category in itself. It may be recognized as a socially constructed category but nonetheless continues to be used by researchers as a way to differentiate between certain groups of people. Also in this chapter, the terms of white, colored and black are employed in order to indicate self-described identities. These should always be considered as social and deeply politicized constructions rather than predetermined group indications.[13] Somers' discussion of narrative identities is helpful in this respect.[14] Seeking to move away from the a priori categorization of persons, she looks at identities as embedded within time, space and relationships, and above all within stories that change through time and space. The communities in which people live and the places where they end up working determine the ever shifting narratives through which they perceive themselves and the world around them. Which narratives predominate in turn depend according to Somers to a great extent on the distribution of power in society. In the South African context with its long history of white dominance, the narrative of a racial hierarchy that favors white communities over black thus remains prevalent even as individual narratives have begun to shift away from a strict division into racial categories.

Also notable in current debates about race and religion is the absence of the religious change theories discussed earlier in this section. Focus is given to traditional expressions of religion through church institutions and congregations. Evidently, both retain significant influence on their members. The increasing versatility of these members as they move between different worldviews and identities is however also changing the ways in which they relate to members from other faith communities, and consequently other racial or ethnic communities. People might not meet each other inside the church, but find common ground in their beliefs during secular activities, whether at work, during voluntary activities or in school. A useful term here is what Nancy Ammerman describes as spiritual tribes. It relates to any space in which "a spiritually inclined person finds another person who is at least open to talking about the world in terms that include religious dimensions."[15] In a complex and increasingly

---

13　In the South African context these terms are not only very common but also often written with capitals. In this study I have, in adherence to current American scholarly debates about race and religion, chosen not to use capitals.

14　Margaret R. Somers, "The Narrative Constitution of Identity: a Relational and Network Approach," *Theory and Society: Renewal and Critique in Social Theory* 23.5 (1994): 605–649.

15　Nancy Ammerman, "Finding religion in everyday life," *Sociology of Religion* 75:2, (2014): 199.

secular context, people with different backgrounds build unlikely alliances on the basis of vaguely shared spiritual topics, values or perspectives on society. Such perspectives are still informed through particular religious institutions but not necessarily limited to their immediate members. The notion of spiritual tribes helps understand religion as one element of people's cultural package. It provides a cue to others with similar elements that they can connect on the matter of faith if not on other matters. In South Africa, where people remain separated at so many levels, whether through racial categories, language or class, such cues can be essential to contribute to the country's prolonged reconciliation process. Discussing a variety of cases, this chapter is aimed at uncovering instances in which religious connections emerge and what they imply for the potential of the churches to help overcome South Africa's well-known divides.

4.2   Faith and Frustration on the Cape of Good Hope

4.2.1   *In Relative Proximity*

Historically, both URCSA and the DRC have had a strong presence in South Africa's Western Cape province. URCSA's founding meeting took place in one of the many suburbs around Cape Town, the provincial capital, seat of the national Parliament, as well as South Africa's second largest city. Both churches send their theology students to nearby Stellenbosch, a central academic hub and stronghold for Afrikaans speakers. Furthermore, the DRC regional synod of the Western and Southern Cape as well as URCSA's regional synod in the Cape traditionally hold significant sway in the churches' respective national leadership bodies. Especially the former is known for proposing key initiatives for the larger church family, notably on church unification. These initiatives cannot be understood outside of the particular regional context of the Western Cape, or simply the Cape.

Despite being among the wealthiest regions, the Western Cape faces the same type of problems that keep tormenting the rest of the country. Two decades after apartheid, its communities remain largely segregated by race and increasingly by social-economic position. Income gaps are sharpening and poverty has been unrelenting, particularly in the vast slums surrounding Cape Town. Whites tend to live in affluent neighborhoods, colored communities inhabit lower middle class areas while black South Africans are still overrepresented in the impoverished townships. That said, the Western Cape tends to fare better economically than most other provinces and has made some strides towards residential integration. It stands out as the only province in South

Africa not dominated by the African National Congress. Since 2009 the opposition party of the Democratic Alliance governs the region. The party finds its electorate mainly among the Cape's proportionally high number of white and colored communities, 48.8 and 15.7 percent respectively versus a national percentage of 8.9 for both in 2011.[16] Among either group, Afrikaans is the main household language, followed closely by English. If any racial mixing occurs in the Cape, it is primarily between these two communities. Several of Cape Town's suburbs today show a gradual integration of white and colored South Africans.[17] The latter have been moving upward on the social ladder and some can now afford middle class housing and private education for their children at schools offering both English and Afrikaans programs. The poorest areas meanwhile continue to be almost homogeneously black, just as the richest neighborhoods remain white.

With most people preferring to worship at a site nearby, churches in the Western Cape as much as elsewhere tend to reflect the racial composition of the neighborhood in which they are situated. The vast majority of Reformed churches in this region appears either white, black or colored. Residential segregation, and its persistent association with class and racial divisions, thus remains one of the most pivotal factors here keeping the various church communities apart from each other. However, as neighborhoods gradually change, so do the churches. A 2014 report on multicultural congregations showed some level of interracial mixing among 21% of Reformed churches in the wider Cape region (including the Eastern and Northern Cape provinces).[18] Another 19% claimed they would like to be more multicultural. Among the key integrating factors, the report indicated the increased diversity of the community in terms of racial background and language within the church's residential boundaries. While recognizing that most Reformed congregations still served a single ethnic group with its own language and traditions, the report suggested a rising level of diversity among churches participating in the study, or at least support for diversity. This support is significant. It emerges throughout surveys conducted among especially DRC church members in the Cape, asking them about their attitudes towards church unification and *Belhar*. Notwithstanding

---

16   *Census 2011*, 16

17   L. Hill and S. Bekker, "Language, Residential Space and Inequality in Cape Town: Broad-Brush Profiles and Trends," *Etude De La Population Africaine* 28.1 (2014): 661–680.

18   M.A. Van der Westhuizen, W. Van der Merwe and R. Van Velde, "Multicultural churches in intercultural ministries." Report presented at the *Multicultural Conference* at Belville, South Africa, 22–23 July 2014. Accessed at 3 March 2015, http://communitas.co.za/taakspanne/gks/multikulturele-konferensie/.

the broad critique that also exists here, these attitudes generally tend to lean towards a positive appreciation of both issues.

Such appreciation seems in line with, and is constantly nourished through, the wide ranging unification initiatives Reformed church leaders have been undertaking in the Cape over the past two decades. Well before the DRC's General Synod entered official unity talks with URCSA, the regional DRC Cape synod had already begun structural collaboration with URCSA's predecessor, the Dutch Reformed Mission Church. In 1991 the two churches jointly established the Commission for Witness (CFW, in Afrikaans: Kommissie vir Getuienisaksie in die Wes-Kaap) to coordinate their mission activities in the region. The DRC Cape synod was the only regional synod to submit a report to the Truth and Reconciliation Commission about its role in the apartheid era in 1997, the same year in which URCSA submitted its own report on behalf of the entire Uniting Reformed Church. The DRC Presbytery of Stellenbosch had made a similar submission one year earlier. These regional church bodies acted independently at the time and far ahead of the national DRC leadership that refused to cooperate with the Truth and Reconciliation Commission.[19]

In more recent years the Western Cape sections of the DRC as well as URCSA have continued to spearhead matters of unity and reconciliation in the church family. While the general synods of both churches remained bogged down by complex procedures, regional leaders established joint synod committees, merged presbyteries and gradually expanded other forms of cooperation across racial divides. One of their most significant initiatives in this respect comprised the Cape Convent on Unity in the early 2000s.[20] Another noteworthy partnership is found at the Stellenbosch University Faculty of Theology. In 2000, URCSA moved its theological education from the University of the Western Cape to the DRC's Seminary at Stellenbosch. Today, students from both churches might follow their individual tracks to prepare for ministry in either the DRC or URCSA, but they do so in the same building of the Stellenbosch Theology Faculty, with professors from across the different population groups, sharing daily classes and extracurricular programs. Nico Koopman, an URCSA trained theologian, has since 2010 been serving as the Dean of the Faculty. Difficulties abound in determining responsibilities and balancing financial resources. The DRC generally dominates the faculty in terms of numbers and resources. It nonetheless serves as a site for unprecedented collaboration

---

19   Christo Thesnaar, "Reformed churches' struggle for justice. Lessons learnt from their submissions before the TRC," in Mary-Anne Plaatjies and Robert Vosloo. *Reformed Churches in South Africa and the Struggle for Justice*, 385–399.
20   For more on the Cape Convent, see section 2.3.2.

between URCSA and the DRC as well as a basis for other church organizations to tag along and pursue inter-church educational partnerships.[21]

These strides towards church unity attest to the distinct situation of the Cape. The presence of a relatively large colored and white population comprises another vital factor contributing to integration efforts in this region. It has made unity processes different here than in other parts of the country where you find only small white and colored pockets among a majority black African population. The two communities share the Afrikaans language as well as a more formal expression of their faith than is common among black Reformed communities. This is partly due to the history of the church family. Where black Reformed churches used to be allowed, if not encouraged, to maintain their own customs, the colored churches were expected to mirror the DRC as much as possible. Current disparities also play a crucial role here. Colored and white South Africans tend to display higher levels of income and schooling than black population groups.[22] In the context of the Cape, the two communities increasingly meet at the work place, in middle class neighborhoods and at school.

In addition to the many church unification projects of the region, the social-economic and demographic context hence plays an important part in bringing the long divided DRC and URCSA communities closer together. They are evidently far removed from each other as a result of both past and present inequities, but nonetheless appear in relative proximity, especially in comparison with the other population groups present within the Reformed family. It is therefore all the more remarkable that the Cape's Reformed family continues to be organized largely along the lines of the old apartheid categories. Despite the many unity initiatives and proclaimed support for integration, URCSA and DRC congregations across the Western Cape tend to have little to no contact. How have local churches and their leaders been approaching this challenge, and what hampers their efforts?

4.2.2   *The Story of Stellenbosch: Uniting Structures, Not Communities*

Arriving in Stellenbosch, visitors often wonder whether they are still on the African continent. The picturesque university town boasts freshly painted buildings from the Dutch era that have been turned into hotels, restaurants and boutiques for the many tourists who are touring the nearby wineries. Students,

---

21   These include the Ecumenical Center for Leadership, Development and Congregational Studies (Ekklesia) and Communitas, a service center for congregations inside both URCSA and the DRC in the Cape region.

22   *Census 2011*, 26–42

most of them white and Afrikaans speaking, flock the sidewalk cafes and well-kept parks. Neat middle and upper class suburbs surround the city on one side. On the other side, and far out of sight for the tourists, the impoverished township of Kayamandi sprawls into the farmlands. URCSA maintains a small congregation here, led by a white minister whose salary is largely paid for by other Reformed churches in town. Among them is the DRC Moedergemeente [literally "mother community"] and DRC Welgelegen, both situated in wealthy white neighborhoods with a strong presence of professors, university staff and their families. Besides supporting Kayamandi, the two DRC churches partner with the URCSA congregations of Idas Valley, Cloetesville and Rynse. Rynse is the only church left in the city center with a majority colored membership. Others were pushed out during the apartheid era as part of the Group Areas Act. The neighborhoods of Idas Valley and Cloetesville evolved during this era as specifically designated areas for Stellenbosch's large colored community, which in 2011 amounted to 52,2 % of the entire city population.[23] Most of the residents here are poor or lower middle class, working in the service industry if they are employed at all. Drugs and crime are major problems in Idas Valley and Cloetesville as well as in the predominantly black township of Kayamandi.

The church partnerships formed amidst these disparities have since 2006 been coordinated through the Uniting Presbytery of Stellenbosch (UPS). UPS is one of the few presbyteries nationwide in which the DRC and URCSA have merged their organizational structures. Presbyteries of the two churches in most instances oversee the congregations in their area separately, each being responsible for disciplining their own ministers and church council members, coordinating as well as closing existing congregations, or establishing new ones. By integrating these activities into one presbytery, the Reformed churches of Stellenbosch have taken a major step towards unification at a local level. They meet each other on a regular basis, discuss common concerns and foster direct collaboration between the DRC and URCSA congregations under their jurisdiction. During my research in South Africa, Stellenbosch was often mentioned as a unique success story of church integration. For many church actors on the ground however, the story had arrived at an unsatisfactory impasse. Years of partnership and extensive projects to overcome racial divides had done little to change the reality of a deeply segregated city and church life.

The disillusion I encountered in 2012 and 2014 stemmed from a long history of high-minded though often ineffective unity efforts within the boundaries

---

23   Statistics South Africa, *Stellenbosch*. Based on *Census 2011*. http://www.statssa.gov.za/
      ?page_id=993&id=stellenbosch-municipality. Retrieved at 3 April 2015.

of the Stellenbosch Presbytery. They still garnished appreciation among the churches involved but also increasing doubts as to how much a formal approach to integration could really achieve. Robert Vosloo, a Stellenbosch theologian, and Theunis Botha, a minister at one of the city's DRC congregations, have both described the Presbytery's unification process as a treacherous road.[24] As early as 1976, Stellenbosch presbyteries of the Reformed Church family began meeting each other in an official capacity through the so-called Liaison Committee. This Committee had been established in response to the Soweto uprisings in order to offer the churches a space for conversation to help mitigate tensions between their respective communities. Although the Liaison Committee had little direct impact in the increasingly dire social-political situation of the late seventies and early eighties, it did pave the way for further cooperation. 1987 saw the constitution of the first Combined Presbytery in which the DRC and URCSA's predecessor, the Dutch Reformed Mission Church, would regularly gather to discuss immediate common concerns of both their presbyteries. This stage also died a slow death and by the early nineties all joint operations were suspended.

From here, it took another fifteen years for the current Uniting Presbytery to take shape. During those years Reformed church leaders of Stellenbosch gradually expanded their personal relationships, moving from deep mutual suspicions to a slowly emerging sense of trust and partnership.[25] This resulted not only in the ultimate merger of the once racially divided presbyteries. It also generated a host of initiatives to stimulate interaction between Stellenbosch' black, white and colored church communities, from minister exchanges to joint bazaars or mutual visits to each other's communities. Significant limitations remained in place though. Until the churches would officially unite their national leadership structures, UPS could only make recommendations on matters of congregational oversight. Final decisions were left to the individual DRC and URCSA presbyteries that still gathered separately in addition to

---

24   R. Vosloo, "The presbytery and church reunification in the Dutch reformed family of
      churches in South Africa: the story of the United Presbytery of Stellenbosch," in Allan
      J.A. Janssen *Collegial Bishop?: Classis and Presbytery at Issue* (Grand Rapids, Mich: W.B.
      Eerdmans Pub. Co, 2010); Theunis Botha, *Ons sal mekaar nie los nie: 'n kwalitatiewe onder-
      soek na die aard van die onderlinge verbondenheid van leraars binne die Verenigde Ring van
      Stellenbosch* [We will not let go of each other: a qualitative study on the connectedness of
      ministers within the Uniting Presbytery of Stellenbosch] (Thesis. Stellenbosch University,
      December 2014). Accessed at 17 February 2015, http://hdl.handle.net/10019.1/95986.
25   Vosloo, "The presbytery and church reunification in the Dutch reformed family of church-
      es in South Africa," 10–12.

the Uniting Presbytery. The very word "uniting" indicates that UPS had come a long way, but that its process of integration was far from complete.

In recent years the UPS has, despite the ongoing struggle to complete its trajectory, boasted several accomplishments in gathering URCSA and DRC communities through concrete structures and activities. For the attending ministers the Presbytery first of all constituted a platform for conversation and relation building. Its frequent meetings formed an opportunity to address pragmatic matters inside their congregations, from finances and vacant minister posts to the planning for joint celebrations. Beyond such practicalities, UPS was proudly presented as a model of reconciliation for the rest of the church and the broader society. "[The church] family of Stellenbosch is established to put the past squarely on the table."[26]

Above all, ministers across the involved churches stressed the UPS's importance for engaging with the broader Stellenbosch community today. It offered them a space to share their concerns for the city and develop functional agreements away from church- and national politics. A DRC minister depicted UPS as a "ground level alternative to frustrating unity efforts at synodical level."[27] As an example, the minster referred to the consensus the Presbytery reached on the *Belhar Confession* and the incorporation of its core principles of unity, reconciliation and justice into its faith basis and daily work. According to an URCSA colleague, the Presbytery had crucially helped improve interracial relationships by in his case changing the way he viewed white communities and particularly the old mother church.[28] Being able to connect with DRC ministers on a regular basis had mitigated his long held suspicions of racism in the church. Ministers on both sides claimed they felt comfortable to reach out to each other and address personal problems as well as issues related to their congregations. They aired their challenges of convincing congregations to be more socially engaged, or asked for help in dealing with the detrimental conditions for congregants working at the farms around Stellenbosch. The direct communication channels were furthermore used to ask direct support for certain community initiatives, like the realization of a new youth center in the neighborhood.

As a second key accomplishment, and strategy to expand such direct contact, church actors involved with the UPS pointed to its twinning program. The

---

26   UPS Press release in Eikestadnuus, December 2010. Quoted in Botha, *Ons sal mekaar nie los nie*, 82.

27   Interview, DRC minister, 12 March 2014.

28   Interview, URCSA minister, 19 February 2014.

program encompassed close partnerships between specific congregations, such as URCSA Rynse with DRC Welgelegen, and DRC Moedergemeente with URCSA Cloetesville and Idas Valley. In most cases, the congregations in question shared a history of contact, dating back to the apartheid era. Unlike in the past, the UPS emphasized in a 2010 meeting report that the twinning partnerships were built on equal terms and with respect for each church's individual input.[29] Ministers of twinning congregations met periodically, in some cases every month, to exchange news about their communities. They initiated activities together like a joint Easter service or pulpit exchanges in which the ministers take turns in preaching at each other's congregation. At community level, members were encouraged to join in social works and fundraising events of each of the participating churches. They invited each other to their annual church fairs, to volunteer together in soup kitchens or jointly visit other communities in need. One URCSA member told of her experiences with an inter-church prayer group in which women from various Reformed churches and other denominations in Stellenbosch developed a food program to help out impoverished families in cases of emergency. The experience she said not only helped build trust among the women. It also took them into situations they would otherwise avoid. "I would never go to Kayamandi on my own. The church takes initiative and that is how we meet and get to know one another."[30]

Members as well as ministers praised such partnerships, especially when they translated to tangible poverty relief. "Contact works better," a member at the twinning DRC congregation explained, "when we create something together ... We need exposure to each other to help change perceptions." Often times, the joint initiatives took place in the context of a broader ecumenical effort. A particular favorite was Stellemploy, a church-based non-profit organization that provided career training and opportunities to Stellenbosch' many unemployed. DRC Moedergemeente and its twinning partner URCSA Cloetesville both supported the NGO along with half a dozen other churches. They did so financially or in kind by for instance advertising the skills of unemployed church members in local papers and helping to link them up to Stellenbosch businesses. Stellemploy exemplified for one URCSA minister the kind of project the churches truly needed: one that required an "external vision for the community, not just for yourself."[31]

Opportunities for direct interaction between the different racial communities remained scarce though. Church involvement with programs like

---

29　　Botha, *Ons sal mekaar nie los nie*, 81

30　　Interview, URCSA Rynse member, 24 March 2014.

31　　Interview, URCSA minister, 26 March 2014.

Stellemploy tended to be coordinated by a small number of ministers and lay leaders who liaised with the social works program on behalf of either the DRC or URCSA separately. They asked members to volunteer, but few members were engaged in the further implementation of the program, and even less collaborated across the still prevalent racial boundaries.

Agape is considered one successful example of member engagement. It evolved under the umbrella of the UPS in the early 2000s as a dialogue initiative primarily run by individual churchgoers. Members from DRC Moedergemeente and URCSA Idas Valley and Cloetesville had begun the initiative of meeting at each other's homes to "eat together, pray and talk."[32] Agape, a New Testament word for love, gradually turned into a regular activity, engaging up to 100 members in small group dinners and occasional celebrations throughout the year. Participants described Agape primarily as a vehicle to get to know each other. "Through Agape," an URCSA member recalled, "I made friends inside the DRC. I still easily pick up the phone to call them and drop by."[33]

Besides friendship, the dinners were meant to engage church members from various racial and social-economic backgrounds in faith-based dialogues about topics of general concern. Minutes of the meetings that were held, reveal extensive discussions about local youth unemployment, drug abuse or the larger state of South Africa after twenty years of democracy. The intimacy of each other's houses was considered to help churchgoers speak freely about their points of view on these matters. The major goal was not to find agreement, but to "expand comfort zones."[34] In a context where communities seldom meet, this exposure in itself constituted a significant accomplishment for many participants. Reports of the Agape meetings accounted of members' emphasis on their joint prayers and concrete activities. They rarely connected with the UPS' greater attempts towards structural church unity. Members recognized the "disillusion of these attempts in the past, in the eighties when the process failed and we had status issues." These days they still felt persistent "prejudice and alienation" hampering their daily contact but stressed their ability to overcome these challenges through faith.[35] With broad references to the belief in Jesus Christ and the Bible's message of love and reconciliation, the

---

32   Interview, Agape participant, 24 March 2014.

33   Interview, Agape participant, 24 March 2014.

34   *Agape Fees, 14 April. Verwagtinge soos gelys teen die muur* [Agape Party, April 14. Expectations as listed at the wall.] Meeting document obtained from Agape member and organizer, author and date not included.

35   *Agape 2010*, Gedagtes waaroor ons kan gesel by die Agape vergadering [Thoughts about which we can talk during the Agape meeting], 22 April 2010.

Agape initiative appeared determined to overcome the divisions of the past and the present on an individual level. Sharing food also comprised a crucial spiritual element in participants' interpersonal reconciliation. "It reminds of the ordinary meals that Jesus had with his disciples. When we have an Agape meal together, it is a celebration of our love and communion."[36]

After a range of meetings and informal get-togethers, Agape quite suddenly came to an in end in 2013. Some of the involved URCSA and DRC congregants continued to meet as friends, but no longer as part of a church based activity. When asked why Agape ceased to exist, those involved chiefly pointed at the moment that ministers took leadership of the initiative. "We needed them [the ministers] to steer it, but they did things differently … they looked at it too critically and seemed afraid to just do it."[37]

The last comment signifies a greater problem at stake throughout the unity programs in Stellenbosch. After years of trying to bring the different communities closer together, the city's Reformed churches remained as divided as ever. Ministers claimed their members continued to resist integration. The members themselves said they were waiting for the ministers and other church leaders to take charge and initiate new unity programs. Underneath these mutual accusations, a more complex picture emerged. It comprised two different worlds inside the same church family, the same presbytery, the same town. Race and class distinctions still determined these worlds, and as such shaped the major issues occupying the various congregations. URCSA congregations based in the largely colored neighborhoods of Cloetesville and Idas Valley confronted among the highest unemployment levels in the city. Their primary concerns included school dropouts, teenage pregnancies and alcoholism. A short drive away, DRC congregations found themselves in predominantly white neighborhoods dealing with what Theunis Botha has called the "bad fruits of luxury."[38] Its middle to upper class membership was becoming more individualistic and losing commitment to the church community. Their children were leaving the DRC all together, hopping from charismatic church to a center for Buddhist spirituality, or to no religion at all.

Whenever DRC and URCSA members and ministers met within or beyond the context of a unity initiative, they had to face up to these stark divergences. For the ministers inside the Uniting Presbytery, this implied a constant struggle to align their priorities and coordinate efforts. At DRC Welgelegen for instance,

---

36   *Agape 2008,* Fees VG Cloetesville saam met NG Moederkerk Stellenbosch [Agape Celebration URCSA Cloetesville together with DRC Moederkerk Stellenbosch], 16 April 2008.
37   Interview, Agape participant, 24 March 2014.
38   Botha, *Ons sal mekaar nie los nie,* 88

the major focus had been for years on how to invigorate the congregation and bring in a younger generation to compensate for its declining numbers. The church for long enjoyed a reputation of being rather "snobbish and stiff," a church mostly for academics and theologians affiliated with Stellenbosch University.[39] These days, Welgelegen provided separate services for its youth with lively music and activities, as well as the possibility to choose between a traditional early morning service or the significantly more popular and relatively informal late morning service. At URCSA Cloetesville conversely, an emptying church was the least of the minister's problems. On most Sundays, the church was bursting at the seams as all members, young and old, joined with the band in singing and worshipping. Many of these members though were not able to pay their annual dues and were in need of food services to supplement meager salaries or government benefits. During one of the interviews, the minister had to cut the conversation short to talk to a member about his drug addiction. The poverty in his congregation, the minister conveyed, was often "invisible for white people."[40]

While the Uniting Presbytery offered an important platform to share these problems, it also confronted the ministers with the present inequality amongst themselves, primarily in terms of finances. DRC employees generally earned higher salaries than their URCSA colleagues in similar positions. Time and again, tensions flared up about what caused this unevenness as well as the right way to handle it. A particularly delicate topic constituted the Presbytery supported salaries of white ministers inside colored or black URCSA congregations. Should they be based on URCSA standards or rather follow the higher DRC rate? The Presbytery lacked clear guidelines from the churches' national leadership about how to respond to such questions. As one of the first Presbyteries to unite, the UPS was still experimenting with the practical implications of the inter-church collaboration. Financial aspects were especially complex given the fact that the DRC side of the Presbytery remained significantly wealthier than the URCSA side. With its middle to upper class membership and historic capital, the DRC in Stellenbosch presided over vastly more funds and as a consequence contributed more to any joint venture of the two churches. Support from the Uniting Presbytery for a minister's position in fact meant the DRC paying out his or her salary. The unequal distribution of resources not only caused tensions but also confusion among the ministers about the correlation between race and money. URCSA ministers suspected that their white colleagues were receiving more support from the DRC than colored and black

---

39   Interview, DRC Welgelegen member, 10 March 2014.
40   Interview, URCSA minister, 17 March 2014.

ministers. DRC ministers meanwhile feared, and preemptively resisted, the day they might have to surrender parts of their income to the black and colored ministers inside the Presbytery as part of a national unity agreement. Neither had a clear idea of what would or should happen to arrive at more equal terms.

Despite their different financial situations and concerns, the ministers found common ground on a personal level. Where the new arrivals benefited from a common educational background at the Stellenbosch Theological Seminary, the older generation was able to build on years of joint meetings and other opportunities to get to know each other. Church members lacked such opportunities. They rarely encountered people from the other Reformed churches. When encounters did occur, they involved a significant effort on the part of the visiting congregation to overcome both physical and psychological distance. A joint Pentecost service held for the twinning congregations DRC Welgelegen and URCSA Rynse one evening in May 2012 epitomized this. On their way to Welgelegen, members from URCSA Rynse first had to wait for an arranged bus service to take them to a neighborhood on the other side of town. Upon arrival, the congregants entered a large modern church, sharply contrasting with their own small 17th century building that once served enslaved communities. They joined a service in formal Afrikaans, different from the dialect most were used to, with unfamiliar songs and rituals. At the end of the service, members from each congregation grouped together separately for tea and soup before heading back to their own respective neighborhoods. On the way home, URCSA members noted they had hardly spoken with people from the other church, as both sides had seemed unable to cross the worlds keeping them apart.

Noteworthy in this example is that relatively speaking, the members from Welgelegen and Rynse were not that far apart in terms of for instance language, lifestyle and to an extent income, especially when compared to much poorer communities such as Kayamandi. Despite such commonalities, members from both sides said they experienced the gatherings as difficult confrontations. Rynse congregants talked about how they remembered a time in which the people at Welgelegen were their bosses for whom they had to step aside on the streets, or avoid direct eye contact. One man recognized the freedom to enter the "white man's church" as a significant achievement of today's post-apartheid South Africa, and that this should continue to be the major premise for future unification in the church family. The member nonetheless admitted, "I do not feel this freedom today."[41] On the side of Welgelegen, churchgoers also

---

41   Interview, URCSA Rynse member, 26 March 2014.

expressed a deep sense of discomfort with the prearranged unity meetings. In the words of a local business owner and longtime Welgelegen member: "I do not want to engage with diversity in the church. ... I already do so every other day of the week through my work. On Sunday I want a break."[42] "They [the joint activities] are too forced," another more elderly congregant insisted. "It does not work."[43] The woman along with several of her fellow congregants also described the positive encounters they experienced with Rynse. Many praised the faithfulness of Rynse's sizable membership and said they felt true inspiration during its worship service. A random Sunday at Rynse continued to attract some people from Welgelegen who have kept coming on their own account after the planned pulpit exchanges ended. Most interviewees however admitted that once the initial excitement had worn off, they felt more comfortable staying within the boundaries of their own church and that they had not returned to Rynse.

Conversations with other congregations inside the Uniting Presbytery reflected the overall experience of Rynse and Welgelegen. They revealed support for the fundamental idea of church unity, but not for what many referred to as forced contact. URCSA as well as DRC members described unification as a central obligation of the Reformed churches. It involved for both an active role on the part of the churches to foster love among their communities and joint works to improve their social-economic wellbeing. DRC members particularly expressed the hope that unity between the churches could strengthen their relief efforts in destitute parts of the city by engaging committed volunteers from URCSA who knew poverty first-hand. Among URCSA members, unity was more often thought of as a chance to raise awareness in the larger white community, above all the business and farm owners among them, about the disparities facing Stellenbosch' colored and black communities.

On either side however, members conveyed little faith in the existing unity programs to fulfill these hopes. Rather, the programs appeared a source of disillusion. Across the Presbytery, congregants lamented the near complete lack of interaction between them and the lack of visible integration despite the many efforts to merge church structures at national and local level. "There has been no deep change." "We are still homogeneous, monocultural. We are too white and too rich."[44] With this last comment, a woman at Welgelegen specifically referred to the low DRC turnout at joint activities with other church communities. She felt that living in wealth and comfort had made it "easy to just

---

42   Interview, DRC Welgelegen member, 10 March 2014.
43   Interview, DRC Welgelegen member, 10 March 2014.
44   Interview, DRC Welgelegen member, 10 March 2014.

give money … and not make contact."[45] During a group conversation at Idas Valley, congregants also wondered about the use of such activities, especially when the few whites who attended could "return to their farms or businesses afterwards only to continue the repressive treatment of colored workers."[46] Several claimed to have friends on "the other side" and acknowledged the vital sponsoring of their twinning partner DRC Moedergemeente to keep Idas Valley afloat. But they appeared torn about the extent to which their church should expand its contact with the DRC. Local friendships and financial support had not changed the structural inequalities between their communities. "The church leadership should first move ahead [with unity]. Until then we are wasting time."[47]

Considering Stellenbosch' disparate social-economic context, the frustrations emerging throughout the UPS' unity programs are not surprising. The resistance ministers detected among members suspicious of integration builds on a long history of geographical, class and racial distinctions. But the story depicted here is not black and white. Many members who claimed to be disappointed with the churches' unity process also stated their belief in its necessity. They generally valued initiatives like Agape and the twinning programs as a chance to meet each other and satisfy their curiosity regarding the various expressions of their Reformed tradition throughout the church family. Problems arose with expectations about the possibility of actual unification. Congregants often told me they craved such a larger vision towards one integrated institution. They deplored the churches' failure to catch up with the rest of the country and demanded strong leadership to overcome their apartheid legacy.

Especially interesting here was the increasing awareness among URCSA and DRC members that further collaboration could generate mutual advantages. With the decline in members and commitment, DRC congregations looked at well-attended URCSA communities as source of inspiration as well as potential volunteers for their social works. Meanwhile the DRC no longer constituted a mere financial donor in view of URCSA members, but also a pool of experts and powerful business owners they hoped to involve in sustainable development efforts. In some twinning partnerships, ministers had begun to explore community activities in which the DRC offered skills and connections while URCSA members brought in the numbers and the knowledge of needs on the ground. Still, progress in this kind of collaboration remained slow and often barely visible for the communities involved. Without clear results nor

---

45   Interview, DRC Welgelegen member, 10 March 2014.

46   Interview, URCSA Idas Valley focus group, 5 March 2014.

47   Interview, URCSA Idas Valley focus group, 5 March 2014.

perspective on national church unification, many URCSA and DRC members lost confidence in the entire process, whether it comprised formal unity talks or local partnerships. Awkward situations of formal togetherness seemed to reaffirm rather than bridge differences between the segregated church communities of Stellenbosch. The joint structures of the Uniting Presbytery perhaps inspired leaders across the Reformed Church family. They, so far at least, failed to galvanize church members, including those in favor of integration, to physically step out of their comfort zones.

4.2.3 *The Wynberg Affair: Grassroots Integration, Structural Barriers*

The town of Wynberg, one of Cape Town's southern suburbs, has become synonymous in the Reformed Church family with high hope as well as deep despair of church unification. In 2008, the DRC and URCSA congregations of Wynberg did what their General Synods had been talking about for years. They established the Wynberg Collaboration Agreement to merge the two congregations into one multiracial church. This merger never materialized though. Following a chain of events, including the death of one of the involved ministers and various legal ramifications, the Wynberg integration process fell apart. Today, the two congregations once again pray separately, just across the road from each other. There is one notable exception though. Part of the URCSA members, most describing themselves as colored, moved in with the still predominantly white DRC congregation, leaving behind their former church and community.

The story of Wynberg not only constitutes a case of unification gone astray. It is also a particularly well-documented story. The path towards the Wynberg Agreement, its clash with church orders and bureaucracy, and the ultimate collapse have drawn vast attention from Reformed church media and beyond. The DRC minister in question wrote a detailed report in addition to multiple articles about the process.[48] The Presbytery of URCSA Wynberg kept track of each relevant decision and meeting between August 2007 and April 2009.[49] A quick search online reveals dozens of news articles, blog postings and Facebook

---

48   Reverend Danie Nel of DRC Wynberg shared this report with me: Danie Nel, *Die Herenigingsprocess van Wynberg* [The Reunification Process of Wynberg]. The undated and unpublished document covers the period from 2007 to 2010. Most of it can also be found on the DRC Wynberg website: http://www.ngkerkwynberg.co.za/Kerkeenheid.htm. In conversations with URCSA Presbytery of Wynberg the report was validated as an accurate presentation of the facts despite being written from the perspective of the involved DRC minister.

49   *URCSA Capeland 2009.* Verloop van die Wynberg aangeleentheid [Order of events of the Wynberg affair]. Presented at URCSA Cape regional synod meeting, 15 October 2009.

discussions about the sad turn of events that had initially seemed so promising. What drove the communities of Wynberg to engage in these events in the first place, and how can we understand their apparent failure?

As with the Stellenbosch Uniting Presbytery, the Wynberg unification process is intricately linked to its local context. Designated as a colored neighborhood during the apartheid era, Wynberg today is still home to a significant colored population of about 46 percent, while whites make up another 24 percent.[50] Poverty numbers are clearly higher among the first group, but recent years have seen the rise of a colored middle class that tends to be more educated and enjoy higher incomes than in the surrounding areas. The Afrikaans speaking and largely colored URCSA Wynberg illustrates this trend as one of the richest congregations in the greater URCSA Presbytery of Wynberg it is subject to. For long, the congregation stood in the shadows of the neighboring DRC Wynberg with its impressive historic church building and upper-class membership that comprised major leaders of the white Afrikaans speaking community in the Cape. Since the 1990s however, DRC Wynberg has steadily been shrinking. Members are leaving and new arrivals, primarily from a nearby military base, tend to stay for only short intervals before they move out of the area again. Even though the congregation retained some of its powerful community leaders, the high turnover and unpredictability has spawned serious financial difficulties. It does not help that the congregation forms part of a troubled DRC Presbytery of Wynberg. The Presbytery was categorized in 2013 among the most stagnant in the region, struggling with finances, membership decline and overall isolation.[51] Amidst these altering circumstances, the DRC and URCSA Wynberg came closer than any other Reformed community in the country to an actual merger.

In conversations during my 2012 and 2014 visits about how the near merger had come about, members and ministers on both sides marked their long commitment to break with the churches' past of segregation. As early as 1991, when the anti-apartheid struggle was still in full swing, the DRC and URCSA Wynberg church councils[52] agreed to start meeting on a regular basis. Their aim according the DRC minister was to "talk openheartedly about the estrangement of the past."[53] The councils set out a path towards collaboration through

---

50   *City of Cape Town – 2011 Census Suburb Wynberg,* July 2013. 2.

51   Frederick Marais, *De stand van gemeentes. Sinode van de NG Kerk Wes Kaapland.* [The status of congregations. Synod of the DRC Western Cape], October 2013.

52   These councils usually comprise of the minister and a small group of active members who take up responsibilities as deacons, elderly and treasury of the congregation.

53   Nel, *Die Herenigingsprocess van Wynberg,* 10

a range of small scale and bottom-up initiatives. By the early 2000s, the two congregations held services together at least once a month, sent their youth on joint church camps and had begun to merge the functions of their church councils. Members, especially council members, actively participated in many of these programs. Commemorating this period, many recounted the joy of getting to know each other as well as the powerful experience of interracial worship. "Such contact goes much deeper than interaction at work."[54] On the side of the DRC, members indicated their urge to "become less white."[55] URCSA members in turn talked about the excitement of "being accepted by whites."[56] The notion of bridge building, taking action at the forefront of the country's transformation rather than staying on the backseat, also surfaced throughout these conversations. As we saw in Stellenbosch, DRC Wynberg congregants highlighted their eagerness for unity with their URCSA neighbors as a way to strengthen the church's position in the community and enhance the effectiveness of their social programs. "They [URCSA] know what we in the rich suburbs don't know and they are more active than we are."[57]

Motivation to end segregation was one thing. Its practical implementation stood, and fell, by the Wynberg ministers and their personalities. These included from the beginning Reverend Dani Nel at the DRC along with his URCSA colleague and later president of Stellenbosch University, the late Reverend Russel Botman. Another powerful URCSA leader, Reverend James Buys, succeeded Botman in 1994. Buys also served as moderator of URCSA's General Synodical Committee in these early years and became known as a strong, be it critical, proponent of unification with the DRC. Building on years of joint meetings and services, Buys and Nel together led their congregations, and particularly their respective church councils, into the unification process. They encouraged council members to work together, invited each other to their church activities, developed a thorough strategy and presented this to their respective Presbyteries.

A 2007 Statement from Buys to the URCSA Presbytery of Wynberg revealed a pragmatic plan for the two congregations to merge their structures, including the full integration of Sunday services that would alternately be held at either of the two church buildings and led by one of the ministers.[58] The statement

---

54   Double interview, Wynberg members, 1 April 2014.

55   Double interview, Wynberg members, 1 April 2014.

56   Interview, Wynberg member, 28 March 2014.

57   Double interview, Wynberg members, 1 April 2014.

58   J.D.S. Buys, *Vertoe aan die Ring van Wynberg* [Statement to the Presbytery of Wynberg]. On behalf of the URCSA Wynberg Church Council, 22–23 August 2007.

made for a groundbreaking moment in the national history of the two churches. For the first time an URCSA and DRC community committed to a tangible
arrangement of church unification. An official Agreement of Collaboration expounded the congregations' "decision to combine" with minute details, from
the integration of minister responsibilities to a joint financial account.[59] According to a closely involved DRC member, the Agreement merely constituted "a natural next step." "We had already done everything else we could do in
terms of cooperation. Becoming one congregation just made sense."[60]

To the regional leadership of both churches, the Agreement made far less
sense however. The URCSA Presbytery of Wynberg rejected it as inconsistent
with URCSA's national church order. Objections were also raised on the side of
the DRC, particularly regarding the fulfillment of pastoral duties. Could DRC
members still count on house visits by their own minister or enjoy baptisms in
their own tradition once the two congregations were united?[61] In 2009, the DRC
and URCSA jointly expressed their reservations about the Wynberg Agreement
in an official statement by their two Law Commissions. The Commissions denounced Wynberg's proposition to conduct all Sunday services together. "This
really is not possible." (...) "Of course there can be joint services. Even at a regular
basis. But this cannot replace the congregation's own service."[62] Their statement
came at a time of deep distress for the two Wynberg congregations and particularly for URCSA Wynberg. Its minister, Reverend Buys, had committed suicide a
year earlier in 2008 and had been replaced by a new minister, Rev. Samuels, who
appeared far more skeptical about the unity process and lacked the level of personal contact Buys had nurtured with the DRC Wynberg minister.

With both congregations, their ministers, Presbyteries and Law Commissions haggling over the details of the Agreement, Wynberg evolved into a
church political quagmire. Its rapidly unfolding debacle became the topic of
heated debates across the Reformed Church family and even in the national
press. "Wynberg's dream has shattered."[63] "Congregations 'divorce'."[64] "Church

---

59   Ooreenkomst tussen NGK Wynberg en VGK Wynberg [Agreement between DRC Wynberg
      and URCSA Wynberg]. Original version, 2 September 2008.
60   Double interview, Wynberg members, 1 April 2014.
61   Kommentaar van die Sinodale Regskommissie (NGK) en die Permanente Regskomissie
      (VGK) op die ooreenkomst tussen die gemeente Wynberg (NGK) en die gemeente Wyn-
      berg (VGK) [Commentary of the Synodical Law Commission (DRC) and the Permanent
      Law Commission (URCSA)], 9 March 2009.
62   Kommentaar van die Sinodale Regskommissie (NGK) en die Permanente Regskomissie
      (VGK), 9 March 2009.
63   *Die Kerkbode,* 3 September 2010
64   *Rapport,* 14 August 2010

triumph rather becomes tragedy."[65] "Unification process not to the honor of God."[66] As Wynberg hit the media headlines, relationships between the two congregations and their regional leaders soured. Finally, the URCSA Presbytery of Wynberg pulled the plug and in August 2010 issued a moratorium on any further collaboration between URCSA and DRC Wynberg.

What caused this sharp turn of events remained at the time of this research a matter of great division inside the church family. Both URCSA and the DRC blamed each other for turning a genuine local effort into a battleground about national church unity. Both also emphasized the uniqueness of Wynberg. Things would have gone very differently if one of the central figures had not passed away early on in the process. Indeed, the tragic death of Reverend James Buys severely interrupted the relationships cultivated over time between the communities. But it occurred as problems were already unfurling.

First among them was the deep attachment between the congregations and the specific communities in which they were rooted. The DRC's and URCSA's Law Commissions hinted at this attachment when they warned Wynberg about undermining the primary responsibility of each congregation to tend to its "own."[67] Services might be open to all and joint services were encouraged. But they should according to the law experts, never come at the cost of each individual community's services as prescribed by church regulations. At leadership level, this involved a rather bureaucratic if not financial argument about the need for a congregation to conduct its own Sunday mass and ensure the income from weekly collections. For members at the two Wynberg congregations, the Law Commissions' statement tuned in with deep underlying emotions about "their church" and its specific communal identity. Integrating organizational structures did not appear to be an issue here. But the prospect of worshipping every other Sunday at a different church, with a different minister with his own style, dialect and rituals, offset congregants on both sides.

This became painfully apparent as the number of DRC members attending joint services at URCSA Wynberg began to dwindle after 2008. Interviewees explained that their numbers were never big and that resistance to integration had from the beginning caused several DRC members to leave for other churches in the area. When a new minister took over the URCSA congregation

---

65   *Die Burger*, 6 November 2008

66   URCSA *News*, 1 October 2010.

67   The Afrikaans term for one's own, "eie" returns throughout the Law Commissions' Commentary in reference to church services, community finances, duties, regulations etc. Commentary of the Synodical Law Commission and the Permanent Law Commission,. 9 March 2009.

from Rev. Buys, this trend accelerated. "We became more aware of our cultural differences when the new priest arrived."[68] During the long services, one and a half or even two hours versus the traditional one hour they were used to, DRC members said they missed their community, their minister and his calm way of preaching in comparison to the "screaming" of the new URCSA minister.[69] Even the most motivated for unity eventually retreated to their own church, attending joint services only when they took place at the DRC congregation. Meanwhile URCSA members kept visiting DRC services and continued to participate in activities at the white church. The ensuing unevenness reaffirmed what some critics had anticipated all along. Rather than integration, the unity process was creating a situation of domination by the DRC Wynberg, its overall style and membership. In his report, Rev. Nel quoted one URCSA member expecting early on in the process that "a future combined church could find certain people alienated or a congregation dominated by intellectuals or affluent or eloquent. ... I fear that many of our people would join up with the white church on their (DRC) terms."[70]

The concern for domination this URCSA member voiced, points at a second major impediment to Wynberg's unity process regarding the deep contrast between the narratives with which the two congregations sought to explain their unfolding difficulties. On the part of the URCSA congregation and especially its Presbytery leaders, emphasis was put on the persistent racism inside the white DRC that inhibited the church from accepting the colored Wynberg community as an equal partner. According to Presbytery leaders, Reverend Nel did not share but rather took over the care of the congregation after Reverend Buys died. Without prior agreement and before they had appointed a new URCSA minister, Rev. Nel was believed to have looked after the funerals of some of its members, conducted house visits and continued to work out the details of the unity process without consulting URCSA. The new URCSA minister Rev. Samuels lamented that at the joint URCSA-DRC Wynberg gatherings "the superiority feelings of the whites and the 'submissiveness,' if that is the correct word, of the so-called Coloreds" still operated.[71] During interviews, Presbytery leaders corroborated the deep resentment surfacing in Samuels' remarks towards the DRC and stressed the need to view them in the context of their apartheid past.

---

68   Double interview, Wynberg members, 1 April 2014.

69   Double interview, Wynberg members, 1 April 2014.

70   Nel, *Die Herenigingsprocess van Wynberg*, 12

71   Reaksie van Ds. W.J. Samuels op die samewerking tussen die NGK en VGK Wynberg [Reaction of Ds. W.J. Samuels on the cooperation between DRC and URCSA Wynberg], 8 April 2010. Capital for "Colored" in original text.

Decades of paternalistic relations they claimed, could not be transformed overnight. "I do not trust the white man. We are together in the church, but not outside."[72] For these local URCSA leaders, the Wynberg unity process did not represent the reconciliation Reverend Nel described in his report, but rather an effort to "expand his own congregation and turn ours into a museum." The baggage between the two churches was considered too big to be overcome through a local integration effort. "First we need to change our attitudes towards each other." "We need unity from above, along with equal conversations at the bottom, between cleaners and their bosses."[73]

The views inside URCSA's local leadership sharply contrasted accounts at DRC Wynberg, including above all the URCSA members who had transitioned to the DRC. This unforeseen transition occurred after the Collaboration Agreement of Wynberg had collapsed in 2010. Since then, a growing number of usually well-off URCSA congregants have been leaving their former community for the white church on top of the hill. In 2014 about forty of them had become full members at the DRC Wynberg, joining in with its Sunday services, Bible classes, coffee hour and outreach activities. These members along with their fellow DRC congregants generally attributed the fissure between their churches to social-economic and particularly cultural factors rather than racial domination. Deep sorrow was expressed about this fissure as well as motivation to still make work of integration by turning DRC Wynberg into a multicultural congregation, with or without a partnership with its URCSA neighbors. One former URCSA couple indicated that they still sensed the pain of the failed unity process, but that this did not prevent them from feeling welcome and at home at their new community. It was their own decision to come to the DRC and they never regretted it. "We appreciate the deep intellectual sermons of Reverend Nel and the intimacy of our Bible group."[74]

DRC interviewees across the board underscored the importance of the spiritual and personal connections in their new congregation, above politics and history. Conversations about apartheid or racial hierarchies were rather shunned so as not to obstruct the much valued interaction across color lines. "When Reverend Samuels brought up old feelings from the past, it made people close up again."[75] Neither white nor colored congregants at DRC Wynberg appeared very concerned with race issues in general. URCSA members who switched, referred to their own middle class status and higher education as reasons for their transition. Many no

---

72   Interview, URCSA Presbytery Wynberg, 27 March 2014.
73   Interview, URCSA Presbytery Wynberg, 27 March 2014.
74   Interview, Wynberg member, 28 March 2014.
75   Interview, Wynberg member, 28 March 2014.

longer felt at ease with the traditional and collective character of the poorer section of the URCSA community that they felt still dominated the congregation. The DRC's abbreviated services and focus on one's individual relationship with God held more appeal to them than the hierarchal style associated with URCSA Reverend Samuels. "He came in as a young minister who still had to prove himself." "He frightened the children and often acted as school teacher telling the group what to do."[76] Much frustration was expressed at the complaisance with which the remaining URCSA members had followed their new minister in his critique on the unity process. The lack of perseverance indicated for new and old DRC members that their neighbors had never been truly committed and lacked the mental preparedness for a merger of their congregations. "They [URCSA members] sometimes seemed like children. They said they wanted to get together but in the end did what the minister said. They were in awe of him."[77]

Issues of personality, class and culture might have mattered more to these members than the inequalities mentioned by URCSA Wynberg's leadership. Imbalances in power and resources undoubtedly affected the congregations' unity process though. This third pivotal barrier surfaced primarily in the convoluted debates between the various stakeholders in regional and national church bodies and in personal leadership reflections on the Wynberg case. Between the lines, the detailed elaborations by either church's Law Commissions revealed a deep concern among leaders for the example Wynberg could set to other congregations. Over and again the URCSA Law Committee warned of the increasing influence of Wynberg's zealous DRC minister.[78] Reverend Nel had come to symbolize a greater threat of well-trained and resourceful white ministers drawing members from colored URCSA congregations. Wynberg was not the only case in point here. Across the country URCSA had in the years of the Wynberg affair seen its colored congregants transitioning to nearby white DRC churches where they enjoyed services in roughly the same language but from a minister with more time and money on his hands than the average underpaid and overworked URCSA minister could provide.

On a larger scale, Wynberg according to some key actors involved, met resistance from URCSA leaders because it presented a dangerous sidetrack on the course to church unification.[79] Central in this course for URCSA was the

---

76 Interview, Wynberg member, 28 March 2014.

77 Interview, Wynberg member, 1 April 2014.

78 Uitspraak van die Aktuarius VGKSA [Statement by the Actuary URCSA], 15 September 2009.

79 Interviews, Wynberg member, 28 March 2014; minister, 6 March 2014; minister, 27 February 2014.

adoption of the *Belhar Confession* by the DRC's General Synod. When congregations merged before such adoption had taken place, it potentially jeopardized the entire process. URCSA feared that the DRC would no longer see the need for either *Belhar* or structural unity when communities locally achieved the racial integration the DRC sought to parade towards the rest of society. What complicates this account, is the fact that DRC leaders did not seem too keen on Wynberg's unity either. They were ill prepared for the practical implications of local integration, despite their often repeated support of such efforts. The prospect of a DRC congregation to lose income from or influence over its own community raised all sorts of bureaucratic barriers that, along with URCSA's concerns, drained the Wynberg process of its energy. With national unity talks collapsing in September 2008, few URCSA or DRC leaders remained willing to move the process ahead. On that point at least, the churches agreed.

In many ways the story of Wynberg's failed unification is extraordinary. The combination of factors facilitating its initial progress, the presence of two communities that broadly shared geography, middle class incomes, language and powerful leaders on both sides, rarely occurs simultaneously. Its collapse was also unique in the sense that it so closely coincided with the collapse of the national unity process. The unfortunate suicide of Reverend Buys occurred only a few months before the 2008 decision of URCSA's General Synod to cease all talks. Wynberg nevertheless contains many elements characteristic for the churches' overall unification trajectory. The communities both struggled to set aside their specific church identities and grew over time increasingly divided in their narratives of what was keeping them apart. On the side of URCSA, leaders blamed the unequal distribution of power between their churches in the past and the present. DRC members and the URCSA congregants that ended up joining them, rather stressed their different backgrounds and how these had shaped diverging needs for worship.

The gap between leaders and members is conspicuous here, as well as complex. At multiple occasions, members of the two Wynberg congregations took the initiative in furthering interaction between their communities, whether through their church councils or later as individuals sharing prayers and Bible discussions at DRC Wynberg. By and large though, members followed the path their leaders set out, also when that path changed. What took URCSA members to drop their support for unity after the arrival of the new minister, and to what extent did they? These questions are difficult to answer at this time. While visiting Wynberg in 2014, the URCSA congregation was in deep morning over yet another premature death of a minister, this time Reverend Samuels. Few knew what the future would bring to their congregation, let alone to their relationship with the DRC neighbors. If anything, members in both communities indicated they were "moeg," tired of unity, of disunity and of all the events and attention it had generated. Those who still expressed hope, did so quietly and only in modest terms. Some joint projects and a spiritual journey of "reconciliation in our hearts" were mentioned as potential next steps.[80] But not much more.

4.2.4   *Bridging Communities, Their Leaders and Members*

For all their frustrations, it is hard to deny that the Reformed churches of the Western Cape made at least some progress towards unification. Their regional DRC and URCSA synods along with local church leadership bodies jointly established a vast network of partnerships and organizational structures that have allowed increased contact between their communities. After the Wynberg fiasco, both churches took pain to expand these structures and include concrete regulations for congregations that wish to merge. In addition, guidelines were developed on how presbyteries elsewhere on the Cape can follow the example of the Uniting Presbytery of Stellenbosch. Granted, many of these structures were in 2014 still in their early stages, crucially lacking support from the churches' national leadership. They did however offer a basis for communities to foster inter-church and interracial partnerships. The question remains why so few communities utilized these possibilities.

Persistent racial, social-economic and geographic divisions had an obvious role here. But they played out quite differently among church leaders and members. Where leaders tried to build a narrative of interracial unity through organizational collaboration, members struggled with the actual diversity this could bring. Regarding the leaders, the Cape area exhibits a rather unique multiracial church establishment, especially since the integration of the two Reformed seminaries at Stellenbosch University in 2000. It comprises professors and students, newly trained ministers and key organizers in the regional and local leadership bodies of both churches. Within this group, all of the above divisions remain present, but traditional boundaries are fading. DRC and URCSA Cape elites regularly encounter each other at seminars and leadership meetings, in middle class neighborhoods or at the outdoor cafes of Stellenbosch. Throughout my conversations with both groups, the majority claimed to support a future unity. It formed a crucial element of their self-description as progressive church leaders.

---

80   Double interview, Wynberg members, 1 April 2014; Interview, minister, 27 February 2014. See also Danie Nel, "Lesse uit die herenigingsproces van Wynberg" [Lessons from the reunification process of Wynberg], 2012.

In these conversations as well as in meeting reports and documents of re-cent years, the leaders often jointly warned of the profuse obstacles in rec-onciling the churches' disparate financial situation and power imbalances. Amidst these warnings, stories of apartheid took a pivotal position. A repe-tition of past inequalities had to be avoided at all cost. Detailed frameworks outlining formal responsibilities and rules in any new partnership were thus considered essential to prevent one church from dominating the other and ensure that each could maintain its own constituency as well as authority over this constituency. As they cautioned for unity, the church elites raised all sorts of barriers, often with strong references to the theology and organization of the church. Local URCSA leaders demanded each joint agreement to include clauses about the *Belhar Confession* as expression of the DRC's remorse over the past and a true change of its ideological doctrine. DRC leaders stressed the need for democratic decision making, reluctant to agree with anything that could generate a loss of members or resources. Both carefully designed their joint projects so as not to upset anyone and to guarantee fair treatment.

Such formalities perhaps responded to the anxieties of theologians and leading ministers. However, they undermined the often precarious efforts ma-terializing within Cape communities – as happened in Wynberg – or offered scarce opportunity or inspiration for members to join in. Similar to their lead-ership, members of the studied congregations in the region tended to convey overall support for unity. They saw fewer impediments in its organizational dimension, urging their leaders to simply get on with it. What concerned ordi-nary congregants more, was how to face diversity on their own premises. Many found it hard to imagine a Sunday service that attended to the churches' widely diverging race, class and language groups in ways that all understood and ap-preciated. The stories of Stellenbosch and Wynberg showed DRC and URCSA congregants struggling to envision themselves in the pews with respectively their cleaning lady, or their company director. They agreed that such interac-tion might be the future goal of the church. Today however, too much luggage from the past and the present set the communities apart, and with significant-ly sharper edges than among their church elites.

Part of this luggage constituted memories of the apartheid era. More im-portant in the cases of Stellenbosch and Wynberg however appeared the type of narrative identities Somers describes and their divergences among URCSA and DRC communities. In both communities, these narratives weaved in still predominant views on racial hierarchy and white dominance with ideals about post-apartheid unity and changing class identities and relationships. The prev-alent association between a higher social-economic status and whiteness was particularly pointed in Wynberg. Having moved up the social ladder gave

URCSA members a sense that they were now closer to the worship styles and expressions they associated with their DRC neighbors than with the colored church they used to identify with. White DRC members meanwhile not only expected the newcomers but also the overall integration process to follow their ways. Such expectations parallel Edward's critique of the persistent whiteness of multiracial congregations in the United States. Nonetheless, neither URCSA nor DRC members attached much value to the racial categories involved here. Emphasis was put on the broad spirituality and social engagement that united them as well as their increasing proximity in society as middle class families with similar concerns about their children's education, the failing economy and persistent crime and poverty in the country. Any differences were attributed to culture or class, not race.

In general, Western Cape churchgoers in this study reiterated that race was not the problem. Explaining their challenges with integration, congregants rather referred to their discomfort with other cultures that were in turn associated with different social-economic positions. A common narrative among DRC and URCSA members comprised the predisposed incompatibility between their communities' values and customs. One would be too formal, the other too loose. One involved too much intellectualism, the other too much clapping and dancing. Although they outwardly denied the role of race, members did not hesitate to relate the supposed cultural differences with distinct groups and places, such as the black communities of the townships or the wealthy white suburbs. As we saw in the discourse chapter, the term "culture" appeared to function as a euphemism here that members employed to avoid accusations of racial prejudice. It covered both class and race in a way strikingly reminiscent of the categories of the apartheid era. Besides the literal overlap between these past categories and current group divisions, the notion of culture was used in a similarly essentialist manner as race used to be.

On neither side of the color line, did members indicate enthusiasm for the pre-arranged moments to cross their supposed cultural differences. Nor did they express eagerness to initiate spontaneous activities along the lines of Agape or even Wynberg before clearing them with the leadership. The Cape Reformed churches thus arrived at an impasse in which leaders hoped to engage members in formal joint projects for which the latter had little gusto. Members meanwhile waited for their leaders to guide them towards new bottom-up initiatives that leaders however believed should be launched without involvement from the top. Few doubted the reasons why their churches should ultimately unify. Decades of pro-unity discourse from the national and regional Cape leadership had generated a broad consensus on the spiritual value of unity in the eyes of God, its necessity in view of the apartheid past, as well as the opportunity it would create for the churches to play a greater role in contemporary South Africa. Without a sense of urgency though, it appeared exceedingly difficult to bridge the narrative gaps among communities, and between their church leaders and members.

4.3   Stuck Together in the Free State

4.3.1   *A Daunting Backdrop*

"Church is not a therapeutic space in which people can withdraw from a society in which they are struggling to adapt. Church is missional, focuses on the greater world, to mediate and embody some of the promises of the Trinity God."[81] In an effort to reposition itself, the DRC regional synod of the Free State in 2013 touched a raw nerve in the church family. The Reformed churches in the Free State, whether affiliated with the DRC, URCSA or the dissident black synods of the DRCA, have over the past few decades seen their communities diminish and retract in the shadows. Those members who remain, tightly hold on to their congregations, suspicious of any effort to change what for many constitutes a last bastion of familiarity. Reformed churches, especially DRC communities, in the Free State tend to be more conservative in their social values and with respect to race relations than their brothers and sisters in the Cape. Unity bears a negative connotation here with the perceived failure of the post-apartheid transition to bring security and wellbeing for all. Reconciliation has become a dirty word. A small group of regional church leaders are trying to change attitudes by advocating for a more outward directed church. Against the daunting backdrop of the impoverished Free State, few are optimistic about their chance of success.

In contrast to the Western Cape, the central region of the Free State is fairly representative of much of South Africa. Its population is majority black African while the number of white communities is decreasing. The presence of colored and Indian or Asian population groups is almost negligible, respectively 3 and 0.1 percent.[82] Poverty rates are high, as is unemployment and school failure.[83] Once known as the "bread basket" of South Africa, the Free State today is urbanizing. Small towns and farms see their youth leaving for the cities

---

81   DRC Free State Regional Synod 2013, Handelinge [Minutes], 31.

82   *Census 2011 Municipal Report Free State*, 10

83   Jaana Puukka, Patrick Dubarle, Holly McKiernan, Jairam Reddy and Philip Wade, *Higher Education in Regional and City Development: The Free State, South Africa* (OECD, 2012), 65–83.

to look for work outside the dwindling agricultural and mining sector. The state is showing some progress in terms of education and income among black communities, but generally scores below the national average on both.

Beyond its contemporary struggles, the Free State is famous, or more infamous, for its contradictory history. Established as one of the two original Boer Republics and a major battleground in the South African wars, the Orange Free State long comprised a stronghold of Afrikaner politics, culture and language. It symbolizes for many white Afrikaans speakers their suffering as well as survival as a people. For black communities, the region is rather synonymous with the apartheid era and black resistance. The National Party commenced its white supremacist journey in the Free State Capital of Bloemfontein in 1914, only two years after the founding of the African National Congress in the same city. Besides their conflicting pasts, white and black Free State communities continue to live in deeply segregated worlds today. Both experience hardships due to the region's flawed economy and deteriorating government services. As elsewhere in the country, black Africans largely bear the brunt though. Many continue to live in the overpopulated townships or homelands created during apartheid, while most of the land remains in white hands.

In this context the DRC and URCSA are scrambling to maintain their presence in the region. The DRC remains prominent among white Afrikaans speaking communities, but suffers from the overall decline of its rural constituency as a result of migration and urbanization. In cities like Bloemfontein, DRC congregations encounter stiff competition from other churches on top of overall trends of secularization especially among youth. They retain a small number of members who often stay primarily because of a sense of historic belonging to the old mother church. Grace Davie's phrase "belonging without believing" appears appropriate here.[84] During my visits in 2012 and 2014 Free State ministers told me about the engrained anxiety they found among congregants for the "flooding" of their churches by other communities and cultures.[85] Members' attachment to the church, one young minister explained, had less to do with belief than with the memory of the former "volkskerk" and a time in which they felt in control of events and not, as today, at the mercy of a failing government.[86]

A 2013 DRC Free State synod report pronounced the resistance among its congregations to church unification, and specifically to the *Belhar Confession*,

---

84   Davie, "From believing without belonging to vicarious religion."
85   Interview, DRC minister, 16 April 2014.
86   Interview, DRC minister, 17 April 2014.

a direct consequence of the region's harsh circumstances.[87] Unemployment, farm attacks, land reform and deteriorating public services were mentioned as factors severely obstructing interracial conversations. They had turned any initiative on collaboration with the other churches in the Reformed family into a political debate about South Africa's post-apartheid transition. Many DRC congregations had according to the report lost faith in this transition and preferred focusing the church's attention on their own issues. Piet Strauss, a former moderator of the DRC, theologian and minister in the Free State, referred to such issues as "the mini-morality of problems in the immediate community or in their families."[88] They involved marriage and old age, raising children and protecting against violence in the neighborhood. Unity talks or any talk of integration appeared miles removed from this mini-morality.

URCSA confronts similar tribulations in addition to the damaging impact of its conflict with the DRCA and internal divisions. The Free State synod of this traditionally black African church, was among the few synods that refused to dissolve in 1994 and join the newly established Uniting Reformed Church. Its refusal generated more than thirty court cases between DRCA and URCSA communities fighting about church properties. Millions of Rand have been spent on lawyers while the embattled congregations can often barely afford basic amenities. Poverty and its coinciding problems of unemployment, drugs and crime, define URCSA communities across the Free State, whether or not they are mired in court cases. Particularly challenging has been the situation of its Afrikaans speaking colored congregations. Few can collect enough funds to cover a full-time minister and thus depend on so-called tentmakers or consulenten, ministers who stretch their time between multiple congregations and other lay occupations.

In the Free State today, URCSA has 91 congregations served by 43 ministers. These ministers not only have to balance their time and attention, but also the languages and styles in which they serve the many different population groups inside URCSA. Few master the Afrikaans language still predominant in colored communities. They preach in English or Sesotho[89] or in a mix of both languages, but hardly ever in Afrikaans. Colored URCSA congregations have in recent years increasingly voiced their grief about this situation. They complain about being ignored by a Sesotho dominated regional synod that does not value their

---

87   DRC *Free State 2013, Belydenis van Belhar*: Gespreksdokument [*Confession of Belhar*: Conversation Document].

88   Interview, Piet Strauss, 17 April 2014.

89   Sesotho is the main language spoken in the Free State and the mother tongue of the majority of the region's black African population.

language, nor their culture or identity. "We want someone to serve us in Afrikaans, and who does not look down on us."[90] "We don't exist. We are not recognized. We are seen as a branch." Representatives from Afrikaans speaking URCSA congregations expressed these sentiments in front of their regional synod leaders during a 2014 meeting in Bloemfontein. They admitted, with regret, that many of their constituents left for nearby DRC churches that were serving in their language. These churches had been welcoming them, but often by creating a separate "section" through which the new members received their own space and time for worship, apart from the church's traditional and still mostly white Sunday service.

Not surprisingly, relationships between the DRC and URCSA in the Free State tend to be strained. The former has kept close, and invariably one-way, financial ties with the dissident black synod as it continues to support DRCA congregations with minister salaries and other in-kind services. The rapprochement between colored communities and the DRC provides additional ammunition to the claim that the old mother church is trying to meddle with URCSA's internal affairs. The latter has accused the DRC of luring these members to leave URCSA and of obstructing efforts towards reconciliation between its black and colored constituents. With little motivation on either side, collaboration among the Reformed churches of the Free State has been limited to the bare minimum. A pulpit exchange, perhaps a joint meeting of the regional synods or two local presbyteries might occur every now and then. Such initiatives generally come from individual church actors though, a junior minister or an inspired community member. They seldom last beyond the individual's tenure.

Since 2011, there appears to be some detente as a DRC brokered settlement between the DRCA and URCSA is gradually bearing fruit. With a 1 million Rand fund from the DRC, the other two churches have, after almost two decades of dispute, been able to negotiate an end to several court cases. A 2013 greeting message from URCSA to the DRC described the fund as "a sign for us that the DRC accepts co-responsibility for the conflict between the sister churches in the Free State and actually wants to do something about it."[91] Other signs of improvement are emerging at the Theology Faculty of the University of the Free State (UFS). Similar to Stellenbosch, this university and above all its theology department used to be Afrikaner bastions. The university as a whole changed but the faculty remained behind. Today, a majority of the UFS' students are

---

90   Conversation between the URCSA Management and representatives of Afrikaans speaking congregations of URCSA in the Free State, URCSA Heidedal South, 1 May 2014.

91   Ds Mokone Tswabisi John Letsie. Quoted in: *DRC Free State 2013*, Handelinge [Actions]. Bothaville, 14–17 June 2013, 118.

black, except at the Theology Faculty. Nonetheless, the still mostly white Theology Faculty has been making efforts to attract academics and students from other churches and population groups. While diversity is sparse, the Faculty these days boasts a nominally integrated student organization and constitutes one of the few platforms in the Free State where ministers, students and theologians of both URCSA and the DRC can interact, whether through class, seminars or in the common coffee room. Some of them have quietly been uttering support for church unity and even for the adoption of *Belhar* in the DRC, often with great skepticism regarding the probability that either will succeed. Many are frightful to bring their changing opinions into congregations they believe to remain deeply antagonistic towards any effort of integration. What is really happening inside these congregations?

4.3.2   City Tales: "We are Open"

The literal translation of Bloemfontein, "fountain of flowers," can be quite deceptive. Once a year, usually in October, the city indeed prides itself with abundant flowers and especially roses covering its gardens and green spaces. For much of the year however, Bloemfontein is as arid as the countryside surrounding it. Apart from a few well-tended parks and the gardens of its wealthier suburbs, the capital of the Free State, as well as the seat for the national Supreme Court of Appeal, resembles an urban jungle with broken pavement, large pedestrian-unfriendly intersections, fast food restaurants and inner city decay. The center offers a contrasting sight of homeless people camping out in front of monumental buildings that reflect the city's history as the judicial capital of the country during the apartheid era and a legislative center of the earlier Boer Republics.

Racial and social-economic disparities sharply divide Bloemfontein's majority poor black population from its middle class white and mostly Afrikaans speaking community, but with notable deviations. More than Stellenbosch, Bloemfontein is also home to impoverished whites as well as upwardly mobile blacks in addition to a small lower to middle class colored community. Illustrative of the latter is URCSA Heatherdale, a booming church located in the crime and drug-ridden township of Heidedal. It tends to a mix of poor and somewhat wealthier congregants who speak mostly Afrikaans, but also Sesotho and English. DRC De Bloem in turn represents those associated with "the new poverty among Afrikaners" on the edge of the city center.[92] After a long period of decline, De Bloem's membership today consists of a small community of white

---

92   NG Gemeente De Bloem 75 Jaar [DRC Congregation De Bloem 75 Years], 2010, 11.

single parent families, elderly and intellectually disabled inhabitants of a lower class neighborhood, in addition to a number of colored and black members who have recently joined the once homogeneously white Afrikaans congregation. Heatherdale and De Bloem will serve as case studies in the rest of this section to explore the often ambiguous trajectories of inner-city churches as they navigate changing neighborhoods and identities.

Both Heatherdale and De Bloem are based in struggling parts of Bloemfontein. Where the URCSA congregation presides over a long history of deprivation among its members, the DRC community still tries to come to terms with the more recent transition of its constituency from middle class to increasingly poor. Neither congregation signaled much interest in unity. Altering circumstances however, and the ways in which the two churches tried to tackle these changes, were gradually generating more diversity in their midst.

Starting with URCSA Heatherdale, it is important to first note its history as one of the main colored congregations within the Free State's Reformed Church family. This history is deeply entangled with that of the neighborhood.[93] During the apartheid era, Heidedal became a designated colored group area, and a stronghold for this relatively small population group in the region. Today the area is still largely colored, but community boundaries are blurring. Heidedal borders the predominantly black township of Bochabela that harbors its own URCSA congregation. While interactions between the two communities remain limited, they occasionally cooperate on the vast social problems both share. It is also increasingly common for Heidedal's residents to mix some English and Sesotho into their Afrikaans home language. Many have family relationships with someone with a Sesotho background. Others have gradually been moving up the social ladder and work or study in English speaking environments together with people from other population groups.

When visiting URCSA Heatherdale in April 2014, the congregation appeared at the forefront of these developments. At that time, ministers and members alike celebrated the outcome of a nine year internal renewal process that was said to have transformed Heatherdale from a stagnant and aging community of around five hundred souls, into a vibrant church with over a thousand members. Many continued to live on or below the poverty threshold. Nonetheless, URCSA Heatherdale claimed to have raised sufficient funds to finance a new building with plenty of space for church offices and activities, particularly for its newly established charity organization. This organization, the Bloemfontein Life Change Center, had just been set up with the specific purpose to help

---

93   URCSA Heatherdale describes this history at its website: http://www.vgkheatherdale.co
      .za/index.asp?PID=78. Visited at 30 March 2014.

Heidedal as well as neighboring communities improve living standards. Besides the provision of basic necessities, the Center was aimed at building youth capacities to have a better chance at job opportunities and break vicious cycles of school failure, unemployment, drugs and crime. Early 2014, the Center was still in its infancy. But according to interviewees, it had already served as a catalyst for members in the congregation to become more involved with social projects, from knitting workshops to prisoner support or vocational training.[94]

The Life Change Center formed a cornerstone of Heatherdale's renewed identity to be an active player in its community. Under leadership of the charismatic Reverend Pienaar, the church adapted to suit the needs of a younger and changing constituency. Instead of the Afrikaans-only services of the past that members felt mimicked the white church's rather formal style, Rev. Pienaar preached dynamically and often at least partly bilingually.[95] During a special Good Friday service the Reverend went back and forth between English and Afrikaans without translating particular words or phrases. The church choir similarly switched from songs in Afrikaans to English to Sesotho. Some joined in enthusiastically with the Sesotho songs and clapped and danced in a manner reminiscent of the nearby URCSA Bochabela congregation. Others were carried away by traditional Afrikaans songs one might also hear in churches like De Bloem. The sermon explicitly mentioned the importance of inclusivity. Referencing a Biblical story in which Jesus Christ granted paradise to his fellow prisoner at the cross, the Reverend urged the congregation to reach out to everyone in their community, also to those "who have gone wrong." "It is never too late to turn to Jesus."[96] The minister team itself exemplified another form of inclusivity, involving a female white minister recently ordained in URCSA. Heatherdale strongly marketed itself as an outward focused church. An elaborate website and large banners on church walls explicated Heatherdale's mission to make a difference in the world, take care of the vulnerable and collaborate with other churches, particularly in the Reformed Church family.

Notable in URCSA Heatherdale's renewal process was its emphasis on self-reliance. It offered a sharp contrast with other colored congregations in the Free State that greatly depend on the regional synod or even the DRC for the continuation of their church services. URCSA Heatherdale also received financial support from the DRC to for instance sustain Reverend Pienaar's salary. But its members and ministers reiterated throughout conversations that the congregation worked hard to expand its own resources. Outside funds were raised, members grouped

---

94   Interviews, URCSA Heatherdale members, 29 April 2014.
95   Interview, URCSA Heatherdale member, 29 April 2014.
96   Reverend Pienaar during Good Friday service, 18 April 2014.

together to collect the annual dues or encouraged each other to volunteer in the construction of the new building. "We did not pay anything when we were still the Mission Church. The DRC was our big daddy. ... Now we pay ourselves!"[97]

Talks with the DRC about a future merger did not figure particularly high on Heatherdale's agenda. Reverend Pienaar expressed his disappointment with the process thus far. Having been involved in local conversations about collaboration between the two churches for several years, he said he had lost confidence in the DRC's commitment to unity. "Some [DRC members] still call us 'kaffir' ministers." "It is hard to acknowledge for them that their grandpa was heretic."[98] Implied in this last point was the 1980's denouncement by the black Reformed churches of racial segregation as sinful, especially through the *Belhar Confession*. The minister explained that this era still shaped his attitudes towards the DRC and that it would take a new younger generation of leaders and ministers for the churches to transcend their historic divisions. Until then, the Reverend along with his fellow ministers felt they should focus on getting their own house in order. The DRC needed to sort out its internal divisions regarding *Belhar* while URCSA still had work to do in settling with the DRCA and gaining financial independence.

URCSA Heatherdale's leadership appeared especially reluctant to enter into any small-scale agreements on pulpit- or other exchanges with the DRC before both churches were ready to sign up for the national unity it remained deeply devoted to. Such agreements were considered a soothing tool and an excuse to evade tough decisions about the *Belhar Confession* or finances. Past joint projects had only engendered disillusion as few from the DRC turned up and the projects had slowly bled to death without any tangible results. The one form of viable partnership still valued by the minister, constituted concrete cooperation on for instance the Life Change Center. DRC donations and other forms of support were welcomed here, even with the recognition that just giving money formed yet another easy way to avoid commitment.[99]

The frustrations apparent among Heatherdale's leaders did not necessarily resonate with its members. Among the congregants I spoke with, all expressed high appreciation for a chance to interact across racial boundaries through the small-scale arrangements their ministers dismissed. At Heatherdale, they said they had experienced the importance of engaging with people from different social-economic backgrounds. Members who had moved up the social ladder

---

97   Interview, URCSA Heatherdale member, 29 April 2014.
98   Interview, Reverend Pienaar, 11 April 2014. – Kaffir is considered a gravely derogative term stemming from the apartheid era when it was commonly used to refer to a black person.
99   Interview, Reverend Pienaar, 11 April 2014.

often continued attending the otherwise poor congregation and provided significant financial backing for its activities. In the end though, "class is an issue, but color is more of an issue." Members stressed the importance of learning from and about the different communities still separated by race. Many were deeply concerned about the persistent troubles inside their own neighborhood, especially with respect to the youth. They hoped that through collaboration with the DRC, their community could gain more expertise in effectively organizing activities at the new Life Change Center.

For such contact, structures were widely believed to be inevitable. These could include anything from prearranged mutual church visits to joint youth camps and church council meetings.[100] An older member and teacher said he looked back favorably to events that had been organized together in the past with a nearby DRC congregation. The joint initiatives would have ceased not because of a lack of interest or racial divisions, but rather because "people got busy." Issues of race, prejudice and apartheid traumas were perhaps recognized. In general, URCSA Heatherdale tended to downplay them as matters they felt ready to leave behind. One congregant made it explicit that there was really no need to talk about the past as it would likely upset white people and cause them to stay away.[101] He rather focused on having exposure, something he and other members agreed, had to be initiated by local church leaders and ministers on either side.

Compared to Heatherdale, De Bloem's problems seem relatively modest. Its members reside in affordable rental apartments in a central part of the city that might have seen better days, but that remains far ahead of the destitution found in Heidedal. Some thirty families rely on the church for weekly food packages. Many others receive government benefits to supplement meager incomes and pensions. The community totals around 730 confessing and 100 baptized members, about half of the 1600 attending De Bloem in the mid-seventies. This decline has for decades been a source of deep disturbance to the congregation. A 75 year anniversary publication described the impoverishment and diminution of De Bloem's community in close relation to the country's transition after 1994. With the arrival of a black majority government, the community was said to have experienced the "integration of residential areas" and the "verswarting," literally "blackening," of neighborhood industries. With this last controversial phrase, the publication referred specifically to the increasing numbers of blacks working at the local railway services, a long-time

---

100   Interviews, URCSA Heatherdale members, 29 April 2014.
101   Interview, URCSA Heatherdale member, 29 April 2014.

major employer of De Bloem's traditionally white congregants.[102] Due to these circumstances, the publication asserted, many of the congregation's Afrikaner membership left the area while those who stayed faced increasing poverty. White newcomers tend to stay only short periods of time before moving on to a better place to live. A more consistent group of newcomers is made up of the black and colored residents who moved in the neighborhood and of whom several have in recent years turned to De Bloem as their spiritual home. The arrival of black and colored churchgoers forms part of a rather unintentional transition at the once homogeneously white church which has everything to do with its decline.

The steep drop in membership is far from unique to De Bloem congregation. Across South Africa, city centers have seen vast changes since the end of apartheid as white residents moved to the suburbs, taking with them businesses, schools and infrastructure. The small city congregation of De Bloem developed a rather singular strategy to cope with its new reality though. In the early 2000's it started to supplement the dwindling collections from its members through a catering initiative that offered services at events outside the church, from weddings to corporate parties. Instead of, or in addition to paying their dues, members volunteered by cooking or serving food and as such helped make money for the congregation. The pragmatic and dedicated Reverend Smith professionalized the initiative to the extent that it counted, according to his own estimates in 2014, for a good fifty percent of De Bloem's annual income.[103] The catering service provided essential funding for social works in the immediate community. It paid for the soup kitchen or for an outing for the children to a nearby garden.

Above all, the catering service was often mentioned during conversations with members and in the congregation's documentation as a source of inspiration for everyone to engage with the neighborhood and the church. Deeply engrained was the notion that anyone could contribute regardless of their social-economic status or background. At the annual fundraising bazaar, elderly ladies prepared pancakes while single mothers helped clean up in exchange for a food parcel. The anniversary publication told their story: "[The members'] greatest concern would become their greatest blessings. They do not have much money, but there is nothing wrong with their hands! (...) Especially the 'gatherings' around the stove often amount to the most profound pastoral conversations."[104]

---

102   *De Bloem 75 Jaar*, 4.
103   Interview, Reverend Smith, 30 April 2014.
104   *De Bloem 75 Jaar*, 1.

With the gradually expanding catering service, De Bloem changed its position in the neighborhood. Beyond a congregation that merely served its immediate members, the church began to reach further outwards. Eager to draw in new clients, members engaged people outside the neighborhood and welcomed whoever could contribute to service, regardless of their background. One unexpected development in this transition story comprised the arrival of a still very small but nonetheless surprising number of black and colored churchgoers. In 2014 around ten non-white families were regularly attending the sermons of Reverend Smith and joining in with local congregational events like the bazaar or the catering project. Rev. Smith proudly pointed out the spontaneous nature of their arrival. "I welcomed black families just like I welcomed white people – no worse, no better."[105] According to the minister, most of these newcomers have thus far involved residents in De Bloem's immediate neighborhood with slightly higher incomes than its regular members. Some transferred directly from an URCSA congregation, where others previously attended different denominations across the city. One woman told her story of leaving URCSA Heatherdale for DRC De Bloem five years ago after she moved closer to the city center and the car with which she had still been driving to Heidedal broke down. "We decided to give Bloem a try." "I feel welcome here, it is like family."[106] She appreciated De Bloem's community engagement for which she arranged donations through her work at a major supermarket chain. Similar comments were made by a mixed race couple that visited De Bloem's annual bazaar with their newborn baby. "We live close by and just decided to drop by."

Evaluating the changes in their congregations, members and ministers emphasized that De Bloem had in fact stayed the same. It remained a conservative congregation, far removed from the transformation processes happening in their larger Reformed family, or their country for that matter. Preoccupied with the mere survival of the church as well as the direct needs of its members, De Bloem just like Heatherdale, indicated scarce interest in topics of racial integration or church unification. Where Heatherdale still mentioned the goal of collaboration among the Reformed churches on its banners and websites, De Bloem refrained from even nominally supporting such collaboration.

Congregants mostly conveyed their satisfaction with having gained congregational autonomy through the catering project. Few appeared keen to spend their energy on inter-church partnerships of which they did not see any direct

---

105   Interview, Reverend Smith, 30 April 2014.
106   Interview, DRC De Bloem member, 1 May 2014.

benefit. The main priority, members said, constituted their ability to preserve the congregation and to practice their faith by helping the vulnerable in their neighborhood. "We do mission work in our own community, not outside, as so much happens right here."[107] This woman clarified that she did not oppose the idea of unity per se. She felt rather indifferent towards a merger between the DRC and URCSA or towards racial integration in the church, especially since in her view the congregation was already a place of inclusion. "It is not about the DRC. It is about Jesus Christ." Reverend Smith added to this the overall suspicion among his members and himself towards any institutional change or so-called reconciliation enforced from the top. "The plan for one united General Synod is being associated with the transition of South Africa," he explained. "The idea back then was that everyone could stay themselves. That did not happen and that hurt a lot."[108] People in the congregation were according to Rev. Smith unlikely to go along with official unity structures, fearing they would be overwhelmed and become a diminished minority just like in the rest of society.

The minister's sermons as well as conversations with members left little doubt as to how they understood 'themselves.' The congregation stood firmly for a conservative view towards church tradition, moral values as well as national politics. The Sunday service comprised for most interviewees a place of quiet and formal worship in which the minister did not shy from uttering sharp critique on current affairs, from *Belhar* to corruption or the so-called reverse discrimination against whites. In the week leading up to the twentieth anniversary of South Africa's democracy, Rev. Smith raised the question whether, in the past two decades, "the people of the country have truly become more free, or have the oppressors rather changed faces? … Have we withdrawn in a dark corner, too careful to name the evils of violence, murder, rape, the injustice of restorative action, corruption and poverty?"[109]

Besides Smith, congregants at De Bloem have been served by the outspoken theologian and former General Synod moderator Piet Strauss. Strauss is not only known for openly voicing his opposition to adopt the *Belhar Confession* in the DRC. He has also led one of the last Afrikaner bulwarks, the youth organization of *Die Voortrekkers,* and enthusiastically shared the organization's central goals to promote Afrikaner culture as well as the "good parts of Afrikaner

---

107　Interview, DRC De Bloem member, 6 April 2014.
108　Interview, Reverend Smith, 30 April 2014.
109　Reverend Smith. "Aan wie is jy eintlik gehoorsaam?" [To whom are you really obedient?]. Sunday Sermon. 20 April 2014.

history."[110] For the congregants I interviewed, De Bloem's Afrikaans character was usually taken for granted. No one, not even Piet Strauss, spoke of an Afrikaner ethnicity, nation or "volk." Instead, emphasis was put on the Afrikaans language as prime identity marker. Several realized though that in the future even De Bloem might switch to English. If that were to be the case, they were not sure they would stay with the church.[111]

The presence of black congregants and the increasingly outward focused activities of De Bloem had thus done little to change its perceived identity. Conservative values and politics in addition to Afrikaans and a sense of care for the entire community remained persistent markers of the congregation's self-perception. Congregants recognized that some of these traits, especially language, formed reasons for why non-whites rather stayed away from their church. Why some had decided to make De Bloem their church was little accounted for. In general, churchgoers, whether identifying as white, black or colored, did not made much of their interaction across the color line. Some articulated appreciation for the minister and the way he welcomed people regardless of their social-economic or racial background. The fact that the church had over the past years become a home for people with intellectual disabilities also emerged as a factor preparing the congregation for diversity and was said to have further enhanced their belief in being a church for the entire local community. As long as racial integration, if that word was even used, happened locally and spontaneously, without undermining the congregation's core values, congregants claimed to "have no problem with it."[112]

Despite their many differences, Heatherdale and De Bloem represent similar dynamics occurring on either side of the Reformed Church family. The congregations both portrayed themselves as first and foremost a community church. Neither was keen on institutional collaboration whether within their own denomination or with others. Instead, the two congregations developed strategies to enhance their independence. These strategies effectively combined member participation with local projects to expand the financial resources necessary for gaining more autonomy. Members who could not pay their dues were invited to volunteer. Those in wealthier positions were asked to invest not merely in the church, but in their community.

---

110   Die Voortrekkers Strategiese Plan vir 2013–2017 [Die Voortrekkers Strategic Plan for 2013–2017], 2. Accessed at 12 August 2015, https://www.houkoers.co.za/Dokumentasie/Literatuur. NB. Die Voortrekkers comprises an organization specifically meant to preserve and foster Afrikaner language, culture and history among youth.

111   Interview, DRC De Bloem member, 25 April 2014.

112   Interview, DRC De Bloem member, 25 April 2014.

The focus on the local elucidated the congregations' disinterest in official unification processes. Members nor ministers saw how this could advance their own goals and in general exhibited suspicion towards initiatives coming from the churches' national or regional leadership. At De Bloem members admitted they had not read the extensive materials from their General Synod about the *Belhar Confession* and its importance to church unity, but that they were nonetheless convinced that it amounted to propaganda for a politicized document meant to destabilize the DRC. At Heatherdale, congregants had long distanced themselves from the regional URCSA leadership which they felt did not represent their interests. Copies of *URCSA News* or other national church documents on issues like unification were also scarce if made available at all.

Such indifference may be little surprising. More remarkable was the lack of greater resistance as often presumed by national leaders in both churches. For members at Heatherdale, a merger of the DRC and URCSA constituted something inevitable that would happen perhaps not in their lifetime, but in that of their children. They realized the impediment their past formed to any reconciliation within the Reformed family. Still, they claimed to be willing to set this aside for the sake of more contact in the future. De Bloem's congregants largely dismissed the past as a problem. Their focus was on the present. New church structures, including even *Belhar*, were in the end not believed to make much of a difference for De Bloem's daily struggle to tend to its neighborhood. Besides, De Bloem as well as Heatherdale signaled pride in implementing on ground level the inclusiveness their national leaders advocated, even, or especially, without committing to the broader vision of church unity. In both cases, close affiliation between the church and its traditional community had not prevented people from different backgrounds joining and being welcomed. Diversity was appreciated, if not in terms of race, then in terms of class or social status.

Here we should note a significant divergence between the two congregations. Where Heatherdale sought to accommodate differences among its members, De Bloem rather expected new members to adopt its established church culture. Heatherdale turned the changes deemed necessary to attract people from the Sotho-Tswana community into a success story of internal renewal. Its ability to adapt had made the congregation stronger and bigger as new members started to join the church. In the meantime, URCSA Heatherdale continued to present itself as the historic home for colored people in the Free State. It remained deeply invested in this particular constituency and protective of its language and minority position.

De Bloem conversely, had been resisting any form of change until change literally appeared at its doorsteps. Members almost ignored the presence of black and colored families in their midst, claiming they were no different than themselves and that their church stayed the same. This perception was facilitated through the fact that most newcomers comprised middle class residents of the neighborhood. They formed less of a threat to the lower class white community than poorer blacks from the townships perceived to be stealing jobs or bringing crime. Congregants also seemed eager to evade references to their own racial or ethnic background and instead stressed other elements of their identity, namely conservative morals and Afrikaans language. However limited the actual diversity at DRC De Bloem, it tuned in with the congregation's self-description as a nonetheless inclusive community. In this description, the idea of one united and multiracial church was not necessarily denounced, but rather dismissed as pointless. As one church council member explained, "society wants churches to come together but in the meanwhile we are open to other people."[113]

4.3.3   *In the Country: "People Can No Longer Avoid It"*

Despite decades of urbanization, a vast segment of the Reformed Church family remains based in small agricultural communities. These village congregations, made up of mostly farmers, farmworkers and their families, are often idealized as situations in which the church is occupying a central position instead of competing with others at the fringes of a diverse urban religious landscape. Rural churchgoers are known to be tightly knit and committed to their congregation as they jointly seek to stave off problems of poverty and disease.[114] For a growing number of rural congregations, these difficulties mount to a sheer struggle for survival. No longer able to sustain themselves, they are forced to find alternative strategies to continue worshipping in the tradition and style they are accustomed to. Among these strategies has been collaboration with different Reformed churches, across the color line. Throughout the Free State and in other remote parts of the country, black, colored and white Reformed congregations increasingly share buildings and resources, not because they want to but because they feel they have no choice. Cooperation has become the only way towards preservation of one's church community. Interracial contact occurs here as an unintentional side-effect rather than a conscious strategy towards unification.

We will be looking at two examples. One involves the story of Ladybrand in which an URCSA community moved in with a local DRC congregation. The other pertains to Philippolis where a DRC congregation called in the help of its

---

113   Interview, DRC De Bloem member, 25 April 2014.
114   See Christina Landman, "Klein is Lekker" [Small is Nice], *Kruisgewys*, June 2014.

URCSA neighbor and asked to share the URCSA minister's time and services. In both cases, communities opened up once strictly homogeneous and racially exclusive church identities and began unusual partnerships with long-time adversaries. How did these transitions, if one can describe them as such, occur?

On the border with the Kingdom of Lesotho, Ladybrand has managed to steer off some of the worst effects of rural decline by operating as a hub for local businesses and tourists on their way in or out of Lesotho. Still, the roads are filled with potholes, crime is up and unemployment high. The town used to have two DRC congregations, a DRCA and an URCSA congregation based in the township of Mauersnek. In 2003, the latter officially closed down after years of mismanagement and financial woes. Different narratives circulate about how and why this closure occurred. Fingers have been pointed at the largely absent part-time minister who had to drive two hours from Bloemfontein and was scarcely invested in the congregation.[115] Poverty played a role as the community could not afford a full-time minister nor keep up its building. Above all, former congregants blamed the DRC that had owned their building ever since apartheid and unilaterally decided to sell it to the American non-profit Hope International Missions. This organization turned the URCSA church into a multipurpose building that included an Evangelical church and a school.[116] Some congregants stayed at the new church, but many drifted away. They tried out the nearby DRCA and several other congregations. Ultimately, a small group began attending the very DRC congregation, Moedergemeente Ladybrand, that had sold their building. By 2014, this group had grown to around thirty members who now formed a steady colored presence at what had thus far been a homogeneously white church of just around 500 congregants.

When asked about why they made this transition, people in the Mauersnek community first of all highlighted motives of faith. "I spiritually grow here," one woman stated.[117] She had visited a range of different churches before turning to the DRC and had found little resonance there. Especially the DRCA had been a disappointment as she could not relate to its charismatic style and constant demand for money to pay for church services. The formality and conservatism characterizing the DRC's services appealed more to the Mauersnek community than the DRCA's "born-again dancing."[118] Many also appreciated the fact that

---

115   Interviews, DRC Ladybrand members/former URCSA Mauersnek members; Reverend Kleynhans, 24 April 2014.

116   "Hope Christian Academy," *Lesotho Letters,* January-February 2007. Accessed at 15 July 2015, http://www.gsgault.com/Newsletter_Archive/2007iJan.pdf.

117   Interviews, DRC Ladybrand members/former URCSA Mauersnek members, 24 April 2014.

118   Interviews, DRC Ladybrand members/former URCSA Mauersnek members, 24 April 2014.

they were not compelled to pay their dues and rather received support, including a bus service especially arranged by Moedergemeente Ladybrand to pick them up at the township each Sunday and drive them to the central location of the DRC. They were realistic about the fact that they could not afford their own minister. Moving in with the DRC had become the second-best option to allow the Mauersnek community to preserve, or rather revive, its Reformed tradition. It moreover presented an opportunity to challenge the white community. Interviewees expressed pride in having pushed comfort zones. "I'm going to church. I don't care what people in church think about me, whether they like me or not. We sit in the middle of the pews when whites move to the corners." They recalled text messages they had initially sent to DRC members, saying that "God loves us all." These days, Mauersnek members claimed, more people, white and colored, were attending the church. "We made a change at DRC Moedergemeente."[119]

This change however occurred far from smoothly. It took churchgoers from Mauersnek close to two decades to make the transition and their presence at the DRC has remained humble. They initially received a lukewarm welcome, with white congregants not merely moving to the corners of the pews, but threatening to leave at the prospect of an increasingly diverse congregation. This fed existing suspicions among the Mauersnek community that the DRC was prejudiced against them. For years, people preferred to attend the Hope Missions Evangelical church, or no church at all, over joining their supposed sister congregation. Only recently members said they overcame the grave insult caused by the DRC when it sold off their building without consulting any of the former URCSA members. After a joint conversation with the DRC minister in 2013, "it was forgiven and forgotten."[120]

At Moedergemeente, congregants meanwhile appeared far less eager to forgive and forget the grievances they claim to have experienced in the past and present. These included the broadly felt deterioration of their living conditions since 1994 in addition to a long history of strife to protect their Afrikaner minority identity against dominant powers, whether British in the past or black today. "It's bigger than racism," a theology student familiar with the congregation explained. "It's in our blood."[121] The arrival of people from outside the traditional DRC membership base triggered, according to the student as well as the involved minister, deep anxieties inside the congregation. Colored people were feared to soon be arriving in bus loads and take over the church just as black Africans had taken over the country.

---

119   Interviews, DRC Ladybrand members/former URCSA Mauersnek members, 24 April 2014.
120   Interviews, DRC Ladybrand members/former URCSA Mauersnek members, 24 April 2014.
121   Conversation, DRC member, 24 April 2014.

In this tensed context, any talk of unity or interracial collaboration seemed futile. The deeply committed minister of DRC Moedergemeente, Reverend Kleynhans, stressed that he hardly ever addressed either topic explicitly and in general avoided references to politics or current affairs. Instead, the minister developed a careful strategy of coaxing both sides into sharing their worship space, no more and no less. Towards the Mauersnek community he extended throughout the years multiple invitations to visit his congregation. He arranged the bus service and made sure the children could join the Sunday school either in separate Sesotho or in joint Afrikaans classes. Notably, he made time for pastoral care for the new members, which several lamented they did not receive in the other churches they attended. Simultaneously, Rev. Kleynhans prepared his own congregation for the change that he felt was bound to happen. This involved the constant repetition of one of his main beliefs that "if we follow Jesus, we must be a warm community."[122] Along with his wife, a social worker in Ladybrand and surroundings, the minister encouraged the congregation to not only love their neighbors but find out who their neighbors were. He showed pictures depicting the shacks of townships like Mauersnek, collected money and engaged in employment projects for the black community in town. A central motto guiding these actions figured prominently on the congregation's website: "I stand up today to make a difference in God's world."[123]

Beyond seeking to inspire his constituency on the basis of faith, the minister did not shy from addressing their concerns. In a 2013 letter to all members, he acknowledged their distress with changes in the congregation, "especially in light of the falling apart of the rest of the country and [of the fact] that the church is in reality the only place where we can keep things together."[124] Rev. Kleynhans assured the congregation that as soon as the number of newcomers increased significantly, he would be looking into possibilities for a separate worship facility in Mauersnek. "Still, I want to share with you that these events [the presence of colored members] in many ways enhanced the credibility of the congregation as follower of Jesus."[125]

---

122 Interview, Reverend Kleynhans, 24 April 2014.

123 Website DRC Moedergemeente Ladybrand. Visited at 10 July 2015, http://www.ladybrand .gcehosting.com/www.ladybrand.info/default.html.

124 Reverend Kleynhans, "Aan die lidmate van NG Moedergemeente Ladybrand" [To the members of DRC Moedergemeente Ladybrand],13 November 2013. Important to note here is that the minister began his letter by discussing the country's problems primarily in terms of climate change, high gas prices and economic crisis. More contentious issues such as corruption and crime were not mentioned.

125 Ibidem.

The DRC minister thus positioned himself at the center of his congregation's path towards change. How much change actually occurred is however dubious. The move of the Mauersnek community towards DRC Ladybrand can hardly be seen as a step towards integration. As in the case of De Bloem, it rather comprised the adoption of members with a different racial and social-economic background into a white congregation and its predominantly conservative Afrikaans identity. Little of this identity altered upon or after their arrival. Trying to sooth members' concerns, the Reverend in fact reaffirmed the sense that diversity posed a serious threat to Moedergemeente's historic constituency. Installing separate worship services for the white Moedergemeente and colored Mauersnek communities was presented as a natural solution to prevent the former from losing its position as a "place where we can keep things together." It should be noted that where the term "colored" regularly surfaced, neither the minister nor members made much reference to "white" or "Afrikaner." They rather assumed both characteristics as implicit markers of Moedergemeente Ladybrand's identity that were unlikely to disappear anytime soon, whether or not the population of the congregation became more heterogeneous.

Change for the congregation came down to the acceptance of this new reality, and its gradual normalization. These days, the minister was convinced, members no longer felt confronted by the presence of people from Mauersnek in their sanctuary. They did not talk about it, nor did they resist it. He also believed their presence had crucially helped transform DRC members' stereotypes about the township community from angry poor to joyful worshippers in their midst. For the colored worshippers themselves, change meant first and foremost pride. They did not see themselves as merely adapting to the DRC. They claimed to symbolize the transition their entire country had made after apartheid by praying and singing freely along with people who used to dominate them.

Ladybrand illustrates an intriguing development across the country in which small numbers of colored and at times black Reformed communities have begun to approach nearby DRC congregations for immediate support with their church services. In several cases, the former evolved into separate sections of their neighboring DRC, with perhaps the same minister, but with their own worship times. The case of Ladybrand is unique in the sense that the community actually moved in and, thus far at least, did not evolve into a detached section or "wijk" of Moedergemeente Ladybrand.

The opposite almost happened in Philippolis, a small picturesque village surrounded by vast empty plains and farmlands in the south of the Free State. The two Reformed churches of Philippolis, the centrally located DRC Philippolis and URCSA Bergmanshoogte in one of the townships on the edge of the village, have both at different moments in their recent history endured deep crises. The DRC initially helped out Bergmanshoogte by establishing a fund to pay for a new minister in the late nineties. Several years later, it was DRC Philippolis that could no longer afford a full-time salary. In 2007 it turned to URCSA to request a special partnership in which both churches would share the time and services of the minister of Bergmanshoogte. Since then, Reverend Van Schalkwyk has been tending to both churches in addition to a third DRC congregation a few miles further south. The three congregations continue to function as autonomous entities, tending to their respective colored and white communities separately. But they have done so on the basis of a quite extraordinary interdependent relationship in which the DRC no longer constitutes the dominant player that supports a poor URCSA community, but both need each other to keep afloat.

Before discussing how this relationship manifested itself, it is important to address the circumstances. DRC Philippolis forms the smallest congregation within the dwindling Presbytery of Fauresmith. Between 2000 and 2010, the Presbytery lost over twenty percent of its members as many moved to the cities, abroad or for other reasons no longer felt at home in the DRC. In 2013, DRC Philippolis was estimated to have a mere 230 members left.[126] The congregation along with the town itself epitomize the degeneration of the countryside we see across South Africa. Besides rising unemployment, the breakdown of public services and security, Philippolis suffered significantly from the HIV AIDS epidemic and the failure of local health services to cope with it. The epidemic arrived here in 1998 and lasted throughout the 2000s. It primarily hit the townships. Here, an average of 17 funerals per month comprised HIV AIDS related deaths, to the extent that the cemeteries could barely cope with the number of burials at the height of the epidemic.[127]

In a town of just 5000 inhabitants, few remained untouched. Orphans roamed the streets and burial grounds became awkward meeting points where white farm owners would visit black and colored communities to pay respect to a housekeeper or gardener. Both URCSA and the DRC actively responded to this crisis.[128] The Bergmanshoogte congregation in particular took up a key

---

126   Kobus Schoeman and Carin van Schalkwyk, "Klein plattelandse gemeentes as ruimtes om brûe na die hele gemeenskap te bou: 'n Prakties-teologiese ondersoek" [Small rural congregations as spaces to build bridges for the entire community], *LitNet Akademies* 10(3) (2013): 787.

127   Kate Groch, Karen E. Gerdes, Elizabeth A. Segal & Maureen Groch, "The Grassroots Londolozi Model of African Development: Social Empathy in Action," *Journal of Community Practice* 20:1–2, (2012): 168–169.

128   Schoeman and Schalkwyk, "Klein plattelandse gemeentes," 793–796.

position as the only church in town that from the beginning of the epidemic conducted burials of the heavily stigmatized HIV patients within and outside of its own community. It developed a training program to raise awareness about HIV AIDS. Congregants openly talked about sex and encouraged others in the communities to get themselves tested. The DRC community in turn engaged with a so-called teddy bear project in which members knitted stuffed animals for orphaned children in the townships. Besides a source of comfort, the teddy bears became, according to Rev. Van Schalkwyk, a way for the DRC members to actively engage with the township communities.[129] Many remained committed to the children as they grew up, at times supporting them with money for education or clothes. Ultimately, the DRC congregation turned to the township for assistance with its own problems and initiated the partnership with URCSA Bergmanshoogte.

Upon my visit in 2014, this partnership comprised an arrangement in which Reverend Van Schalkwyk dedicated forty percent of her work to URCSA Bergmanshoogte, another forty percent to DRC Philippolis and twenty percent to DRC Gariepdam. The minister traveled back and forth between these congregations as she offered each separate worship and pastoral services. For the times she was serving at one of the other communities, Bergmanshoogte hired an assistant while DRC Philippolis and Gariepdam relied heavily on lay leaders to help with or even conduct services and other church related activities. In the words of Rev. Van Schalkwyk, the congregations thus "chose to collaborate ..., but always kept their own identities."[130] Each retained its own style of worship as well as its traditionally homogenous white or colored membership. The minister highlighted the various manners in which contact between URCSA Bergmanshoogte and DRC Philippolis expanded over the years. Ever since the HIV AIDS crisis, the two communities began reaching out to each other through spontaneous small-scale initiatives. Farm owners helped out building a daycare center for the children of Bergmanshoogte. URCSA members visited elderly DRC congregants once a week to help clean the house and keep company. All prayed together when the village was without water for five consecutive days. In joint conversations, they shared frustrations about the excessive power of the ANC in their region and the need for ANC membership to get anything done, even to find a job.[131]

---

129   Interview, Reverend Van Schalkwyk, 23 April 2014.

130   Carin van Schalkwyk. "Kerkhereniging in die Suid-Vrystaat – 'n alternatiewe verhaal" [Church reunification in the South Free State – an alternative story], *Die Kerkbode*, 16 May 2008. 15.

131   Conversation, DRC-URCSA Focus group Philippolis, 28 April 2014.

An increased awareness among the two congregations of their common faith had, in the eyes of members as well as the minister, facilitated these interactions. They could not imagine themselves at integrated Sunday services, but were nonetheless convinced that their churches should and would ultimately be together.[132] Partaking in the same religious tradition was meanwhile considered a crucial factor in building trust between the colored township and Philippolis' white population. Rev. Van Schalkwyk said that members were aware of the fact that they all heard the same sermon and received similar guidance on values and morality. It helped generate a common frame of reference unique for two communities whose worlds remained far removed from each other. A DRC member gave the example of the increasing fear among white communities of farm attacks and the damage this had done to relationships with colored and black farm workers. In such situations, she stated, "it helps us trust each other, when we know we are all Christians."[133] Above all, members and minister agreed that they did not need to be physically together in church on Sunday to be united. "We pray where we feel safe." "Worship does not only happen on Sunday. It occurs when we work together, building a daycare or renovating the church building."[134]

The course of events at Philippolis should not be romanticized. The HIV AIDS crisis and subsequent developments between the two churches scarcely altered the disparate reality of white farmers owning most of the surrounding lands and black and colored communities scraping by in impoverished townships. The minister servicing the two congregations had to balance the needs and expectations of two vastly different congregations. On both sides, hierarchal patterns, in which whites support and rule over the town's non-white communities, remained embedded. Resistance to break with such patterns has continued to run deep, particularly in the DRC congregation.

Notwithstanding its decrease in numbers and finances, DRC Philippolis maintained in the eyes of the other communities as well as its own constituency, an emblem of white dominance. DRC members still held powerful positions in the town, and the church, with its high steeple and historic building, continued to symbolize this. Reverend Van Schalkwyk is white herself and has been occupying an important position as scribe of the DRC Free State regional synod. Her assistant Ms. Vermeulen at Bergmanshoogte is also white and studied to become a DRC minister at the Stellenbosch Faculty of Theology.

---

132   Conversation, DRC-URCSA Focus group Philippolis, 28 April 2014; Interview DRC member, 28 April 2014.

133   Conversation, DRC-URCSA Focus group Philippolis, 28 April 2014.

134   Interview, Reverend Van Schalkwyk, 23 April 2014.

Vermeulen remarked that "prejudice, racism and segregation are still facts in Philippolis."[135] Members on either side openly conveyed their difficulties with changing these attitudes. A colored URCSA member and community worker said she was still afraid to enter the white church she associated with the apartheid days. A white woman shared what she believed to be a prevalent notion in DRC Philippolis that people from the colored townships worshipped under the influence of alcohol and would as such feel uncomfortable in the DRC's formal church environment.[136]

On a personal level though, small changes seemed both feasible and desirable to the two congregations. Members from both sides said they interacted on increasingly equal terms, taking for granted that each had an obligation, and an opportunity, to help out the other in case of need. The symbolism of the DRC requesting help from URCSA Bergmanshoogte had made an impact. Rev. Van Schalkwyk believed URCSA members had gained confidence as they no longer comprised the only congregation holding out its hand for support. In general, churchgoers here felt more independent now that they had shown to handle a crisis as devastating as the HIV AIDS epidemic. DRC members meanwhile, had quietly come to terms with being tied to a colored congregation. Together with URCSA Bergmanshoogte, they appeared relatively content with their partnership and the small initiatives it had engendered, especially because neither had undermined the congregations' individual identities. Expectations of collaboration remained low, but the improvement of personal relationships was valued.

The assistant minister at Bergmanshoogte presented herself as example of how such relationships helped mitigate congregants' general fear for change. Being openly gay, Vermeulen had been refused an official position as minister or even assistant minister at either the DRC or URCSA.[137] Rev. Van Schalkwyk took her on as employee at a small non-profit associated with Bergmanshoogte and gradually involved her in more pastoral tasks. Over time, DRC and URCSA members became used to her presence.[138] I am no longer strange for them."

---

135   Interview, Ms. Vermeulen, 28 April 2014.

136   Conversation, DRC-URCSA Focus group Philippolis, 28 April 2014; Interview, DRC member, 28 April 2014.

137   At its General Synod of 2015 the DRC resolved to allow same-sex marriages and the ordination of ministers in a same-sex relationship.

138   This interestingly affirms the finding of Andrew Whitehead that US congregations with a positive stance towards female leadership often also tend to be more positive towards gay or lesbian membership or leadership. See: Andrew L. Whitehead, "Gendered Organizations and Inequality Regimes: Gender, Homosexuality, and Inequality Within Religious Congregations," *Journal for the Scientific Study of Religion* 52.3 (2013): 476–493.

With no resources to pay for someone else, the communities had little choice but to accept what had initially appeared a radical departure from their conservative social values. Vermeulen perceived a similar development on issues of race. Neither of the congregations had been particularly eager to engage across group boundaries. But in face of Philippolis' harsh reality, "people can no longer avoid it."[139]

The absence of the term church unification in the above discussion on Ladybrand and Philippolis is no accident. In neither case, did the communities express interest in national conversations about an official merger between their churches, nor did they engage with any broader effort towards racial integration. There appears to be some irony here. To an extent, the two rural stories epitomize the kind of church unity national leaders have long insisted on. Both comprised bottom-up initiatives in which the communities themselves chose to collaborate across the color line without being forced through official structures. At least in Philippolis, the evolving partnership included the often called for preservation of each community's local character. In Ladybrand white and colored congregants managed to actually join in worship, not a small feat in South Africa's deeply segregated church life. The involved churches nevertheless persisted their deep historic affiliations with a single racial community as well as their distrust of diversity. Their major purpose constituted survival as a community church, just as we saw with Heatherdale and De Bloem. Decisions for collaboration in Ladybrand and Philippolis were chiefly motivated by pragmatic concerns about local conditions. The rural congregations had fewer options for financial autonomy than the two city churches. Forging interracial partnerships formed in either case a last resort to ensure their own survival rather than an attempt towards reconciliation. Each community retained its own carefully constructed comfort zones, with but small cracks for individuals to interact on specific occasions, like a new church building or cleaning project.

The small-scale partnerships between the two rural DRC and URCSA communities might have generated little tangible change. They did offer a chance for these communities to engage on relatively equal terms. On the countryside, such interactions have continued to be scarce. Where urban dwellers meet each other at nominally integrated businesses, public institutions or facilities, agricultural communities often remain embedded in patriarchal patterns of the past with white farm owners on one side and black and colored farmworkers on the other. Engaging with each other in church or through church related activities constituted for members in Ladybrand and Philippolis a rare moment to step out of these traditional roles.

---

139   Interview, Ms. Vermeulen, 28 April 2014.

Faith helped level the play field. Ministers employed terminology from the Reformed churches' unity discourse to prepare congregants on either side for their inevitable contact. They presented diversity as a cause for celebration rather than fear, and inclusiveness as an expression of belief in Jesus Christ rather than a liability to conservative church identities. Individual congregants similarly made an appeal to Christian beliefs and rituals to reason why they should be together. The notion of divine unity appeared particularly import- ant among URCSA members to help overcome their deep suspicions of the white church. DRC members primarily valued the possibility to share worship, whether in church or through joint community works, as an unthreatening way to engage with black and colored neighbors on their own turf or on neu- tral territory. Both signaled strong appreciation for spontaneous opportunities to translate their beliefs into practical efforts and help improve local living conditions for all villagers.

Ultimately, few appeared impressed with these efforts. DRC members strug- gled to disassociate their URCSA partner from the deep sense of loss many still experienced since the end of apartheid. The emerging mutual dependency symbolized the painful transition from a powerful majority, political, religious and social-economic, to a minority that for its own survival now had to rely on the people they used to rule. The partnerships furthermore triggered fears for reverse domination. The little realistic yet powerful image of "busloads of coloreds" knocking at the church doors eclipsed both religious and pragmat- ic motives for cooperation. DRC members in Ladybrand as well as Philippo- lis seemed to rather accept their churches' decline than being confronted by outsiders. On URCSA's side, members put more emphasis on the gains made through their interaction with the old mother church. Expectations remained low however and barely rose above the mere fact of sitting next to a white per- son in the pews and not feeling frowned upon.

4.3.4 *Diversity, but Only on My Turf*

The four discussed case studies in many ways exemplify the backlash among Reformed communities particularly in the Free State against official efforts towards church unity. In the region's unfriendly conditions, the idea of mak- ing the church a more diverse place is rather associated with threat than with progress. Communities prioritize internal solidarity over integration, surviv- al of their own people over reconciliation with others. The churches' prima- ry function involves the ability to offer one's own community refuge from the outside world. Uniting into one church would undermine this ability. Amidst their resistance to change, congregations in the Free State have however made greater steps towards visible integration than many of their church brothers and sisters in the Cape. Willingly or unwillingly, DRC and URCSA congregations across the arid state are sharing buildings, services and ministers. They tend to include churchgoers from different backgrounds than their traditional membership even while persisting in their historic attachment to one single population group.

Underlying this paradox appears once again the growing distance between local congregations and their national as well as regional leadership. Members in the above case studies placed little trust in the institutions of either the DRC or URCSA. Both were considered to be too preoccupied with church battles around unity and *Belhar* to care about the daily realities of their constituencies. The antagonism towards these issues followed the overall disappointment with the church as a source of tangible support on top of a larger sense of disillusion with the country's failing government. Emphasis was thus put on the autonomy of the local congregation from institutional power, whether church or political, and its ability to care for the immediate community.

At De Bloem and Heatherdale, this urge for independence emerged as the congregation's top priority. In their search for greater financial autonomy and a stronger position in the neighborhood, both congregations ended up loosening deeply engrained racial affiliations. Perceptions of who belonged to the immediate community were widened to include non-whites or Sesotho speakers. A similar opening up could be discerned in Ladybrand and Philippolis where local partnerships across the color line gained appreciation as strategies to survive as a congregation and better care for the entire village.

Compared to the Cape, the Free State case studies thus display an alternative and quite contradictory route towards overcoming church divisions. Apart from small-scale agreements to for instance share a minister's time, the route seems void of formal structures. It built largely on grassroots initiatives among individuals who tended to pick and choose from the various religious discourses available to them. They wholeheartedly denounced the *Belhar Confession* as a politicized document and simultaneously stressed the importance of its three major themes, unity, reconciliation and justice. Ministers developed entire sermons around values of diversity and inclusiveness, only to reiterate the congregation's key responsibility to safeguard its distinct culture and language. The reverends at De Bloem, Heatherdale, Ladybrand and Philippolis each employed strong references to the Bible that congregants claimed were influential in creating a sense of social cohesion across race and class distinctions. Rarely, did ministers couple such language with a call for structural efforts of interracial collaboration. It primarily served as inspiration for members to spontaneously reach out to one another at the local level. Anything above this level was rather discouraged as at best a waste of time, or at worst a risk to the community. Diversity was better considered to remain within boundaries that could be controlled. Inside De Bloem's sanctuary or during social works in Philippolis, individual interactions with people from the village or the neighborhood presented less of a danger than the idea of greater church integration and its anticipated ramifications for the future of the community.

This unstructured and hesitant approach might have triggered gradual processes inside Free State congregations towards more inclusivity. But in each of the discussed cases, change remained limited to short term alliances between specific groups of individuals. Among them were primarily ministers from the DRC and members from URCSA. Both held pragmatic interests in interracial collaboration as a way to sustain their communities. Both also sought to bolster these interests through strong religious motives. Such motives often turned out to be insufficient though to persuade others. DRC ministers across the four cases encountered steep resistance from their constituencies to alliances that were perceived as but one more defeat for the Afrikaner people. On the side of URCSA, members confronted ministers and regional leaders highly skeptical of any cooperation that would provide white churches a sense of victory over the past. This discrepancy between ordinary churchgoers and their ministers appears emblematic for the Reformed churches' struggle with unity. As one Bloemfontein minister asserted: "just URCSA members and DRC leaders together would work well."[140] Now, neither finds backup for their efforts to cross boundaries. Consequently, such efforts barely moved beyond local, or even just personal relationships.

The limited scope of the discussed cases raises questions about whether the Free State's grassroots approach generates any substantial progress in integrating communities. It might further interracial contact on a personal level, whether as a result of sheer pragmatism or on the basis of religious principles. In the end, the same problem emerges as Becker, Emerson and Smith among others have noted in the United States. Focus is given almost exclusively to individuals while structural inequalities are kept in place, if not reinforced. At this personal level diversity is moderately tolerated, but only under the condition that it does not interrupt the ways in which the community and larger society are organized. The stories of Bloemfontein, Ladybrand and Philippolis appear exemplary of this dynamic. Whether black, white or colored, faith communities generally shunned tough discussions about institutional discrimination or legacies of the apartheid past as these were feared to upset the already precarious balance inside a neighborhood or village with multiple identity groups present.

---

140   Interview, DRC minister, 16 April 2014.

The conscious avoidance of structural change however did not prevent the unfurling of a different type of transition. Through their emphasis on the local and the individual, the churches of the Free State appear frontrunners of the de-institutionalization scholars of religion have noted worldwide. Particularly, they show the evolution of an alternative approach to faith and community. While the churches remain cultural bastions of single identity groups, faith is increasingly employed in the secular domain to connect across group boundaries. The farmers and farmworkers of Philippolis often found more spiritual meaning outside their congregation while working together on a social project, than inside their own congregation, just like De Bloem's congregants connected over their stoves and catering services rather than during Sunday service. At these informal instances they were able to develop the unlikely alliances Ammerman speaks of in her discussion on spiritual tribes. Rather than establishing a new institution to express these alliances, congregants preferred to keep things low profile. Broad religious values, loosely inspired by their respective church traditions, on top of concern for the local environment offered material for a sense of common belonging. Or rather a common mission to alleviate disparities in the name of God. The question emerging here is what this sense of mission then implies for the cause of unity?

4.4   Serving God Together, Separately

4.4.1   *"Mission in Unity and Unity in Mission"*

The previous two sections discussed efforts to integrate local church bodies and leadership structures. We saw an attempt towards the bottom-up merger of two congregations and strategies of self-sustenance versus interracial partnership to adapt to changing circumstances. This last section reaches beyond the experience of specific church communities and explores initiatives across the Reformed family to collaborate on social programs. They involve mission and evangelization work as well as poverty relief efforts, orphanages, elderly homes and educational development, in and outside of South Africa, within and well beyond the churches' immediate constituencies. Historically, social programs formed a major pillar of the DRC as part of its efforts to consolidate the church's public function in society. Within URCSA, they have been gaining a similarly important position.

In either church, the social programs constitute a unique intermediate level of cooperation between leaders and members, and between different Reformed communities. The various stakeholders tend to allude to a higher goal motivating their programs beyond one's own church agenda. It comprises a joint calling to "contribute to the healing of the land, in humility, together with one another – 'mission in unity and unity in mission.' "[141] This sense of calling is quite recent though and clashes regularly with prevailing counter-narratives in which the white DRC is expected to help out black and colored congregations through short-term relief activities rather than partnering together towards broad community development objectives.

Tensions between the churches' ambitious unity discourse and a reality of paternalism and segregation become highly visible here. Also pertinent is the reoccurrence of nationalistic ideals in the churches' presentation of their joint social calling. These dynamics will be discussed on the basis of four social programs through which URCSA and the DRC have been seeking to offer relief services at home and abroad. The first two programs, the Western Cape based Commission For Witness[142] and the Free State based Partners in Witness[143] illustrate the ongoing transformation of the two churches' long segregated mission policy. Secondly, the local non-profits of Badisa and Towers of Hope[144] exhibit the increasing distance between the social programs and Reformed church institutions.

Before elaborating these initiatives, it is crucial to address the historic evolution of social programs in the Reformed Church family, and particularly inside the DRC. This history begins with the mission policy of the mid-nineteenth century, the era in which the DRC significantly expanded its evangelization efforts in Southern Africa. As indicated in chapter two, the DRC mission policy overlapped to a great extent with the church's apartheid policy. Servicing each racial community separately was considered essential to answer God's wish for preserving distinct cultures and nations while disseminating the message of Jesus Christ. The Mission Secretary of the Free State even spoke of "our mission policy of apartheid."[145] The black Reformed churches formed the primary subject of this policy. They embodied the segregation that the DRC claimed to be consistent with God's will. Black congregations moreover relied on the DRC's

---

141   Dawid Bosch, *Transforming Mission, Paradigm Shifts in Theology of Mission* (New York. Orbis, 1991), 463–467. Quoted in *United Ministry for Service and Witness*, "Our Calling to Service and Witness. A Theological Basis for the DRC Family's Missional Ministries. Policy Document" (2011): 28.

142   Afrikaans: *Kommissie vir Getuienisaksie* (KGA).

143   Afrikaans: Vennote in Getuienis (Vennote).

144   Afrikaans: Torings van Hoop.

145   Rev. J.G. Strydom quoted in G. van der Watt, "Recent Developments and Challenges in Understanding the Dutch Reformed Family of Churches' Missional Identity and Calling," *Dutch Reformed Theological Journal = Nederduitse Gereformeerde Teologiese Tydskrif* 51 (2010): 165–6.

missionary "goodwill" to provide anything, from church buildings to ministers. The DRC not only offered church services, but also general support for these communities. Hospitals, school initiatives and special institutions for the deaf and blind formed an intrinsic part of the DRC's mission policy, thus entangling the goals of evangelization, segregation and development.

For decades the DRC sharply distinguished between these missionary programs and the social works the church organized for its own white Afrikaner constituency. In the period immediately after the Anglo-Boer Wars up until the establishment of the National Party apartheid regime, the DRC invested tremendously in elevating what it called "the poor white problem."[146] It established schools, orphanages, homes for the elderly and adult education centers. Above all, the DRC emerged in this era as the prime advocate of white communities that were struggling to adapt to a rapidly modernizing and urbanizing society. The church successfully recommended state welfare programs and collaborated closely with the National Party on its social works. Central to these works was the DRC's notion of compassion and the clear distinction between white poverty programs and the DRC's black mission policy.[147] Where the latter involved relief programs among non-white population groups as a way to help spread the Gospel in Africa, compassion specifically referred to the DRC's duty to care for its own "volk." It was tied to the perception of the DRC as the Afrikaner people's church and simultaneously tuned in with concerns about black Africans threatening the social-economic position of whites in the cities. The church's primary responsibility was to keep its white membership from further harm and nourish Afrikaner identity.

Church social programs, from missionary to poverty relief activities, thus formed an intrinsic part of the greater apartheid system, and were critiqued as such. Not only did they epitomize rigid racial segregation practices by providing separate services to black, white, colored and Asian communities. They also reaffirmed and consolidated paternalistic thinking patterns. Which whites acted as active participants in their churches' relief programs whereas non-white communities were seen as subjects and dependents of white church charity.

These patterns triggered deep resentment among the black Reformed churches. The *status confessionis* and *Belhar Confession* both emerged partly in protest against the DRC's mission policy of separation and paternalism.

---

146   Robert Vosloo. "The Dutch Reformed Church and the poor white problem in the wake of the first Carnegie Report (1932): some church-historical and theological observations," *Studia Historiae Ecclesiasticae* Volume 37 Number 2, [14] (September 2011): 67–85.

147   Watt, "Recent Developments and Challenges," 177.

In 1986, one of URCSA's predecessors, the Dutch Reformed Mission Church, organized an extensive workshop on redefining mission within the broader Reformed family. A small group of progressive representatives from the DRC also attended the workshop and joined in its sharp protest against the "sinful division" current mission and other poverty relief policies had caused in the Reformed churches.[148] The workshop concluded by stating that the churches' duty of service could only be conducted in union and not in separation. "The unity of the church is the credibility test for the witness about the Kingdom of God."[149] Spreading and living out the Bible's message of peace, justice and reconciliation required the churches to join hands in social programs that crossed rather than reaffirmed racial boundaries.

The vision and terminology conveyed at the 1986 workshop remains crucial in the current social programs of the Reformed Church family, albeit in confusing ways. It forms the basis of a wide range of inter-church organizations and commissions. These involve partnerships between the DRC and URCSA to for instance develop a joint Bible dissemination project in Mozambique or Zimbabwe. Other organizations have been seeking to merge long segregated relief programs into newly established faith-based non-profits. Local DRC and URCSA congregations are encouraged to expand their soup kitchens to include a broader and more diverse group of recipients, or to volunteer together at a church childcare provision or elderly home.

Terms such as mission, compassion and social works have become increasingly intertwined here. Missionary activities rarely focus on evangelization alone, but may also include local homeless shelters or knitting workshops for single mothers. Church social workers and missionaries alike today speak of their commitment to compassion. This term is now associated with care for the vulnerable regardless of their racial or ethnic background, rather than the care for "one's own." To add to the mix, witness is often employed as another comprehensive term for all missionary, relief and development programs within the Reformed family. Understood broadly, it refers to the church's obligation to actively engage with the larger society and calls upon congregations to turn outwards rather than inwards. More specifically, the notion of witness is used to advocate for an outspoken church agenda against racial, economic or other forms of oppression and for the church to act as model of God's Kingdom of justice and reconciliation on earth. In the end though, most social programs

---

148   Phil Robinson and Johan Botha (red.), *Wat is sending? 'n Werkswinkel vir die familie van NG kerke* [What is mission? A workshop for the DRC family] (Swartland Drukpers (Edms) Bpk. Malmsbury, 1986), 164.

149   Robinson and Botha, *Wat is sending?* 164.

comprise short-term initiatives to provide support for struggling communities. Under the motto 'mission in unity and unity in mission,' URCSA and the DRC collaborate on many of these initiatives, at least on paper. Yet, in practice, most programs take place along the divisions of the apartheid past. How can we understand these programs in light of their convoluted history, and what do they have to offer to the current unification process?

4.4.2   *From Daughters to Sisters*

"Partnerships are meant to purposefully move away from the old mission era of "mother" and "daughter" churches which was marked by dependence and prescriptiveness, the handing out of money and consequential tensions; they are meant to join hands in a new way with our sister churches in a common calling to service and witness in context. Partnerships are a purposeful step on the path towards greater visible unity."[150] With these words, the DRC of the Free State mission commission explained its name change from Synodical Witness Commission to Partners in Witness. The quote is illustrative of the broader attempt by the Reformed churches to overcome the connotation of their mission policies with the unequal relationships of the apartheid era.

The DRC as well as URCSA seek to refashion their approach to mission from paternalism towards partnership, and from segregated evangelization towards joint and united projects meant to improve overall living conditions. Partners in Witness and the integrated Commission for Witness on the Western Cape comprise two organizations, also referred to as ministries, through which the churches have been phasing in this transition. What do their partnerships in mission consist of today and to what extent do they reach beyond the churches' historic divisions?

The Commission for Witness (CFW) first of all presents one of the earliest examples of a joint mission program inside the Reformed Church family. It evolved as a practical follow-up to the 1986 workshop. To implement the vision of a united mission, white and colored churches on the Cape decided to merge their regional mission commissions into one new commission. The Commission for Witness was formally established in 1991 and designated as the main

---

150   *DRC Free State 2014*, Vennote in Getuienis – 'n Nuwe Benadering [Partners in Witness – a New Approach], March 2014. Original text in Afrikaans: Vennootskappe wil doelbewus wegbeweeg van die ou sending-era van "moeder" en "dogterkerke" wat so gekenmerk is deur afhanklikheid, voorskriftelikheid, die gee van geld en die gevolglike spanning; dit wil op 'n nuwe manier hande vat met ons susterkerke in ons gesamentlike roeping tot diens en getuienis in ons konteks. Vennootskappe is 'n doelbewuste stap op die pad na groter sigbare eenheid.

church body responsible for organizing missionary projects on behalf of all Reformed churches in the region. Today, these projects range from building new churches in poor parts of South Africa and neighboring countries to providing spiritual support for Christians in Western Cape work places, prisons and hospitals. They moreover include public dialogue initiatives between church actors and local authorities or businesses about burning issues such as land reform, restorative justice and reconciliation.[151] Beyond the various activities, the Commission occupies a special position inside the Reformed family as a model of church unity. Through carefully planned joint finances, staff and programming, it shows what the integration of church structures might look like in practice.

Partners in Witness – Partners in short – barely correlates its service programs with other Reformed churches. As a unit within the DRC regional synod of the Free State, it operates international evangelization and development activities as well as general church support and community development for DRCA and URCSA congregations in the Free State. Interestingly however, Partners has also taken up an active role as mediator within the church family. It facilitates negotiations between congregations struggling with property conflicts and seeks to forge connections between local communities across the four Reformed churches to establish joint development programs. This mediating role is especially notable considering the context in which Partners operates. The commission confronts a regional DRC basis that is deeply suspicious of any kind of unity initiative on top of the enduring conflict between the regional DRCA and URCSA synods. Navigating these tensions, Partners is far removed from the organizational integration at CFW. The DRC remains firmly in control of the various social programs, while URCSA and the DRCA continue to be involved primarily as recipients of aid.

Despite their many differences, Partners and CFW share a rather unique position as church programs actively pursuing inter-racial collaboration. Demonstrating how such partnerships can be done has become a prime activity for the two organizations. With reference to the term witness in their names, both have been taking a public stand in their regional contexts to show how (church) communities might work together on social issues regardless of their racial, ethnic or class divisions.

In the Western Cape, CFW has over the years evolved into a central actor in the churches' effort to develop joint organizational structures. The Commission

---

151   See for instance the website of CWF under the section: Center for Public Witness. Visited at 6 May 2015, http://www.kga.org.za/wp/taakspan-4-publieke-getuienis/.

is in constant conversation with other inter-church partnerships, such as the Theology Faculty at Stellenbosch or the various uniting presbyteries in the region, about strengthening relationships within the Reformed family and with other denominations. It collaborates on an initiative to foster theological training for impoverished congregations across the continent and has played a crucial role in the consolidation of a national network of service and witness programs for the entire Reformed family, called the United Ministry for Service and Witness.[152]

Partners seeks to head a quite different but equally noteworthy transition within its convoluted Free State setting. By involving local communities, government agencies and non-profit organizations in its work, the organization helps build trust and initial contact among the embroiled churches and between congregations and authorities. It takes every opportunity to stress the sister relationships between the churches as substitute for the long prevalent mother-daughter ties. For Partners, the churches have become deeply interdependent as they face persistent and growing insecurity. An April 2014 newsletter elaborated: "Our continent is changing dramatically; we need to learn to think differently about being church and about service. That is how we as sisters come together, earnestly and open-hearted."[153] The fact that the churches need each other should be an incentive for the various churches to work with rather than for each other. According to the director, "[the] church is part of a movement. We need to listen to our context and explore how we can get closer together while living in inequality."[154]

Partners regularly facilitates conversations with church and community actors. It convenes representatives of the four Reformed churches to talk about their own concerns and gain perspective of problems in other communities. For years, the lion share of these meetings focused on finding a settlement for the property conflicts between the DRCA and URCSA. Since partially succeeding with a settlement in 2011, Partners has continued to offer opportunities to "[listen to] each other's stories – heartrending stories of exhaustion, division and expulsion, but also touching stories of reconciliation and hope" among the Free State's Sesotho and Afrikaans speaking communities, in the

---

152   Further details about the theological training initiative NetAct are found at their website: http://www0.sun.ac.za/netact/ to NetAct. The operations of the United Ministry for Service and Witness are elaborated at the DRC official website. Visited at 19 May 2015,   http://www.ngkerkas.co.za/index.php/taakspanne-vir-staande-werk/verenigde-diensgroep-diens-en-getuienis-vddg/.

153   "As susters saamstap" [Walking together as sisters], *Ligdraers* [Bearers of light], April 2014, 1.

154   Interview, Gideon van der Watt, 30 April 2014.

townships and on the farms.[155] Listening is considered a crucial activity also to build awareness among members across the Reformed churches. It would help DRC members realize that other communities share their fear for rising unemployment and farm attacks, or foster understanding among URCSA and DRCA members of the problems both face in their fights over church properties. Members are encouraged to tell hopeful stories of new alliances like the minister share in Philippolis or an emerging multicultural student congregation at the University of the Free State in Bloemfontein.

To bolster their position as models of integration, CFW and Partners both employ a strong religiously infused discourse. In an interesting twist of history, it ties the churches' mission not merely to the land of South Africa or the Afrikaner nation, but rather to the entire territory of Africa. After decades of segregated policies, the two organizations claim to be frontrunners in the transition of the churches and the continent at large towards a more inclusive approach of community development and outreach. On their website, in newsletters and in conversations, they present themselves as the churches' conscience in the "calling to service and witness in unity."[156] Where leaders and congregations struggle to even talk across the color line, CFW and Partners say they effectuate practical black-white relationships to serve the Kingdom of God in Africa. This calling to service constitutes the leitmotiv throughout their work. "[W]e are called as prophets, priests and kings to minister the Gospel of God's salvation to all people through word (kerugma), deed (diaconia) and in a relationship of love and unity (koinonia)."[157] Both organizations point to concrete and often widely varying actions to demonstrate how they are implementing God's will on earth. Their newsletters offer stories of an URCSA congregation hosting a DRC supported leadership course for its youth, a joint trip by DRC and URCSA representatives to a mission project in Malawi or a job creation partnership in Bloemfontein's city center.

Sharing certain beliefs and traditions is often mentioned as crucial factor in enabling such activities. The former director of CFW attributed the advanced level of integration of its services to the fact that the various church stakeholders "concur on ethos and values."[158] This ethos notably comprises the *Belhar Confession* as a core foundational doctrine. Referring to *Belhar's* three themes, the former director explained that "CFW through its united being really is a mission to the heart of the church, a voice for justice, reconciliation, unity."

---

155   "As susters saamstap," 2.
156   CFW Website. Visited at 6 May 2015, http://www.kga.org.za/wp/28-2/.
157   United Ministry for Service and Witness, "Our Calling to Service and Witness," 12
158   Conversation, Johan Botha, 27 February 2015.

"We are not [just] working together, we are one."[159] Partners similarly underscores the importance of a common faith basis throughout its documentation, but avoids any explicit references to the controversial *Belhar Confession*. Instead, it focuses on the broader missional identity of the church and its responsibility to engage actively and equally with the many different communities of the African continent.[160]

Unity tends to emerge in the organizations' discourse as a means rather than a goal in itself. Especially at Partners, references to unity or church unification are rare. The organization instead speaks of collaboration necessary to help the church face the vast challenges of African countries today. Considering the persistent poverty and violence as well as the weakening position of the Reformed family, Partners presents contact between the various churches as an indispensable tactic in the survival struggle of contemporary congregations. "Without partners we simply cannot fulfill our calling anymore. The challenges are often too big."[161] Whether or not such partnerships occur on the basis of an official unity agreement appears beside the point.

CFW alternatively pays more attention to the greater goal of church unification, but interweaves it with its own immediate concerns about the diversity of the communities it seeks to serve. To allow for effective and credible programs, the Commission stresses its priority to engage with the communities' cultural and ethnic differences in a way that none dominate the other. Its colorful bilingual newsletter reiterates "our confession that Jesus is the Lord of every human being in his or her world."[162] Churches are urged to act as "models of the Bible's message about interculturality and multiculturality in our context."[163] Although unity and integration may constitute praiseworthy ideals of the future, CFW concentrates on the present and on demonstrating the sheer ability of black and white to serve God together, without threatening each other's identities but rather mutually enriching them.

---

159   Conversation, Johan Botha, 27 February 2015.

160   *DRC Free State 2014*, Vennote in Getuienis – 'n Nuwe Benadering.

161   *DRC Free State*. Klem verskuif na vennootskapsverhoudinge. [Emphasis shifts towards partnership relations.]. Document published without date on the *Partners in Witness* website. Accessed at 22 February 2015, http://www.ngkerkvrystaat.co.za/documents/wat-doen-ons/vennote/amptelikedokumente/Klem%20Verskuif%20na%20Vennootskapsverhoudinge.pdf.

162   "KGA se drie taakspan-fokusse" [The focus areas of CFW's three task groups], *Getuie/Witness* Semester 2 (2013): 2.

163   "Verskillend maar saam in Christus, gee ons hoop vir die wereld" [Different but together in Christ, gives us hope for the world], *Getuie/Witness* Semester 2 (2014): 2.

Neither Partners nor CFW has escaped the intricacies troubling the church family's process to overcome its historic divisions. Prime among them is first of all the persistent financial disparity between the DRC and the other Reformed churches. It cost the CFW partners almost ten years, difficult debates and tensed relationships to reach a somewhat equal salary distribution for the Commission's staff. The DRC easily contributes sixty times the amount URCSA does to sustain its daily operations. The RCA contributes barely anything. Operations are based at and organized from an office in the Bellville suburb of Cape Town, just a few doors away from the DRC Western Cape regional headquarters. They are overseen and coordinated through an inter-church management team and are usually implemented as joint projects. The former director nonetheless illuminated: "We have to be taking into account that there are traditional relationships that we also have to manage through CFW."[164] Inside the DRC, the Commission is still expected to continue some of the original mission projects that used to be conducted by its Evangelization Commission before it dissolved into the partnership. URCSA also looks to ensure through CFW the preservation of specific relief programs for impoverished URCSA congregations in for instance the KwaZulu Natal region. With each church prioritizing its own separate agendas it is the CFW's constant challenge to carry out its activities in greater visible and credible unity.

The discrepancy between words and deeds forms a second major difficulty for the two mission organizations. It becomes palpable when looking at Partners in Witness' actual list of programs. A 2011 Organizational Audit document shows a majority of its activities involving traditional forms of DRC aid to black and colored church communities and barely any of the inter-church partnerships that Partners pleads for in its discourse.[165] Many of the activities in the 2011 report, primarily the funds to support DRCA and URCSA minister salaries, were still in place during my visit in 2014. The director admitted that money continued to play a key role among the churches. "Black expects money from white, white expects control."[166] Persisting these uneven relationships has appeared for all parties easier than developing new structures of partnership. Ministers involved in such structures indicated they often lacked energy to put in the hard work necessary to collaborate across the color line or reflect on more creative ways to help each other rather than through charity.[167]

---

164   Conversation, Johan Botha, 27 February 2015.

165   *DRC Free State 2011,* Organisatie-Oudit Sinodale Getuieniskommissie [Organizational Audit Synodic Witness Commission], October 2011.

166   Interview, Gideon van der Watt, 18 April 2014.

167   Interviews, DRC minister, 14 April 2014; and URCSA minister, 30 April 2014.

Decades of one-way charity programs have made DRCA and URCSA congregations greatly reliant on Partners' support for their minister salaries and buildings, creating, in the view of one DRCA minister, "a dependency syndrome," in which "some black churches will not pay for their minister even if they have the money."[168]

The case of Botshabelo offers a snapshot example of the obstinacy of traditional aid relationships in the church family. For many years Partners in Witness provided essential support to pay for a minister at the DRCA congregation in this mostly black impoverished township a few miles outside of Bloemfontein. The Reverend Hoffman, with his missionary background, had long been viewed as a key person in the community. "He maintains the organizational structures of the congregation, educates assistant ministers and church council members, helps with the youth service, guides the Sunday school staff, leads the social service program. ..."[169]

In addition to the financial support for the minister, Partners facilitated multiple conversations between the DRCA in question and the nearby URCSA congregation. Both claimed rights to the same church building. In 2011 a settlement was reached that allowed URSCA to take the building whereas the DRCA congregation could make use of a special settlement fund the DRC had set up to pay for a new building. While the DRCA congregation felt it had "sacrificed for reconciliation," actors on both sides said they generally appreciated Partner's role in the mediation and took the settlement as a starting point for improving relationships between the two congregations.[170] Some joined in an inter-church project of public dialogue with police authorities about township crime, while others collaborated in small community development projects. Ultimately though, neither of the involved congregations appeared remotely interested in further unification or even a more formalized partnership at local level. They counted on the continued support from the DRC and meanwhile preferred to remain separate. "We enjoy our own culture."[171]

Botshabelo's story is but one of many. Across the Free State as well as the Western Cape, CFW and Partners in Witness and other mission initiatives are primarily known for time-honored services in which the white church offers support to black and colored congregations. Few outside the churches' establishment appear aware of the joint activities these organizations also conduct. Partners has through the years become associated with relatively neutral

---

168   Interview, DRCA minister, 23 April. 2014
169   *DRC Free State 2011,* Organizational Audit Synodic Witness Commission, 9.
170   Conversation, DRCA Botshabelo member, 23 April 2014.
171   Conversation, DRCA Botshabelo member, 23 April 2014.

mediation services that enjoy appreciation across the Reformed family. These services are still initiated by the DRC though and carry little weight as an inter-church effort. CFW might present a model of organizational integration, but the involved black and colored partners remain primarily on the receiving end of this model. In both cases the images of the organizations' bright newsletters are telling. They show white missionaries or social workers amidst poor black and colored communities. The former are quoted in saying they welcome the rare moments of exposure, whereas the latter state their gratitude for the help their government has failed to provide.

As such, the churches' partnerships seem to persist rather than break patterns of paternalism. The key difference with the past is that they increasingly do so on the premise of integration and inclusivity rather than segregation and exclusivity. At CFW, a joint DRC-URCSA staff decides about the relief activities. Partners builds its programs on the conversations it is facilitating with the various communities on the ground. In another departure from decades of mission work, both organizations are careful to avoid any association with the once deeply felt Afrikaner duty to evangelize Southern Africa. The attachment to the African continent however appears stronger than ever before. Rather than reinforcing the DRC's Christian-nationalist heritage, the territorial connection is now used to indicate the churches' broadened commitment to all peoples of Africa, with equal respect for their cultures, languages and ethnicities. It forms a crucial line of argumentation CFW as well as Partners use to demonstrate their acceptance of the new South Africa, the rainbow nation and its predominantly black African rather than white Afrikaner population. The territorial connection is moreover, once again, used as a unifying motive. Transcending class and racial divisions, it would tie the various communities to one overarching mission of implementing God's word on their land. It appears a revisited form of nationalism, or rather continentalism, both the DRC and URCSA stakeholders can contend with, allowing them to concentrate on their own needs while remaining committed to the common good.

4.4.3   *From Church to Non-Profit*

One peculiar side-effect of the Reformed churches' effort to disassociate their social programs from the loaded past is the simultaneous separation of such programs from their church origins. Over the past years they have increasingly evolved into autonomous non-profits that collaborate more with local authorities and other non-governmental organizations than with the DRC or URCSA. Some maintain members from the two churches on their boards and stress their faith-based mission and values. Many others seem to avoid overt affiliations with the Reformed church family even while the latter strains to keep the non-profits under its wings. The organizations Badisa and Towers of Hope illuminate this development. Both were initially established to implement church social services on behalf of respectively the Cape regional synods of URCSA and the DRC, and the DRC Free State regional synod. Today, they are registered as non-profit organizations under South African public law and raise their own funds for immediate relief programs that cut across racial, ethnic, social and denominational divisions.[172] They do so largely independent from the Reformed churches. The churches nonetheless continue to presume ownership and claim the organizations' interracial achievements as their own.

Badisa is well known in the Cape for its vast and inclusive network of services, primarily directed at children and elderly. An integrated team of DRC and URCSA representatives coordinates day care and health care services, food and cloths distribution and centers for drug addiction treatment. Programs reach all communities, regardless of background or ethnicity.[173] In many ways, Badisa bears resemblance to CFW. Where the latter fused the two churches' mission organizations, Badisa comprises an amalgamation of the regional poverty relief commissions of the DRC and URCSA in the Cape. It was established in 2003 with the expectation that the two would soon merge into one new church. When they did not, Badisa continued its services with and for both churches under the heading "joint projects." Unlike the Commission for Witness, Badisa today is set up as an organization outside of official church structures and with an independent legal status. Core funding comes from government subsidies that require Badisa to adhere to state rather than church legislation. It offers direct aid to local communities, whether or not related to one of the churches, and generally refrains from evangelization or foreign mission projects.

The Free State community service organization Towers of Hope is far removed from the level of integration at Badisa. Founded as a DRC initiative to reach out to Bloemfontein's city poor, the non-profit nonetheless displays a rare story of black and white communities jointly reshaping church social programs. At first sight, Towers of Hope appears yet another faith inspired organization that offers support to the needy in South Africa. It hosts soup kitchens and needle workshops, helps homeless people in finding work and

---

172   The South African law allows for faith-based organizations to apply for state funding once they are officially registered as non-profit organizations. Especially important is to obtain approval as Public Benefit Organization. Out of the two organizations discussed here, Badisa has achieved this so-called PBO status and has subsequently been able to apply for and receive significant government subsidies.

173   Badisa explicates the communities it reaches and involves in its projects by these four officially recognized population categories. See for instance. *Badisa Jaarverslag/Annual Report 2012/2013*, 13. Accessed at 14 March 2015, http://www.badisa.org.za/downloads.

engages with prostitutes to "make it possible for them to exit this lifestyle."[174] Distinguishing the organization is the fact that all its programs are implemented at what used to be one of the most powerful DRC congregations in the Free State. The Tweetoring, literally "two towers," church with its impressive building in the center of town long symbolized the deep intertwining of the DRC with Afrikaner nationalist and political power. Three presidents of the Orange Free State were inaugurated here. The Afrikaner pro-Nazi organization Ossewabrandwag came into being in the Tweetoring consistory on the eve of the Second World War.[175]

As many other city churches, Tweetoring lost the vast majority of its members in the late nineties and early 2000s due to inner-city decay and the white flight to the suburbs. Instead of fully closing its doors, the DRC regional leadership in 2010 handed over the keys to the director of the newly established Towers of Hope organization. It was initially hoped that the organization could help revive the church by reaching out to the poor black residents that had come to dominate the neighborhood in addition to what was left of its historic white membership. In the end, few if any of the old members stayed. Towers of Hope instead consolidated its status as an autonomous non-profit organization. A mixed group of black volunteers and homeless people, white social workers and a small number of white newcomers now use the church chiefly to host social programs. They conduct their own worship with barely any noticeable connection to traditional sober DRC services. Instead, the community draws from a wide range of religious experiences, from the African Independent to the Pentecostal churches, which tend to include significantly more free-style dancing and improvised singing than is common in the average DRC church.

Both Badisa and Towers of Hope take pains to emphasize the inclusive nature of their organizations, often at the cost of their original affiliations with the Reformed churches. References to these churches, let alone their unification process, have been minimized or removed from websites and newsletters if they were ever mentioned in the first place. The two non-profits rather indicate an overarching Christian foundation as source of inspiration. Badisa speaks of Jesus Christ as its role model, where Towers of Hope vaguely expounds its

---

174   Towers of Hope website. Visited at 15 May 2015, http://www.towersofhope.org/ministries/ embracing.php.

175   Christoph Marx, *Im Zeichen Des Ochsenwagens: Der Radikale Afrikaaner-Nationalismus in Südafrika Und Die Geschichte Der Ossewabrandwag* [Oxwagon Sentinel: radical Afrikaner Nationalism and the history of the 'Ossewabrandwag'] (Münster: Lit, 1998), 273–274.

vision to empower the vulnerable "in obedience to the Triune God."[176] Both are also eager to emphasize the racial as well as religious diversity of the staff and recipients of their programs, or at least their effort to ensure that services reach "ALL in need, irrespective of their age, gender, nationality or religion."[177] The emphasis on diversity appears mostly an effort to demonstrate website visitors that their organizations do not discriminate.

Allusions to a larger cause of church unity or national reconciliation tend to be avoided. Badisa's website briefly explains its origins in the merger of the two churches' service organizations, but refrains from any references to current unity talks between URCSA and the DRC. Towers of Hope barely relates its activities to either church, let alone to their efforts to come together. In general, the organizations evade discourse and rather prioritize the practical implementation of service projects for an ever growing number of vulnerable people, black and white, in their immediate environment. Inclusivity in this respect does not so much comprise a high-minded ideal, but rather a condition necessary for the organizations to do their work.

Not only the target group is diverse, but so are the potential donors. Funding from the Reformed churches has been insufficient, forcing Badisa and Towers of Hope to look elsewhere for support. In a 2014 interview, Badisa's director acknowledged the key role financial factors have played in the remodeling of his organization's identity, even beyond its Christian affiliation. To be able to apply for more and different sources of funding compelled Badisa to take a broader approach than signaled by its original tagline of "Christian compassion."[178] Adding the phrase "a neighbor to anyone in need," the organization now highlights its image as primarily a non-profit that might still be driven by religious values but that is not directly church-based. At Towers of Hope, similar emphasis is put on the pivotal role of the non-profit to broaden its base and attract external support from for instance government agencies or nonreligious foundations. Donations are used towards the social programs as well as worship services at the small Tweetorings congregation.

A notable consequence here has been the de facto merging of this congregation with the Towers of Hope non-profit. Its Reverend De la Harpe le Roux simultaneously serves as the organization's director. When the drastically diminished Afrikaner congregation closed down in 2009, the DRC Free State Synod

---

176   Towers of Hope website. Visited at 15 May 2015, http://www.towersofhope.org/missionvision.php.

177   Badisa website. Visited at 15 May 2015, http://www.badisa.org.za/index.php/en/who-we-are/core-business-a-values.

178   Interview, Rev. Rust, 28 March 2014.

gave Reverend De la Harpe le Roux an opportunity to plant a new church in the old congregation for the vulnerable people of the inner city, and meanwhile develop a non-profit organization focusing on the same target group. One year later, this organization was then formally established and named Towers of Hope. In a special arrangement with the DRC, Towers of Hope has been functioning as a fully independent NGO that is responsible for the director De la Harpe le Roux' salary while using the facilities and building of the new Tweetorings congregation also under his leadership. For the Reverend-director, the lines between the church and the non-profit have and should be completely blurred for practical and principled reasons. Both benefit from each other in terms of finances and resources. Notably, they complement each other according to the Reverend-director in a symbiotic relationship and as spaces where everyone can experience God in their own way and through practical service. "[Church] should not just be a Sunday event ... It should be a place where marginalized people feel safe ... where rich and poor can be together without feeling guilty or humiliated."[179]

Increasingly removed from the Reformed Church family, the two organizations exhibit at times unexpected forms of the interracial engagement the DRC and URCSA claim to pursue. For Badisa this is chiefly manifested through its management. On ground level, programs remain as segregated as elsewhere in the churches' service landscape. Each run their own child support centers, elderly homes and education programs. Ultimately however, the program officers running these programs have to coordinate their services with each other and align them with the organization's common budget. Working out finances, managing volunteers and staff, liaising with other non-profits and government subsidies compels the various church representatives to be in constant conversation with each other and accept their interdependency. As the director explained: "we always talk together about everything, and do so on equal footing."[180]

Such equal footing is largely absent at Towers of Hope where a white staff supervises overall operations, including a variable group of black volunteers carefully selected from the dispossessed participants in its social programs. The presence of these participants during worship moments at the Tweetoring congregation has significantly altered its character though. Services currently tend to involve singing, clapping and dancing as lay leaders freely interpret Bible texts and homeless men play the piano. White members constitute a minority in a church that once boasted an Afrikaner membership of at least

---

179   Interview, Rev. De la Harpe le Roux, 14 April 2014.
180   Interview, Rev. Rust, 28 March 2014.

3000. Some attend out of curiosity to see what happened with the old mother church. Others told me they made a conscious choice to help out and attend one of the few places where the "church has changed its structures to adapt to the community, rather than doing something separate for each group."[181] Employees insisted that while the soup kitchen continued to be Towers of Hope's primary function for the moment, it was "not just like any other NGO. Because it is happening inside the church, we bring in the spiritual side."[182] "We engage with people here, listen to their stories without judging."[183]

While Towers of Hope and Badisa are turning away from the Reformed family, they have been receiving extensive appraisal from the churches that launched the two organizations, especially from the DRC. Both got mentioned as models of how the church can truly open its doors to all South Africans. A *Kerkbode* reporter described Towers of Hope as an essential "we say thank you to the Lord" project in the DRC Presbytery of Bloemfontein: "Here there are no Afrikaners or Sothos, rich or poor, black or white, homeless or homeowners. But here Christ is all and in all!"[184] An URCSA Cape synod report expressed its "deep gratitude" for Badisa and its "tireless work to help people in need."[185] During interviews in the Cape, church leaders and members referred to the two organizations as rare examples of how unity can work, because the organizations "have focus" and "prioritize principles."[186]

Rarely did such affirmative stories note the increasing distance between the organizations and the Reformed churches. Nor did they address the all too familiar intricacies Badisa and Towers of Hope encounter as they pursue greater inclusivity. The departure of Tweetorings' traditional white membership was rarely mentioned outside Bloemfontein. The de facto segregation of most of Badisa's service programs was either ignored or dismissed as something only certain people in the church were not prepared to let go of yet. "Some people in the DRC just don't want to change."[187]

---

181 Conversations, Towers of Hope staff, 17 April 2014.

182 Interviews, Towers of Hope staff, 17 April 2014.

183 Interviews, Towers of Hope staff, 16 April 2014.

184 "Ons-se-dankie-projekte" [We say thank you projects], *Die Kerkbode,* 17 January 2014, 15.

185 Verslag van Diens en Getuienis (D&G) aan die 6e gewone vergadering van die VGK streeksinode Kaapland [Report of the Service and Witness (S&W) of the 6th ordinary meeting of the URC Cape synod.] 14–17 October 2014, 14.

186 Interviews, DRC minister, 3 April 2014, and DRC Welgelegen member, 10 March 2014. See also Partners in Witness website. Middestadsbediening. [Inner city service]. Visited at 12 May 2015, http://www.ngkerkvrystaat.co.za/documents/wat-doen-ons/vennote/ons-vennote/Middestadbediening.pdf.

187 Interviews, Towers of Hope staff, 16 April 2014.

Another often dismissed challenge comprises the prevalence of narratives of white charity in the non-profits. The supposed responsibility of white churches to aid powerless black communities still greatly shape the service operations of Badisa and Towers of Hope. At the former, controversies regarding who is in control emerge regularly. URCSA representatives complain about the DRC presuming an automatic position of dominance over programs aligned with the former black mission churches. Since these churches historically lack support structures of their own, the DRC has through Badisa continued to step in as major initiator of local relief programs. The name Badisa would provide rather a politically correct cover for the same old condescending programs the white church has always conducted in black and colored communities.[188] Even when a previously segregated DRC elderly home is forced to fuse with an URCSA home, the DRC home often expects to remain in charge and takes over the URCSA home rather than integrate on equal terms. "Cooperating is one thing," Badisa's director elaborated, "but shared ownership is hard when you confront different capacities."[189]

Diverging capacities appear even more starkly in the case of Towers of Hope. The presence of a predominantly black membership might have altered the outlook of the church, but not its leadership and overall organization. Most of the non-profit's permanent employees have a white DRC background. The building itself is still officially part of the DRC Tweetoring congregation, even while the non-profit covers most of its maintenance costs. A committee of the DRC Free State synod helps coordinate the affairs of the Tweetoring congregation, so far without much involvement of the majority black churchgoers.[190]

Employees stress the problem of class rather than race in Towers of Hope's ongoing transformation.[191] The majority of today's roughly 100 churchgoers peddle between the city center and the townships in which their families live. They tend to stay away from the church for months at the time. Towers of Hope has tried various strategies to foster a more structural relationship with the churchgoers by temporarily employing them for instance as parking guards, cooks or cleaners. The worship services are also meant to engage them more deeply with the life of the community. During a visit at one of the weekly combined worship and lunch services, most participants signaled little fervor for

---

188   Interview, URCSA Presbytery Wynberg, 27 March 2014.

189   Interview, Rev. Rust, 28 March 2014.

190   *DRC Free State 2013*, Regional Synod Agenda. Ooreenkoms met NG gemeente Bloemfontein (Tweetoringkerk) [Agreement with DRC congregation Bloemfontein (Tweetoring church)], 24.

191   Interviews, Towers of Hope staff, 16 April 2014.

the spiritual element of the service though. They enjoyed the ability to sing and play music and in some cases talk with Towers of Hope staff at the end of worship about their search for jobs or difficulties in their families. Most however immediately migrated to the kitchen to receive their one meal for the day, promised to them in return for their attendance.

The church family overlooks the perhaps most interesting contribution of non-profit organizations like Towers of Hope and Badisa to the unity process. Engaging a diverse group of volunteers in their social programs, both organizations allow for the emergence of alternative religious experiences that escape the churches' historic patterns. At Badisa, URCSA and DRC representatives jointly pray about how to keep their organization afloat during the country's harsh economic recession. For staff and participants in the Towers of Hope programs, worship is intricately interwoven with social services. In the old Afrikaner congregation, they form a new community that is neither church nor non-profit, but rather a mixture of both.

Away from church traditions, unity talks and past legacies, different population groups engage here in a practical manner. They draw on a variety of religious discourses and rituals loosely based on Protestant Christianity to build trustful relationships. Contrary to the Reformed church unity efforts, the organizations have few expectations of finding commonalities beyond the broad belief in Jesus Christ. Their programs may do little concrete to further the unification process nor are they likely to change the structural inequalities between the population groups they work with. In their limited capacity though, the service organizations provide rare instances in which faith does not impede but rather facilitates connections among people from sharply different backgrounds. As such they also offer a rather unwelcome message for the Reformed family: the type of interracial prayers the churches hope for, are most likely to occur outside their own institutional and congregational context.

4.4.4 *Between Model and Symbol*

The Reformed churches' social programs take up a pivotal position in the search for unity. They constitute singular manifestations of cooperation between URCSA and the DRC and as such amount to powerful emblems of the churches' potential to overcome the divisions that keep their communities apart. Two factors facilitate this unique position. One involves the presence of the strong common goal the programs assert in serving God on earth through serving the vulnerable of South Africa, or rather the African continent. A second factor comprises the level at which the programs operate between leadership and communities on the ground. This intermediate level has shielded service commissions and organizations from the convoluted debates occurring in the churches' national leadership, as well as from the tendency of congregations to withdraw within their own identity group. Significant problems however occur with both these conditions, hampering the ability of social programs to move their partnerships beyond their so-called "in-between" level.

First of all there is the discourse of the churches' shared goals of service and witness about the Kingdom of God in Africa. As a recycled version of the old Christian-nationalist narrative, the discourse claims a similarly faith-inspired commitment to the land but this time involving all of its inhabitants equally. Notions of diversity, unity and inclusion reoccur throughout the documentation of the churches' service organizations, particularly among those with roots in the mission policy. They present Christianity as an overarching identity that ties the various communities of South Africa together regardless of their race or ethnicity. Simultaneously, strong emphasis is put on the Christian duty to help heal the nation.

The social programs thus reiterate, and sanctify, the type of rainbow nation discourse Habib criticizes. It presumes a nationalist resolution of South Africa's racial conflict while ignoring the class divisions that continue to undermine its democratic transition.[192] Concentrating their efforts on inter-racial partnerships, the social programs overlook the disparate reality of the communities they try to involve. The vast social-economic distance between black and white makes any collaboration bound to end up in paternalistic relationships. Failing to mention this reality in their extensive language about partnering and joint services, the programs allow for the opposite to happen. Jubilant stories of inter-church relief activities primarily show white DRC charity for black and colored communities without acknowledging the apparent consistency of such programs with the racial hierarchy of the apartheid era. The revised narrative of a common Christian African identity does little to change this appearance and rather reaffirms perceptions of white power and black powerlessness.

Exacerbating this situation is the convoluted position of social programs within the organizational structures of the Reformed family. They might function as increasingly autonomous commissions and non-profits with their own budgets and staff. In many cases, organizations like CFW and Partners, still answer to official church rules and traditions. Prime among them is the tradition to provide services to the immediate membership of the church. Orphanages, mission projects and elderly homes that were long ago established to serve either DRC or black Reformed church communities are still expected to be maintained in their traditional context. They remain for members on either

---

192   Habib, "South Africa – The Rainbow Nation and Prospects for Consolidating Democracy."

side the embodiment of the church's function to safeguard its own people first. Organizations that have been able to break with these perceptions, Badisa to some extent and Towers of Hope, tend to break with the church in general as they seek a broader base of recipients and, notably, donors to work with. Engaging with the Reformed family's extensive bureaucracy has not been worth the limited funding the organizations receive from the churches. They might be developing alternative programs in which black and white engage at slightly more equal footing than through the old church relief services, but they do so with little involvement of local church communities. The latter hence barely see the progress made by the non-profits towards a more integrated approach of development through partnership.

An additional problem here comprises the limited concrete value church leaders attach to the social programs. They celebrate the programs' presumed achievements of interracial cooperation, but are reluctant to translate the emerging regional partnerships into formal unity arrangements at national level. Neither are they very effective in involving congregations at local level. Both the DRC and URCSA pride themselves with allowing the service programs to experiment with unity practices. For the DRC, they show its progress in becoming a more inclusive institution, ready to cooperate with others on some of its core services. At URCSA, initiatives like CFW and Badisa present prime examples of how the church seeks to practice the principles of *Belhar* to promote justice, unity and reconciliation for everyone. Meanwhile both churches appear content to retain a status quo of relative inequality. Despite an often angry discourse about DRC domination, URCSA refuses to ask its congregations to share in the financial and administrative burdens of the social development efforts that benefit them, whereas the DRC quietly continues to pay for most of these efforts in exchange for a taken for granted dominance in decision making.

The social programs hence offer rather a symbol of hope for future church unity than the tangible models they seek to be. Still, as symbols and through their discourse, they are playing an important role in reshaping church practice. Especially the mission organizations of CFW and Partners have been fostering an extensive faith inspired attitude of public engagement that pushes church actors out of their comfort zones. Their programs invite disparate congregations to interact, perhaps in paternalistic relationships, but with a growing sense of interdependence.

Importantly, the non-profits allow for alternative forms of joint religious experience. Moving away from the divisions represented by the still segregated churches, the social programs tune in with global dynamics of religious change. They avoid references to the institutions of the DRC and URCSA and their dogged association with particular racial or ethnic communities. Instead, focus is given to a broader sense of faith that can be practiced informally, alone and together, outside the sanctuary and during practical works that benefit the larger society or even continent. The organizations thus relate to a broader development in religious life in South Africa and elsewhere in the world towards more personal and fluid relationships with the divine. It is a development many inside the Reformed churches both fear and admire. Above all, it is a development that is likely to continue and bring about more change than the various unity initiatives might generate all together.

4.5   Conclusion

Throughout this chapter we saw both URCSA and the DRC touting the importance of a bottom-up approach to enable the transition of their long segregated churches towards a new multiracial institution. It emerged in my conversations as one of the main strategies all church actors could agree on, with the notable exception of a few top leaders who preferred an official unity arrangement before any local intervention. A major difficulty with the otherwise highly popular grassroots approach involves the misconceptions about its impact. Rarely did local efforts culminate in the anticipated changes such as the integration of racially different congregations or a greater sense of unity within the Reformed Church family. The changes that did emerge meanwhile received little recognition.

A first misconception the accounts from the Western Cape and the Free State display, concerns the reach of local unity efforts. Not only did ground initiatives to transcend the family's racial divisions remain few and far between here. The sparse initiatives that did occur in places like Stellenbosch and Wynberg also gained little foothold in the communities at stake, if they did not collapse entirely. In the Free State and in the churches' social programs we saw perhaps more tangible cases of interracial partnerships. Without much connection to structural processes of change or the churches' national leadership, these cases appeared drops in the ocean though. They often relied on a single minister or an inspired group of church actors with little sustainability built in if the individuals would leave. Overall, member involvement in interchurch partnerships in either the Western Cape or the Free State tended to be limited to but a few mostly white and colored congregants already at ease with each other due to a proximity in residence or social-economic position. The almost negligible presence of black Reformed communities is emblematic of the churches' struggle to stretch further across their embedded boundaries.

Members were unwilling to step out of their comfort zones and into a poor township except perhaps under the guise of a poverty relief program. Local leaders raised bureaucratic barriers to any collaboration they feared could undermine their influence in the community or harm supposedly distinct church traditions.

Another notable misconception pertains to the presumed virtue of contact between the various racial communities inside the Reformed family. The idea that more interaction would automatically propel positive and equal relationships receives little backing from the discussed cases. In the Western Cape, DRC and URCSA members as well as ministers often ended up more frustrated with their differences after an arranged meeting than prior. Congregations in the Free State dreaded moments of contact as the beginning of the end of their own church identity. Even the celebrated social programs appeared to produce more rather than less unevenness as they persisted one-sided white to black charity.

The experience of local Reformed communities seeking integration thus corresponds with the critique Tranby, Hartman and Edwards among others have expressed towards multiracial congregations in the United States and their lack of deep change. Few efforts allowed for an actual confrontation with diversity. Instead of narrowing the gaps between different groups of people, integration processes in South Africa's Reformed Church family often reconfirmed them by keeping in place paternalistic patterns and prioritizing one particular church culture, usually that of the white community, over others.

Outside the safety of the sanctuary, these patterns did show cracks however. In the neighborhoods and villages surrounding the congregations, members employed their faith to build improbable alliances with people they would otherwise shun or barely encounter. In the Western Cape these alliances emerged through for instance the friendship groups of Agape or the academic establishment at the Stellenbosch Theology Faculty. They continued in Wynberg between DRC and former URCSA members even after the dramatic disintegration of their unity process. In the Free State unexpected connections appeared in the form of joint social projects to improve local living conditions. Without the pretension of elevating inequalities, congregants from vastly different backgrounds appreciated such connections as rare moments in which they could interact informally and on a deeper level than they might experience at work or through school. Faith in these instances provided crucial, be it not sufficient, bonding material. It worked as Durkheim's social glue along with other social-economic factors. The upward mobility of black and colored elites in addition to the increasing sense of despair among white rural and inner city congregations created an enabling environment. Communities realized their growing interdependency, looked for ways to relate and found support in their joint faith.

The Reformed tradition formed a point of recognition among these usually far removed population groups. Above all, it offered a line of justification. To explain what for many remained a big step into the unknown, congregations developed narratives of inclusivity they claimed were inspired broadly by the life of Jesus Christ. Ministers building such narratives consciously avoided the churches' official integration terminology and referred to the need for spiritual bonding with different communities in the public domain rather than through church institutional channels. It allowed for the involvement of even those congregants who expressed deep suspicion towards any process they negatively associated with transformation or reconciliation. It also allowed for the evasion of the Reformed churches' often toxic unity debates, particularly with respect to the *Belhar Confession*. It is remarkable how little attention was paid to this confession in the studied cases. *Belhar* emerged during interviews as a source of inspiration to some or frustration to others. Rarely did church actors indicate the confession as an impediment to their contact with other communities in the church family, nor to any partnerships they had formed. Apartheid and restorative justice were also generally avoided as topics that would only undermine the precarious relationships. The dismissal of race as stumbling block and the disregard of economic disparities fit in this picture of conciliation, though not reconciliation. The latter term carried too much weight.

The circumvention of delicate issues not merely characterizes the few interracial alliances that can be discerned among the congregations of the Reformed Church family. It constitutes a crucial condition for these alliances to function. Staying away from institutional religion, politics and contentious reconciliation debates allowed for diverging communities within the church family to build trust and collaborate. Doing so in a secular public space was equally essential. Here, people expected less adherence to particular communal traditions than inside the church. Moreover, the secular space offered a common enemy against which the various Reformed communities could gather in their mission to spread the word of God among their fellow countrymen. Finally, a revised form of nationalism, focused on the new rainbow nation and the larger African continent, provided the perhaps most controversial platform on which the church communities were able to build alliances as a new and yet all too familiar sense of shared national belonging. A question that remains is how much such alliances are worth for South Africa's ongoing post-apartheid transition when they appear so consciously removed from its harsh reality.

Conclusion: Change or Perish

"Why study a church that is dying?" "What could the Dutch Reformed Church, of all churches, tell about matters of reconciliation?" Such questions were not uncommon among South Africans hearing of this research. Especially those not directly involved with any of the Reformed churches, and even those who were, tended to express doubts about the value of studying an institution still deeply associated with apartheid, and pretty much expired. They have a point. The DRC or any of the other Reformed churches can barely be seen as grand success stories. For the last two decades, the churches each walked their own paths, taking them away from apartheid, yet also keeping them closer to patterns of segregation than most other sectors of society, or even most other churches.

It is the apparent failure here that makes the Reformed churches so interesting though. First of all, this book has tackled questions of how to understand such failure, and of how to then define success. Secondly, the admittedly distinct church trajectories discussed in the above chapters offer valuable insights into challenges that reach far past the context of South Africa's Reformed Church family. Its convoluted responses to diversity reveal deep internal discrepancies between religious leaders and individual believers as both pursue diverging tracks to reach outwards and withdraw inwards. They exhibit the simultaneous need for and insufficiency of religious beliefs to handle complex pluralizing realities on the ground. Most of all, the church family appears emblematic of the persistent entanglements of religious, ethnic and racial identities, albeit in constant tension with the now equally persistent idea of unity in the name of God. The rest of this conclusion expounds this tension and what it signifies for religious capacities in overcoming social divisions in South Africa, and beyond.

The Power of Preaching

For all the debate about religion as an increasingly individual "lived" affair, it is intriguing to note the pertinence of official doctrine and texts in the Reformed churches' unification trajectory. It not only confirms the persistent influence of religious institutions that scholars like Davie and Ammerman have noted. The infinite flood of documents, Bible texts and referrals to specific Reformed

© KONINKLIJKE BRILL NV, LEIDEN, 2019 | DOI:10.1163/9789004385016_007

traditions also signal the struggle of the institutions to adapt to their indi-vidualizing membership base and join the pace of religious change. A single doctrine ordaining certain practices and behavior no longer suffices. Instead, the DRC and URCSA leaderships are scrambling to inform their constituencies with often highly subjective arguments to explain why they propose certain measures, and request members' consent, preferably through personal votes. This tailored approach is not entirely new in churches that share a long Prot-estant tradition of placing high value on congregational autonomy and local church distinctions. Quite different is the emphasis on members rather than congregations. Congregants' opinions as expressed through the abundant formal and informal church media, consultations and meetings, have gained significance at the cost of leaders' authority. The latter's discourse appears in constant exchange with that of believers on the ground. These believers may reside in remote villages once disconnected from the rest of the country, and with at times equally isolated opinions. Through Facebook, Twitter and blogs, they now help forge national church discourse. Conversely, leaders employ these members' heated debates towards their own agendas and defend their call either for restraint or urgency in church unification.

Key is then to see what church members do with the discourse flowing from their institutions, and from amongst themselves. Considering the case stud-ies of chapter four, it would appear that the change in ideas is in fact one of the biggest shifts the Reformed churches can take some credit for. They are clearly not alone in facilitating this shift. The majority of church actors I spoke with did acknowledge the core idea of unity as disseminated by URCSA and the DRC through their official discourse for over twenty years now. The funda-mental belief in interracial contact and collaboration as something good and desired by God received overall acceptance. This in itself constitutes a major contrast with the long prevalent focus on divine divisions as propagated by the Afrikaner civil religion. The discursive transition discernable here occurred on the one hand at a profound spiritual level. From Reverend Kleynhans and the congregants of Mauersnek to the two churches of Wynberg, members and ministers indicated the sense of a unique bond that connected them across racial and class divides and that built on their common roots in the Reformed church as well as the Biblical imperative for inclusivity. It motivated the people from Philippolis to venture into intimidating environments, whether the black township or the white church, and helped De Bloem's Afrikaner community accept and join in once unthinkable interracial worshipping. The principles laid out in the *Belhar Confession*, of justice, reconciliation and unity, returned throughout these instances as core spiritual guidance, regardless of wheth-er the communities involved had accepted the confession. The principles signified a deep commitment among them to ultimately realize the visible unity of what had long been, sinfully, segregated.

On a more worldly level though, this unity mindset often remained problematically shallow. The acquired beliefs in inclusivity did little to alter the structural paternalism or mutual prejudices still prevalent across the church family. Rather, it emerged at times as an excuse to refrain from any more substantial change, especially among DRC communities. Having recognized their common spiritual connection, members felt they had done enough for their fellow black or colored Christians. The latter alternatively spoke of unity in terms of a faraway future ideal that God urged them to strive for. It would in the meantime allow for better relationships on immediate personal terms without risking any further cultural or material losses for one's own community. What we see here is not just the persistence of white dominance in church tradition and leadership despite multiracial symbolism, as critics have noted in the United States. The Reformed congregations, whether or not engaging in fleeting interactions, applied their own unity discourse to justify ultimately segregated lives.

This brings us to an important point regarding the potential of religious discourse to instigate processes of integration. Seldom do ordinary believers act directly upon their faith, at least not in the context of South Africa's Reformed church members. Their religious ideas and doctrines came in when a situation called for explanation, and then helped shape responses. Faced with a changing neighborhood composition in Heatherdale and rising poverty inside De Bloem congregation, members turned to some of the available Christian unity talk to legitimate what appeared an appropriate survival strategy in these specific settings: open up the church doors. In other settings, like Stellenbosch, with far less urgency to change manners, the unity talk often remained without tangible consequences. Here it was rather used to explain the need to reform attitudes, from patriarchal to collaborative, fitting with the city's emergent multiracial academic establishment.

The power of preaching unity among the Reformed churches thus depended greatly on the social circumstances that called for such preaching. It furthermore had little effect unless aligned with secular arguments concerning the immediate benefits for the communities at stake. Grand words about a unification covenant with God crashed into the quickly apparent improbability of materializing such a vision in the near future. Church leaders, members and ministers preferred working with concrete proposals for collaboration that, while always linked to the gospel, concentrated on the tangible realities of church structures and congregations on the ground. In the effort to adapt religious language to mundane realities, the former often lost much of its original message though, or even ended up with contradictory narratives. Eager to convince members of the value of unity in their local settings, leaders highlighted the richness of diverse traditions and cultures, subsequently reinforcing perceptions of communal distinctiveness that should be protected. Church actors on all sides meanwhile employed a religious unity rationale to draw other boundaries amongst themselves, between conservative and liberal, rural and urban, apartheid and post-apartheid. This is where the unity discourse appeared perhaps at its most powerful. It served to create and reinforce constantly evolving forms of exclusion as religious actors tried to position themselves in deeply convoluted debates about belonging, to the church, and to South Africa.

From Preaching to Prayer

Church worship constitutes by far the most contested space over which unity battles have been fought these past two decades. As Riesebrodt and many fellow scholars of religion have noted, liturgy remains the center around which much religious life continues to evolve. It is therefore in the sanctuary, during Sunday service, singing and praying, that unification proponents perceived a particularly visible, and problematic, lack of integration. Critics meanwhile pointed at the paramount importance of preserving the various communities' distinct church liturgies, and at the improbability and above all undesirability of trying to merge them. At first sight, the latter appear to be on the winning side, with the Reformed churches' sites of prayer indeed as segregated as ever. What tends to be dismissed here, is the pertinence of liturgy outside the pulpit. It is often employed in gatherings about rather mundane issues to tie together people with divergent backgrounds and ideas, if only for one moment of joint prayer.

Among the Reformed churches, this use of liturgy emerged frequently as a key strategy to help deal with their past and present divisions. It surfaced in organizational meetings where leaders tried to find consensus on the practical aspects of their collaboration, or during community get-togethers in which ordinary members discussed concerns about what was happening in their immediate surroundings, their cities or country at large. Religious rituals, loosely based on the Reformed tradition, played a pivotal role in both cases to create a common starting point. Simple words of prayer that everyone knew functioned as a reminder that participants shared a broad basis in beliefs, values and principles regardless of the diverse racial or ethnic communities of their roots. Familiar Christian traditions of breaking of the bread and drinking from a shared cup constituted acts that people could perform together and that were remembered afterwards as key moments of communion. They were valued as rare instances in which people could set aside their racial divisions, apartheid traumas and current disparities as they experienced, at least briefly, a sense of unity in Christ.

Interestingly, such liturgy appeared quite a bit more malleable once conducted outside the church. It would involve Dutch Reformed lay ministers saying a prayer in English, with perhaps an isiXhosa proverb alongside songs in Afrikaans and references to the *Belhar Confession*. Notable here are also the stories of church related organizations like Badisa and Towers of Hope. As their staff members sought to forge cross-community collaborations, they often turned to a broad lingua franca of religiously motivated social engagement. Worshipping in these contexts pragmatically merged customs, languages and rituals depending on the people the organizations hoped to reach and with little attention to, or rather evasion of, any specific church identity.

This last finding sheds a different light on discussions about the intertwining of religion with ethnic, national or racial identities. Attachments between a particular church and single population group indeed still characterize South Africa's religious landscape and larger society. This intertwining however takes place predominantly inside the church institutions in question. As individuals increasingly situate their religious experiences away from these institutions, once entrenched religious-ethnic bonds have also begun to shift. Especially the younger generations in this study appeared comfortable in exploring different traditions and putting together their own belief system that was not exclusively Afrikaans or tied to for instance the colored community. Certainly, as the previous paragraph indicated, religious institutions held significant sway over the choices these individuals made. But the churches' presence in people's lives has undeniably diminished and become more reliant on the ability to adapt to members' demands for change, or for no change at all.

An enigmatic situation emerges here, in which religious leaders and members interchangeably push each other towards more or less inclusive worshipping, integration or further segregation. Across the discussed case studies, we discern elites stuck in paternalistic church relationships and patterns of separateness. Their constituents meanwhile seek new alliances across their church's ethnic group boundaries, though not necessarily inside the congregation. Here we can think for instance about the dinners of Agape, the youth exchanges in Wynberg or the catering services at De Bloem. Still, the reverse also happens. Stellenbosch, Ladybrand and Philippolis each showed progressive leadership to promote interracial interaction that encountered resistance from members. The latter tightly held on to the racial or ethnic composition of their church communities as if there never had, or should have been an end to apartheid.

Underlying such apparent clashes is an intricate discrepancy between the interests of communities on the one hand, and leaders on the other hand when it comes to matters of social change and greater diversity. Among the former, deep apprehension existed about any modification in the format of their church services. These services comprised above all spaces of communal solidarity and familiarity. Sharing or even merging liturgy was not a problem in itself. Difficulties rather lay in altering the one place communities sought to protect against the influx of different cultures, viewpoints and lifestyles. Black congregants willing to adopt parts of the traditional white Afrikaans church style were hence welcome in what might at best be called diversity-lite, or at worst a continuation of white hegemony. In a similar manner, communities found little trouble in joining temporary church exchanges or even asked leaders to facilitate joint prayers at a town hall meeting, as long as that did not affect the distinctness of their own congregation.

The attitudes at play here drew to a great extent from sentiments of threat and the fear of any further losses of group identity as a consequence of South Africa's ongoing transition. Equally if not more important however was a growing anxiety about the future of the churches amidst processes of religious change. Many congregants were perhaps church hopping themselves or requesting changes in the service to suit their individual needs. They nonetheless stressed the importance of continuity in the overall identity of the churches of their childhood. Significant elements of this identity, like apartheid theology or a close affiliation with the state, had already changed. A distinct racial, ethnic, or as many preferred to say, "cultural" affiliation constituted all that was left. Without such an affiliation, the various Reformed churches could just as well close their doors. The churches hence not only reinforced ethnic and racial boundaries, but were also believed to depend on them for their own survival.

Much of the anxieties for community survival found an outlet in upheaval about top-down efforts to practically integrate and alter church liturgy. Leaders contrarily tended to consider such efforts in more symbolic terms. They looked for ways to claim for themselves, the nation and God, that the churches had finally broken with the sinful segregation of apartheid. Focus was given to structurally merging what still comprised the most visible aspect of church life: the liturgy conducted inside the congregations. Leaders and the more change-oriented ministers developed alternative services meant for integrated worship, but struggled to do so without eliciting the anger of their constituencies. Rather than subsequently addressing the dreaded changes in church character, they concentrated on how to work out the finances, official doctrines or decision-making powers. Leaders thus often ended up in a double bind with ordinary churchgoers. Preoccupied with bureaucracy and the urge to generate perceptible change, they dismissed if not actively discouraged members' spontaneously formed alliances beyond the church. Simultaneously, elite endeavors to institutionalize such interracial contact aroused the deepest fear of these members: to lose the home base that had been offering them the minimum sense of safety necessary to engage with diversity outside.

From Prayer to Change?

The question we are left with is to what extent the Reformed churches have made an actual break with their past as pillars of apartheid. Clearly, a full answer to this question requires more time to see if any of the discussed unity efforts will bear fruit on the long term. At this stage, several observations can be made though, not only about these efforts but also about what they tell us regarding the broader role of religious actors in rebuilding societies after prolonged communal tensions and strife.

In general terms, this book exhibits the importance of distinguishing between different religious actors and functions in order to better understand their bearing on societies in transition. Religious leaders, ministers and ordinary believers in this research held widely divergent perceptions about the potential threats or rather benefits of the social changes they were confronted with, and took on often contrasting strategies to cope with and generate their own change. Besides debates about structural versus spontaneous processes of racial integration, they differed in their perceptions of what such processes could accomplish. Where elites spoke of mutually beneficial partnerships, elevating inequalities and bridging cultural differences, communities kept their expectations low to the ground. If they endorsed any modifications in the way they were interacting with other communities, members chiefly sought exposure, better understanding or, more importantly, awareness of each other's struggles. Local ministers often found themselves in between, pursuing better relationships without perceiving, or intending, larger alterations to congregational life. The perhaps greatest misunderstanding between religious leaders and members concerned the motivation for change. Throughout the Reformed family, the first have sought to convince their constituents through deeply faith induced rationale about the Biblical call for unity. This might have contributed to a not insignificant normative shift. Ultimately, constituents did not change practical behavior or relationships unless pushed by quite earthly matters. At the end of apartheid, business interests, an urge to connect with global markets and cultures, and fear for the total loss of identity and language crucially undermined Afrikaner support for the regime. Similarly, church communities today are far more likely to change their ways due to social-economic and demographic factors than as a result of religious discourse.

This is not to say that beliefs in the transcendent do not matter for processes of social change. As we have seen, notions of God-willed reconciliation can crucially motivate people to step out of their comfort zones and engage with the perceived other. Such religious motivations however remain isolated if they are not connected with other functions of religion, such as the strengthening of an internal sense of belonging through communal gatherings with singing, praying and worship, as well as social works and exchanges to reach the broader society and address everyday realities. In the Reformed churches, leaders and members operated on all these levels, but in often disconnected ways. Few knew of each other's efforts towards integration or of the alternative routes that were being developed on the spot to not so much bring different racial communities closer together, but at least create opportunities for individuals to cross boundaries on their own accord. The detached ways in which church unification was often approached has significantly undermined an already convoluted transition. It has allowed the churches' prolonged journey out of apartheid to become hostage to heated debates about diversity in general, from issues of homosexuality and gender to race and apartheid, the country's disarray, and the broader future of the church in a changing religious landscape.

Amidst such controversy, the limited changes the churches have achieved, as well as their effects, often appear lost. This is unfortunate, as they offer distinct insights into how a former religious-nationalist movement seeks to address its community's dilemmas of belonging. Beyond a shift in ideas, this has involved among the Reformed churches a little recognized revision of the old civil religion to fit with current paradigms of unity and inclusivity. Rather than throwing away the apartheid doctrine in its entirety, the Reformed churches, especially the DRC, have kept some core elements that still resonate with their membership base. These involve a deep spiritual commitment to the nation of South Africa and larger African continent, combined with close attachments to distinct local cultures and languages and a sense of responsibility to care for all the various communities of Africa. The central element of mission here makes an especially intriguing example of the refashioning of ideas. Still infused with paternalistic notions of white charity, it now also entails a belief in interdependency and partnership. To care for the nation means to act as instruments of God on earth, which can only occur through active cooperation across the color line.

The impact of this religious nationalism revisited is ambiguous. At face value, it appears an effective midway between communal withdrawal, global visions and social outreach. It is from their embeddedness in distinct localities that religious actors step into the world and engage with other localities, whether through joint relief efforts, church exchanges or informal prayers. In practice, this often amounts to a small group of individual ministers, congregants and volunteers representing the outreach part most others prefer to refrain from. The diversity they encounter also remains limited to individuals from different communities who are either on the aid recipient side, or already in closer proximity due to upward social-economic mobility. Meanwhile, essentialist notions of group identity are kept in place, as are entrenched social hierarchies and disparities.

This research has nonetheless revealed an intriguing dynamic in the spread of the churches' revised paradigm. It has not only found resonance among the usual suspects, the mentioned small group of clergy and congregants in favor of change, but also among what we could call the unusual suspects. Churchgoers who described themselves as conservative and in often exclusive ethnic terms conveyed surprising support for the basic premises of the Reformed family's unity discourse. The idea of a common Reformed South African identity expressed through community partnerships found appreciation among those who had turned their back to South Africa's post-apartheid transformation, especially within the country's designated white and colored population groups. It offered them tools to deal with the difficult realities transpiring from this transformation and provided a sense of engagement with society, on their own terms.

By gradually recycling and reshaping the old doctrines, the DRC critically slowed down its own break with apartheid. It has however presented an alternative to those who refuse to let go of past ideas or practices, especially in view of a challenging present and uncertain future. The midway between local identities and national responsibilities poses an option for change without the associated sense of loss. More notable perhaps, it presents an option against further withdrawal or a potential turn to religious-nationalist extremism. The limitations of this option have been well covered throughout this study. Prime among them is the backlash we have also seen among congregants across the church family against anything to do with unification. It leaves little doubt about the persistent divisions that run through the churches and that are continuously reinforced in sites of worship, whether or not they aspire to the current vision of unity.

The conclusion emerging from the unfinished story of South Africa's Reformed churches might then point at an inherent inaptitude of religious actors, especially those embedded in religious-nationalist belief frameworks, to truly transform and contribute to greater social cohesion. If this story shows anything however, it is the subjectivity of change. From the perspective of most faith communities involved in this study, they have made tremendous strides. Many of their leaders, ministers and members have committed their lives to the cause of reconciliation that reaches far beyond the local struggles covered here. Twenty years after apartheid it is considered no small feat that white, colored, black and Indian communities can, and increasingly do, come together in what remains a very intimate place for a majority of South Africans. The churches here not only represent distinct communities and their ethnic identities, culture and solidarity. They often comprise an extension of people's family, where they gather in tightly knit groups for moments of suffering and joy, for professional networking and for the children's education. To share these worship spaces with the perceived other almost constitutes the maximum to be achieved in terms of national unity. Considering the deeply divided nature of South Africa's broader society, it is of little surprise that the churches are far removed from this maximum. It should not be an excuse though to keep it that way.

Reflections towards the Future

Spending quite some years studying a controversial case of churches in transition has led me several times to change my mind about the extent of this transition. Participants in the research regularly asked if I would share these personal opinions. With this last section, I seek to offer some general thoughts, not as clear-cut recommendations, but rather as points for further reflection towards the future of the Reformed churches and South Africa's transition, as well as the broader role of religion in post-conflict reconstruction.

On the Reformed Churches' Unification Process

This book has in many ways been critical about the unification processes of the Reformed churches in South Africa. That does not take away the pertinence of these processes for the church family as institution, its diverse congregations, and for the country at large. Simply put, the Reformed church institutions appear to have little choice but to continue their unity efforts if they wish to retain some position in contemporary South Africa. The weight of the past is too heavy to ignore. The rising competition with the country's wide variety of religious traditions moreover leaves the churches few other options than pursuing at least some collaboration to salvage what is left of the Reformed identity. For all its faults, the attempt to implement an actual merger of the four churches has elicited vital conversations about what this identity entails in a post-apartheid reality, among leaders and ordinary members. Their sharp debates might have been hijacked by concerns regarding South Africa's broader transition. One could also perceive them as a crucial vehicle for communities to address these concerns. Throughout my research, participants often took discussions about unification as valued opportunities to talk about the difficulties in their neighborhoods and towns, reflect on personal struggles with racial prejudice or share thoughts about what the churches could do to make things better.

Important then is to think about how to further unity without doing more harm. Building on the above analyses, it appears that this can only be done by recognizing the distinctiveness of its three equally important dimensions: the leadership and community level, as well as the intermediate role of church social programs. The first inevitably requires some arrangement on the *Belhar Confession*. It might constitute little more than an agreement to disagree, as long as leaders jointly provide clarity. The already prolonged confusion about *Belhar* will otherwise likely continue to offer ammunition for the many animosities within and among the churches. Clarity is also needed towards what local congregations can do within institutional parameters.

Primarily, communities need concrete support. Many more than indicated in this study have over the past decades explored ways to connect with their neighbors across the color line. Too often these initiatives falter on lack of resources, knowledge or sustainable leadership. With their extensive social and professional networks, community works and reach into people's everyday lives, the churches have abundant capacities to bolster grassroots initiatives. These capacities move far beyond the financial aspects on which many efforts tend to concentrate and get stuck. Key is for the churches to leave plenty space for local members and ministers to find their own paths while offering unambiguous directions as to where they are heading. In this sense, the 2015 interim church order seems to be a good step on the way. It offers tangible guidelines for local integration processes, but without imposing a one-size-fits-all unity agreement few appreciate.

Yet, the perhaps most difficult decision facing the Reformed churches, pertains to whom they might lose on the way. It should be clear by now that not everyone is equally ready to engage with unity efforts. Some people might never be. The DRC in particular faces the task of making unpopular decisions if it wishes to implement its discourse. Notably, these decisions might turn out to receive more approval than is often thought. Surveys and popular debates about *Belhar* or unification are misleading in that they bring out antagonistic voices while the many quiet supporters or rather indifferent members remain unnoticed. Either way, the churches, DRC and URCSA, will have to do a better job in grounding their unity vision in practical benefits for the communities at stake, and accept that some will make more of such benefits than others.

Segregation, despised as it is, offers advantages most people know in terms of group solidarity and familiarity. Integration implies many unknowns. It requires the kind of mutual trust that is lacking exactly because of the long separated structures. To build trust, much more attention is required for local collaborations than is currently offered through the churches' social programs or rather vague and paternalistic "joint projects." It is in tangible actions to help employ young people, enhance neighborhood safety, or keep hydraulic fracturing plans in check, that communities often come to value each other's varied contributions. United or apart, the leading principle here must be first and foremost, interdependency.

On South Africa's Dealing with the Past

In the years spanning this research, South Africa faced two particular events marking a new phase in the country's post-apartheid transition. One involved the killings at the Marikana mine in 2012 where 44 people died after police violently cracked down a months' long strike. The other comprised the death of Nelson Mandela in December 2013 that spurred the entire nation into mourning, and into further reflection about what the achieved freedom from apartheid had brought to the country. Reactions to these events epitomize the trend mentioned in chapter one regarding South Africa's shift from reconciling with the past towards seeking economic justice in the present.

Themes of income disparity are obviously not new and are intricately connected with the country's tortuous history. What this research demonstrated is the difficulty of aligning concerns of the past with those of today. Over the last two decades, South Africans have developed an impressive set of discourses about restoration, forgiveness and Ubuntu, along with a range of initiatives to improve interracial relationships among communities on the ground. The Reformed family, especially URCSA, has played its own part in national reconciliation efforts by promoting theologies of social justice and unity, or facilitating dialogues about the churches' role in apartheid. Notwithstanding their intrinsic value, many of these efforts now appear out of touch. Their focus was long on the divisions between black and white, and on healing the traumas inflicted by the National Party regime. Now they need to add attention to the divisions between disparate black communities, or the violent police actions conducted this time by the ANC.

This new phase is still unfolding and remains therefore hard to foresee. It does offer food for thought about what it takes to deal with a history as convoluted as South Africa's. The country appears in desperate need for alternative vocabulary. Notions such as reconciliation and rainbow unity are perhaps considered obsolete. Their old surrogates of segregation and autocracy remain very much alive. What comes after the rainbow? Some say revolution, others call for realism. The story of the Reformed churches exhibits the need for a bit of both. The next step in their, as well as South Africa's, transition demands a radical effort to stem the rampant inequalities, as well as a good dose of pragmatism to prevent a new wave of disillusion when change will not materialize immediately. Above all, South Africa continues to need ideas to help further a common sense of belonging. The churches preside over a powerful package of symbols, beliefs and practices that could be used towards such common belonging. It is unfortunate that so much of this package remains clouded by narratives of the past and by essentialized identities ill suited for South Africa's shifting realities.

On Religion and Post-Conflict Reconstruction

The last point takes us back to the factor of religion in post-conflict reconstruction. This study has given ample material for substantiating the commonly made claim that religion feeds into social divisions and as such exacerbates tensions between different identity groups. It has also become apparent that the role of religious actors is rather elusive, though certainly not absent. Their most notable impact in society relies on their ability to consolidate certain patterns, perceptions and behavior into people's everyday lives. In polarized societies and situations of conflict, these patterns tend to be ones of separation. They linger long after immediate frictions dissipate and can easily resurface when conditions again deteriorate. The case of South Africa's Reformed churches has allowed for at once a greater comprehension of how these structures are kept in place, and of how they might be undone.

Among the most obvious factors sustaining separateness we have discerned the search for internal group cohesion, autonomy and security as well as the various distinct resources, ideas and ceremonies that religion has to offer towards these needs. The Reformed Church family however exhibits increasing ambiguity in the preservation of its group affiliations. The churches show a sharpening of racial boundaries, and their simultaneous blurring, through for instance the incorporation of alternative traditions, languages or people from different backgrounds. These developments might occur gradually and unintentionally. Making them appear as such is often part of an explicit strategy that has everything to do with how religious actors are navigating their strained social and political environments. Persisting exclusivity, or at least keeping up the appearance of exclusivity, in this context has become a pivotal form of resistance against top-down change. It expresses dissatisfaction with religious, political and community leaders that have not brought the improvements promised to come with peace. Authorities would have sold out the idea of national unity and engaged, to employ a common South African expression, in cheap reconciliation.

This intransigence still does not have to imply a rigid persistence of the status quo. Religious communities not only confront social-political tensions, but also and often much more so, the challenge to compete with other religious and non-religious worldviews. Amidst such survival struggles, inconceivable changes become conceivable. Alternate worship services are developed along with discourses that justify engagement with the diversity that can no longer be avoided. Believers form new connections with people who share the conservative religious morale they stand for, or at least broad principles of faith they now feel they have to defend together against pluralization or secularization. The unexpected inter-communal alliances occurring here raise questions about the solidity of the religious-ethnic affiliations visible on the surface. It also points at the need for creativity in engaging ostensibly defiant religious actors in transformation processes. Prime focus is often given to the moderates within a certain faith tradition, or to religious actors already in favor of dialogue. In this book we have however seen fervent supporters of unity wedged in separate structures, where proclaimed reactionaries quietly dismantled them. Which responses ultimately contribute to greater social cohesion remains a question for many more studies to come.

Appendix: Data Analysis Fieldwork

The overview presents the outcomes of an analysis of fieldwork data gathered in South Africa in 2014. These involved conversations and interviews with 62 participants in the DRC and URCSA on various themes regarding unification processes over the past two decades, and particularly since 2006. For each theme, I looked for the extent to which respondents considered it important for unification and distinguished between positive, negative and ambiguous responses. The table shows the percentage of respondents that responded positively. With conditional formatting, a color scheme was applied to show the level of positive responses for one particular theme across different functions in the two churches, with the darker colors indicating a higher level of positive responses. See table next page.

© KONINKLIJKE BRILL NV, LEIDEN, 2019 | DOI:10.1163/9789004385016_008

	Total	DRC	URCSA	A	L	Me	Mi
Structural national church unification	46.2	31.6	60.0	60.0	77.8	46.7	10.0
Bottom-up unity efforts	84.8	90.0	76.9	100.0	50.0	92.9	100.0
Local exchanges	67.6	68.8	66.7	100.0	100.0	75.0	78.6
Integration regional synods and social works	76.5	80.0	71.4	80.0	75.0	75.0	... [a]
Joint social works	91.2	100.0	83.3	83.3	75.0	100.0	100.0
Poverty relief	79.2	75.0	83.3	50.0	75.0	81.8	85.7
Belhar Confession	56.7	33.3	80.0	60.0	77.8	55.6	28.6
Resource inequalities	100.0	100.0	100.0	100.0	100.0	100.0	100.0
Spirituality: God wants unity	100.0	100.0	100.0	100.0	100.0	100.0	100.0
Nation: South Africa needs church unity	94.1	100.0	83.3	100.0	100.0	90.9	100.0
Reconciliation	80.0	69.2	88.2	100.0	100.0	69.2	66.7
Number of participants	62	31	31	9	13	24	16

[a] None of the interviewed ministers mentioned the in-between level of church organizations and regional leadership structures as important to unification processes.

Legend:

A = Academics   L = Leaders   Me = Members   Mi = Ministers

Bibliography

Primary Sources

Achterberg Declaration. Signed by delegates from the DRC, URCSA, DRCA and RCA. 6–8 November 2006.

Agape Fees 14 April. Verwagtinge soos gelys teen die muur [Agape Party, April 14. Expectations as listed at the wall]. Meeting document obtained from Agape member and organizer, author and date not included.

Agape 2010. Gedagtes waaroor ons kan gesel by die Agape vergadering [Thoughts about which we can talk during the Agape meeting]. 22 April 2010.

Agape 2008. Fees VG Cloetesville saam met NG Moederkerk Stellenbosch [Agape Celebration URCSA Cloetesville together with DRC Moederkerk Stellenbosch].16 April 2008.

"As susters saamstap" [Walking together as sisters]. *Ligdraers* [Bearers of light]. April 2014. 1.

Badisa Homepage. http://www.badisa.org.za.

Badisa Jaarverslag / Annual Report 2012/2013. Accessed at 14 March 2015. http://www .badisa.org.za/downloads.

Burger, C. "Wat is aan die gebeur met ons? [What is happening with us?] *Die Kerkbode.*10 November 2006, 9.

Buys, J.D.S. *Vertoe aan die Ring van Wynberg* [Statement to the Presbytery of Wynberg]. On behalf of the URCSA Wynberg Church Council. 22–23 August 2007.

Census 2011. Statistical Release. Statistics South Africa. Pretoria, South Africa. 2012.

Census 2001. Primary Tables South Africa. Statistics South Africa. 2004

City of Cape Town – 2011 Census Suburb Wynberg. July 2013.

Church and Society 1990: A Testimony of the Dutch Reformed Church (ned Geref Kerk). Bloemfontein: General Synodical Commission, 1991.

Cloete, Daan. "New people for a new nation! ... And the church?" *URCSA News.* 13 December 2013, 12.

Cloete, G. D., and D J. Smit. *A Moment of Truth: The Confession of the Dutch Reformed Mission Church. Grand Rapids*, Mich: W.B. Eerdmans Pub. Co, 1984.

Commission for Witness Homepage. http://www.kga.org.za/english/.

Community Survey 2016 In Brief. Statistics South Africa 2016.

Die Kerkbode. Official newspaper of the Dutch Reformed Church. Consulted editions: 2006–2014. http://kerkbode.bybelmedia.org.za.

Die NG Kerk praat saam Afrikaner organisasies?" [The DRC speaks along wit Afrikaner organizations?] *Die Ander Kant Blog* [The Other Side Blog]. 10 May 2012. http://anderkant.wordpress.com/2012/05/10/die-ng kerk-praat saam afrikaner-organisasies/.

Die Voortrekkers Strategiese Plan vir 2013–2017 [Die Voortrekkers Strategic Plan for 2013–2017]. 2. Accessed at 12 August 2015. https://www.houkoers.co.za/Dokumentasie/Literatuur.

DRC Homepage. http://ngkerk.org.za/wp/.

DRC 2015. General Synod Aanvullende Agenda [Supplemental Agenda].

DRC 2013. General Synod Agenda.

DRC 2011. General Synod Agenda.

DRC 2009. WARC Fasilitering/Mediasie NG Kerk en VGKSA [WARC Facilitation/Mediation DRC and URCSA]. 14–15 October 2009.

DRC 2009. Submission by the Dutch Reformed Church to the Plenary of October 14–15. 2009 Meeting Between Task Teams of the DRC and URCSA.

DRC 2008. Letter to URCSA on Application Membership AACC. 4 August 2008.

DRC 2008. Besluite van die uitgebreide moderamen oor kerkhereniging [Decisions from the extended moderamen about church reunification]. 11–12 June 2008.

DRC 2008. Besluite van die uitgebreide moderamen oor kerkhereniging. [Decisions from the extended moderamen about church reunification]. 11–12 June 2008.

DRC 2008. Moderamenvergadering. [Meeting of the Moderamen]. 17–18 March 2008.

DRC 2007. Konsultasie oor Kerkhereniging [DRC Consultation about Church Reunification]. 30 July 2007.

DRC 2007. Konsultasieboek Kerkhereniging [Consultation Book Church Reunification].

DRC 2007. General Synod Aanvullende Agenda [Supplemental Agenda]

DRC 2004. General Synod Besluite. [Decisions].

DRC 2004. Besluite Kerkhereniging 1966–2004 [Decisions Church Reunification 1966–2004].

DRC 2004. Notule van die tweede vergadering van die Konvent vir Eenheid [Minutes of the second meeting of the Convent for Unity].Brackenfell, Bellville, 22–24 June 2004.

DRC 2002. General Synod Agenda.

DRC 1998. General Synod Agenda.

DRC 1994. General Synod Besluite [Decisions].

DRC 1990. General Synod Agenda.

DRC Free State. Klem verskuif na vennootskapsverhoudinge. [Emphasis shifts towards partnership relations.]. Document published without date on the *Partners in Witness* website. Accessed at 22 February 2015. http://www.ngkerkvrystaat.co.za/documents/wat-doen-ons/vennote/amptelikedokumente/Klem%20Verskuif%20na%20Vennootskapsverhoudinge.pdf.

DRC Free State 2014. Vennote in Getuienis – 'n Nuwe Benadering. [Partners in Witness – a New Approach]. March 2014.

DRC Free State 2013. Belydenis van Belhar: Gespreksdokument [Confession of Belhar: Conversation Document]. Bothaville, 14–17 June 2013.

DRC Free State 2013. Handelinge [Actions]. Bothaville, 14–17 June 2013.

DRC Free State 2012. Verslag oor Eiendomdispute tussen Nederduitse Gereformeerde Kerk in Afrika enVerenigende Gereformeerde Kerk in Suider Afrika [Report on Properties Disputes between the DRCA and URCSA]. March 2012.

DRC Free State 2011. Organisatie-Oudit Sinodale Getuieniskommissie. [OrganizationalAudit Synodical Witness Commission.] October 2011.

DRCA 2009. General Synod Attachment 1: The discussion between the DRCA and URCSA concerning the Belhar Confession.

DRMC 1986. The Belhar Confession and Accompanying Letter. Retrieved at 27 January 2015. http://www.vgksa.org.za/documents/The%20Belhar%20Confession.pdf.

Esselenpark Declaration. Covenanting for the Reunification of the Family of DRChurches. Esselenpark, 20 June 2006.

Grove, Pieter. *Groeteboodskap aan NGK Wes en Suidkaap Sinode* [Greeting message to DRC West and Southern Cape Synod], 7 May 2015.

Hanekom, Braam. "Moontlike Redes Hoekom Mense die Kerk Verlaat" [Possible Reasons for Why People Leave the Church]. *Nuusperspektief Blog* [News Perspective Blog]. 17 January 2014. http://www.nuusperspektief.co.za/?p=871.

"Hope Christian Academy." *Lesotho Letters*. January-February 2007. Accessed at 15 July 2015. http://www.gsgault.com/Newsletter_Archive/2007JJan.pdf.

Jackson, Neels. "NG Kerk wil *Belhar* ter wille van homself insluit" [DRC wants to include *Belhar* for the sake of itself]. *Die Kerkbode*, 2 October 2014. Accessed at 24 November 2014. http://kerkbode.bybelmedia.org.za/2014/10/ng-kerk-wil-belhar-ter-wille-van homself-insluit/.

Jacobs, Nico. "Hereniging: kerk verloor geloofwaardigheid" [Reunification: church lost credibility]. *Die Kerkbode*. 21 March 2008, 15.

Kairos Document 1985. Accessed at 12 August 2015 https://kairossouthernafrica.wordpress.com/2011/05/08/the-south africa-kairos document-1985/.

"KGA se drie taakspan-fokusse" [The focus areas of CFW's three task groups]. *Getuie/ Witness* Semester 2 (2013): 2.

Kgatla, Thias. "Where are we with church unity within the DRC family? *URCSA News*, 11 December 2007.

Kommentaar van die Sinodale Regskommissie (NGK) en die Permanente Regskommissie VGK) op die ooreenkomst tussen die gemeente Wynberg (NGK) en die gemeente Wynberg (VGK) [Commentary of the Synodical Law Commission (DRC) and the Permanent Law Commission (URCSA)]. 9 March 2009.

Koning, de, Johannes. "Om te *Belhar* of nie." *Woord-Skatte Gemyn op Tsumeb Blog* [Mining Word Treasures in Tsumeb Blog]. 21 October 2013.http://skattegemynuitgodsewoordintsumeb.blogspot.com/2013/10/om-te-belhar of-nie.html.

Kok, Mynhardt. "Begelei lidmate wat teen hereniging is" [Guide members who resist reunification]. *Beeld,* 18 October 2013. Accessed at 20 October 2013. http://www .beeld.com/opinie/2013-10-18-brief-begelei-lidmate-wat teen hereniging-is

Kriel, Johan. "Waar Vrede Heers" [Where Peace Rules]. *Juig!* December 2012. Accessed at 14 May 2013. http://www.juig.co.za/article.php?id=235.

Landman, Christina. "Klein is Lekker" [Small is Nice]. *Kruisgewys.* June 2014.

Louw, Andries N.E. *The management of cultural differences between congregations who are working together.* DRC Synodical Witness Forum. August 2009.

Marais, Frederick. *De stand van gemeentes. Sinode van de NG Kerk Wes Kaapland.* [The status of congregations. Synod of the DRC Western Cape]. October 2013.

Malan, Charles. "Die NG Kerk se hantering van diversiteit – 'n kritische bestekopname" [The DRC's approach to diversity – a critical assessment." Internal DRC discussion document. Pretoria, 2010.

Mokgoebo, Zack. "Los die NG Kerk (familie) uit" [Leave the DRC (family)]. *URCSA News.* 12 December 2008. 10.

Naudé, Piet. *Opening Sermon at the DRC General Synod Meeting 2013.* 6 October 2013.

NG Gemeente De Bloem 75 Jaar [DRC Congregation De Bloem 75 Years]. 2010.

"NGK en VGK hou saam 'kerkjol' op Groot-Brak" [DRC and URCSA organize church fair together at Groot-Brak]. *Die Kerkbode.* 7 November 2008, 3

Ooreenkomst tussen NGK Wynberg en VGK Wynberg [Agreement between DRC Wynberg and URCSA Wynberg]. Original version, 2 September 2008.

Ons-se-dankie-projekte" [We say thank you projects]. *Die Kerkbode.* 17 January 2014. 15.

Partners in Witness Homepage. https://ngkvrystaat.wordpress.com/category/vennote-in-getuienis/.

Pieterse, H.J.C. and C.S. Steyn. *Terugvoerverslag aan die Moderamen ten opsigte van die kerkhereningingsproses vanuit 'n kwalitatiewe inhoudsanalise uit steekproewe getrek uit die verslae van gemeentes uit die tien sinodale streke se ru-materiaal.* [Report back to the Moderamen considering the church reunification process from a qualitative content analysis based on rough samples from reports from congregations in ten regional synods.] 17–18 Maart 2008.

Plaatjies van Huffel, Mary-Anne. "Twenty years of unity talks. The journey towards the merger of the Dutch Reformed Family." Article submitted for publication in *URCSA News.* March 2014.

"Re-unification: Judges show the legal way." *URCSA News.* 11 December 2007. 5.

Schalkwyk, van, Carin. "Kerkhereniging in die Suid-Vrystaat – 'n alternatiewe verhaal"[Church reunification in the South Free State – an alternative story]. *Die Kerkbode.* 16 May 2008. 15.

Scottsdene shows the way to a truly United Church." *URCSA News.* 28 March 2008, 12.

Smit, Nico. "Die kerk wat ons moes wees" [The church that we must be]. *Die Kerkbode.* 18 July 2008, 8.

Smith, David. "Jacob Zuma goes to court over painting depicting his genitals." *The Guardian*. 21 May 2012. http://www.theguardian.com/world/2012/may/21/jacobzuma-court-painting genitals.

Statement on The Proposed Regulator Framework for Hydrolic Fracturing. Signed by Dawid Kuyler (URCSA), Kobus Gerber (DRC), Ben du Toit (DRC), Victor Pillay (RCA). 7 November 2013.

Strauss, P.J. "Message from DRC to URCSA." Delivered at *URCSA General Synod*. 29 September – 5 October 2008.

"Teenstanders van *Belhar* word afgedreig met die rassisme kaart." [Opponents of Belhar are threatened with racism card.] *Hier Sta Ek Blog* [Here I Stand Blog]. 23 August 2013. http://hierstaanek.com/2013/08/23/teenstanders-van-belhar word-afgedreig met-die-rassisme-kaart/.

Theron, Piet. "Nooit weer synode toe" [Never return to the synod], *Hier Sta Ek Blog* [Here I stand Blog], 25 June 2013, http://hierstaanek.com/2013/06/30/belhar instrument-van-eenheid-of-kerkskeuring/.

Toit, du, Ben. *Muur van skeiding ... oopgeskuif!* [Wall of separation ... opened!]. 21 June 2006.

Toit, du, Ben. *Indrukke uit Achterbergh: Die Here gaan voor ons uit!* [Impressions from Achterberg: The Lord leads us the way!]. 8 November 2006.

URCSA Homepage. http://www.vgksa.org.za/Default.asp.

URCSA News. Official newspaper of the Uniting Reformed Church in Southern Africa. Consulted editions: 2006–2014. [Print only].

URCSA 2012. Compilation of Documents on Church Reunification: Process Between URCSA and DRC 2004–2012. Edition July 2012.

URCSA 2012. Sixth General Synod Acta. Strategic Plan 2010–2016.

URCSA 2012. General Synod Committee 2005. Resolutions Church Unity. Compilation of Documents on Church Reunification. Process Between URCSA and DRC 2004–2012. Edition July 2012.

URCSA 2011. Pastoral letter to URCSA congregations on the decision of the Dutch Reformed Church General Synod's Acceptance of the *Belhar Confession*. 20 October 2011.

URCSA 2009. Minutes of a meeting held with WARC. 4- 6 March 2009.

URCSA 2008. Letter to DRC on Application for Membership of the AACC and Related Matters. 20 September 2008.

URCSA 2008. General Synod Committee. Complete Decision on the Process of Church Unity. Hammanskraal. 29 September – 5 October 2008.

URCSA 2008. General Synod Committee Decisions.

URCSA 2006. Moderator's Address to Joint DRC Family General Synodical Commissions. 6–8 November 2006.

URCSA 2006. Moderator's Address to Joint DRC Family

URCSA Capeland 2009. Verloop van die Wynberg aangeleentheid [Order of events of the Wynberg affair]. Presented at URCSA Cape regional synod meeting. 15 October 2009.

"URCSA Polokwane celebrates God' grace." *URCSA News.* 11 December 2007, 2

United Ministry for Service and Witness. "Our Calling to Service and Witness. A Theological Basis for the DRC Family's Missional Ministries." Policy Document. 2011.

"Verskillend maar saam in Christus, gee ons hoop vir die wereld" [Different but together in Christ, gives us hope for the world]. *Getuie / Witness* Semester 2 (2014): 2.

Verslag van Diens en Getuienis (D&G) aan die 6e gewone vergadering van die VGK streeksinode Kaapland [Report of the Service and Witness (S&W) of the 6th ordinary meeting of the URC Cape synod.] 14–17 October 2014. 14.

VrydagNuus. Official newsletter of the DRC Western and Southern Cape Synod. http://www.kaapkerk.co.za/english/index.php/vrydagnuus/.

Vrypos. Official newsletter of the DRC Free State.http://www.ngkerkvrystaat.co.za/dokumente.php.

WARC 2009. WARC Mediasie/Facilitering NG Kerk en VGKSA Verslag [Mediation/Facilitation DRC and URCSA Report]. Carmelite. 14–15 October 2009

WARC 2009. A Statement by the Delegation from the World Alliance of Reformed Churches, 6 March 2009.

WARC 2009. Notas van die gesprek tussen die NG Kerk, WARC en die VGKSA [Minutes of the conversation between the DRC, WARC and the URCSA]. 6 March 2009.

WCRC 2012. Letter from DRC and URCSA management teams and Dr. Jerry Pillay after conversations on 25–27 February 2012.

Secondary Sources

Adonis, J.C. "Bevryding Tot Eenwording En Getuienis : Die Geskiedenis Van Die Verenigende Gereformeerde Kerk in Suider-Afrika – 1950–2001" [Liberation towards Unity and Witness: the History of the Uniting Reformed Church in Southern Africa – 1950–2001]. *Dutch Reformed Theological Journal = Nederduitse Gereformeerde Teologiese Tydskrif* 43 (2002): 327–341.

Adhikari, Mohamed. "Contending Approaches to Coloured Identity and the History of Coloured people in South Africa." *History Compass* 3 AF 177 (2005): 1–16.

Adhikari, Mohamed. " 'Not Black Enough': Changing Expressions of Coloured Identity in Post-Apartheid South Africa." *South African Historical Journal* 51:1 (2004): 167–178.

Africa Check. "Are SA whites really being killed "like flies"? Why Steve Hofmeyr is wrong." 24 June 2013. https://africacheck.org/reports/are-white-afrikaners-really being-killed-like-flies/.

Akenson, Donald H. *God's Peoples: Covenant and Land in South Africa, Israel, and Ulster.* Ithaca: Cornell University Press, 1992.

Ammerman, Nancy T. *Sacred Stories, Spiritual Tribes: Finding Religion in Everyday Life.* Oxford; New York : Oxford University Press. 2014.

Ammerman, Nancy T "Finding religion in everyday life." *Sociology of Religion* 75:2, (2014): 189–207.

Ammerman, Nancy T (ed.) *Everyday Religion: Observing Modern Religious Lives.* Oxford: Oxford University Press, 2007.

Ammerman, Nancy T and Arthur E. Farnsley. *Congregation & Community.* New Brunswick: Rutgers University Press, 1997.

Appleby, R S. *The Ambivalence of the Sacred: Religion, Violence, and Reconciliation.* Lanham, MD: Rowman & Littlefield Publishers, 2000.

Anderson, Benedict R. O. G. *Imagined Communities: Reflections on the Origin and Spread of Nationalism.* London: Verso, 1991.

Asad, Talal. *Formations of the Secular: Christianity, Islam, Modernity.* Stanford, Calif: Stanford University Press, 2003.

Barnes, L P. "Was the Northern Ireland Conflict Religious?" *Journal of Contemporary Religion.* 20.1 (2005): 55–69.

Becker, Penny E. "Making Inclusive Communities: Congregations and the "problem" of Race." *Social Problems* 45.4 (1998): 451–472.

Beer, J.M. and A.S. Niekerk. "Die Missionêre Waarde Van *Belhar* En Die Ng Kerk Familie Se Herenigingsgesprek" [The Missionary Value of *Belhar* and the Unification Conversation of the Dutch Reformed Church Family]. *Dutch Reformed Theological Journal = Ned. Gereformeerde Teologiese Tydskrif* 50.1 (2009): 50–65.

De Beer, P.J.P. "The Reformed Church in Africa's Laudium Declaration. a Gift to the Ecumenical Community." *Faculty of Theology, Stellenbosch University* (2013): 112–113. Accessed at 13 November 2014. http://hdl.handle.net/2263/21578.

Bhorat, Haroon and Carlene van der Westhuizen, "Poverty, Inequality and the Nature of Economic Growth in South Africa," *DPRU Working Paper 12/151.* University of Cape Town: November 2012.

Blaser, Thomas. *Afrikaner Identity After Nationalism.* Basel, Switzerland: Basler Afrika Bibliographien, 2006.

Bloomberg, Charles, and Saul Dubow. *Christian Nationalism and the Rise of the Afrikaner Broederbond in South Africa, 1918–48.* Bloomington: Indiana University Press, 1989.

Boesak, Allan A. and Curtiss P. DeYoung. *Radical Reconciliation: Beyond Political Pietism and Christian Quietism.* Maryknoll, NY: Orbis Books, 2012.

Borer, Tristan A. *Challenging the State: Churches As Political Actors in South Africa, 1980–1994.* Notre Dame, Ind: University of Notre Dame Press, 1998.

Botha, Johan, and Piet Naudé. *Good News to Confess: The Belhar Confession and the Road of Acceptance.* Wellington, South Africa: Bible Media, 2011.

Botha, Nico. "The voice of protest within the Dutch Reformed Mission Church." In Mary-Anne Plaatjies-Van Huffel and Robert Vosloo. *Reformed Churches in South Africa and the Struggle for Justice. Remembering 1960–1990*, 75–91. African SUN MeDIA, 2013.

Botha, Theunis. "Ons sal mekaar nie los nie : 'n kwalitatiewe ondersoek na die aard van die onderlinge verbondenheid van leraars binne die Verenigde Ring van Stellenbosch" [We will not let go of each other: a qualitative study on the connectedness of ministers within the Uniting Presbytery of Stellenbosch]. Thesis, Stellenbosch University, December 2014. Accessed at 17 February 2017. http://hdl.handle.net/10019.1/95986.

Borght Van der, E. A. J. G. "Sunday Morning – the Most Segregated Hour: On Racial Reconciliation As Unfinished Business for Theology in South Africa and Beyond." Amsterdam: Faculty of Theology, VU University, 2009.

Brewer, John, Gareth Higgins, and Francis Teeney. "Religion and Peacemaking: a Conceptualization." *Sociology* 44.6 (2010): 1019–1037.

Bellah, Robert. "Civil Religion in America." *Daedalus.* 96 (Winter 1967): 1–21.

Berger, Peter L. *The Many Altars of Modernity. Towards a Paradigm of Religion in a Pluralist Age.* Berlin: De Gruyter. 2014.

Berger, Peter L and Anton C. Zijderveld. *In Praise of Doubt: How to Have Convictions Without Becoming a Fanatic.* New York: HarperOne/HarperCollins Publishers, 2009.

Berger, Peter L "Secularization and De-Secularization." In *Religions in the Modern World: Traditions and Transformations*, edited by Linda Woodhead, 336–347. London: Routledge, 2002.

Berger, Peter L *The Sacred Canopy: Elements of a Sociological Theory of Religion.* New York: Anchor Books, 1990.

Beyer, Peter. *Religion and Globalization.* London, U.K: Sage Publications, 1994.

Botman, Russel. "*Belhar* and the white Dutch Reformed Church: changes in the DRC 1974–1990." In *Maintaining Apartheid or Promoting Change?: The Role of Dutch Reformed Church in a Phase of Increasing Conflict in South Africa. Religion and society in transition v. 5*, edited by Wolfram Weisse and C.A. Anthonissen, 123 134. Munster: Waxmann, 2004.

Bourdieu, Pierre. *Outline of a Theory of Practice.* Cambridge, U.K: Cambridge University Press, 1977.

Bruce, Steve. "Cathedrals to cults : the evolving forms of the religious life." In *Religion, Modernity, and Postmodernity,* edited by Heelas, Paul, David Martin, and Paul Morris, 19–35. Oxford, UK: Blackwell Publishers, 1998.

Casanova, Jose. "Rethinking Secularization: A Global Comparative Perspective." *Hedgehog Review* 8 (2006): 7–22.

Casanova, José. *Public Religions in the Modern World.* Chicago: University of Chicago Press, 1994

Chapman, Audrey R, and Bernard Spong. *Religion & Reconciliation in South Africa: Voices of Religious Leaders*. Philadelphia, Pa: Templeton Foundation Press, 2003.

Charmaz, Kathy. *Constructing Grounded Theory: A Practical Guide Through Qualitative Analysis*. London: Sage Publications, 2006.

Chipkin, Ivor. *Do South Africans Exist?: Nationalism, Democracy, and the Identity of the People*. Johannesburg: Wits University Press, 2007.

Chidester, David, Abdulkader Tayob, and Wolfram Weisse. *Religion, Politics, and Identity in a Changing South Africa*. Munchen: Waxmann Munster, 2004.

Cilliers, Johan, and Johan Cilliers. *God for Us: An Analysis and Assessment of Dutch Reformed Preaching During the Apartheid Years*. Stellenbosch: Sun Press, 2006.

Cobbs, R. J., S. L. Perry, and K. D. Dougherty. "United by Faith? Race/ethnicity, Congregational Diversity, and Explanations of Racial Inequality." *Sociology of Religion*. 76.2 (2015): 177–198.

Cole, Catherine M. *Performing South Africa's Truth Commission: Stages of Transition*. Bloomington: Indiana University Press, 2010.

Coleman, John A, and Miklós Tomka. *Religion and Nationalism*. London: SCM Press, 1995.

Corbin, Juliet M. and Anselm Strauss, "Grounded Theory Research: Procedures, Canons, and Evaluative Criteria." *Qualitative Sociology* 13.1 (1990): 3–21.

Davenport, Rodney. "Settlement, Conquest and Theological Controversy: The Churches of Nineteenth-century European Immigrants." In *Christianity in South Africa: A Political, Social, and Cultural History. Perspectives on Southern Africa 55*,edited by Richard Elphick and T R. H. Davenport, 51–67. Berkeley, Calif:University of California Press, 1997.

Davie, Grace. "From believing without belonging to vicarious religion: understanding the patterns of religion in modern Europe." In *The Role of Religion in Modern Societies*, edited by Detlef Pollack and Daniel V. A. Olson, 165–176. New York: Routledge, 2008.

Davies, Rebecca. *Afrikaners in the New South Africa: Identity Politics in a Globalised Economy*. London: Tauris Academic Studies, 2009.

De Fina, Deborah, Deborah Schiffrin and Michael G. W. Bamberg. *Discourse and Identity*. Cambridge. UK: Cambridge University Press, 2006.

De Gruchy J. W. *The Church Struggle in South Africa*. London: Collins, 2005.

De Young, Curtiss P., Michael O. Emerson, George A. Yancey, and Karen H. K. Chia. *United by Faith: The Multiracial Congregation As an Answer to the Problem of Race*. Oxford: Oxford University Press, 2003.

Dijk, van, Teun A. *Discourse and Power*. Houndmills, Basingstoke, Hampshire: Palgrave Macmillan. 2008.

Dijk, van, Teun A "The reality of racism." *Festschrift für die Wirklichkeit* VS Verlag für Sozialwissenschaften, (2000): 211–225.

Dolby, Nadine. *Constructing Race: Youth, Identity, and Popular Culture in South Africa*. Albany: State University of New York Press, 2001.

Dreyfus, Georges. "The end of the Saeculum and global capitalism. Should we be scared? The return of the sacred and the rise of religious nationalism in South Asia." In *Crediting God: Sovereignty and Religion in the Age of Global Capitalism*, edited by Miguel E. Vatter, 117–141. New York: Fordham University Press, 2011.

Durand, Jaap. *Ontluisterde Wereld: Die Afrikaner En Sy Kerk in 'n Veranderende Suid Afrika* [Degraded World: The Afrikaner and His Church in a Changing South Africa]. Wellington. South Africa: Lux Verbi. 2002.

Durkheim, Émile. *The Elementary Forms of the Religious Life*. New York: Free Press, 1965.

Ehlers, Anton. "Desegregating History in South Africa: The Case of the Covenant and the Battle of Blood River/Ncome." *Conference on Desegregating History*. Cape Town. 5–9 July 2000. Accessed at 13 September 2014.http://sun025.sun.ac.za/portal/page/portal/Arts/Departemente1/geskiedenis/doc/esegregating_history.pdf.

Edwards, Korie L., Brad Christerson and Michael O. Emerson. "Race, Religious Organizations, and Integration." *Annual Review of Sociology* 39, (2013): 211 288.

Edwards, Korie L., Brad Christerson and Michael O. Emerson. *The Elusive Dream: The Power of Race in Interracial Churches*. Oxford: Oxford University Press, 2008.

Edwards, Korie L., Brad Christerson and Michael O. Emerson. "Bring Race to the Center: the Importance of Race in Racially Diverse Religious Organizations." *Journal for the Scientific Study of Religion* 47.1 (2008): 5–9.

Eisenstadt, S.E. "Multiple Modernities." *Daedalus* Winter, 129(1) (2000): 1–29.

Elphick, Richard, and T R. H. Davenport. *Christianity in South Africa: A Political, Social, and Cultural History*. Berkeley, Calif: University of California Press, 1997.

Emerson, Michael O, and Christian Smith. *Divided by Faith: Evangelical Religion and the Problem of Race in America*. Oxford: Oxford University Press, 2000.

Erasmus, Zimitri. "Undoing the Yoke of Race." In *Religion, Politics, and Identity in a Changing South Africa*, edited by David Chidester, Abdulkader Tayob, and Wolfram Weisse, 89–95. Munchen: Waxmann Munster, 2004).

Essed, Philomena. *Understanding Everyday Racism: An Interdisciplinary Theory*. Newbury Park: Sage Publications, 1991.

Emerson, Michael O. and Christian Smith. *Divided by Faith: Evangelical Religion and the Problem of Race in America*. Oxford: Oxford University Press, 2000,

Erasmus, Johannes C, H J. Hendriks, and Gerbrand G. Mans. "Religious Research As Kingpin in the Fight against Poverty and Aids in the Western Cape, South Africa." *Hts : Theological Studies* 62.1 (2006): 293–311.

Erasmus, Zimitri. "Undoing the Yoke of Race." David Chidester, Abdulkader Tayob, and Wolfram Weisse. *Religion, Politics, and Identity in a Changing South Africa*. Munchen: Waxmann Munster, 2004. 89–96.

Fakir, Ebrahim. "Politics, state and society in South Africa: Between leadership, trust and technocrats." *Development Planning Division Working Paper Series No.1.* DBSA: Midrand, 2009.

Fortein, Eugene. "Allan Boesak and the Dutch Reformed Mission Church between 1976 1990." In *Reformed Churches in South Africa and the Struggle for Justice: Remembering 1960–1990,* edited by Vosloo and Plaatjies-Van Huffel, 303–315. African SUN Media, 2013.

Frederickson, George M. *The Comparative Imagination: On the History of Racism, Nationalism, and Social Movements.* Berkeley: University of California Press, 2000.

Fredrickson, George M. *White Supremacy: A Comparative Study in American and South African History.* New York: Oxford University Press, 1981.

Friedland, Roger. "Religious Nationalism and the Problem of Collective Representation." *Annual Review of Sociology.* 27 (2001): 125–152.

Ganiel, Gladys. "Is the Multiracial Congregation an Answer to the Problem of Race? Comparative Perspectives from South Africa and the USA." *Journal of Religion in Africa.* 38.3 (2008): 263–283.

Ganiel, Gladys, and Paul Dixon. "Religion, Pragmatic Fundamentalism and the Transformation of the Northern Ireland Conflict." *Journal of Peace Research.* 45.3 (2008): 419–436.

Geertz, Clifford. *The Interpretation of Cultures: Selected Essays.* New York: Basic Books, 1973.

Gensicke, Matthias. *Zwischen Beharrung Und Veränderung: Die Nederduitse Gereformeerde Kerk Im Umbruchsprozess Südafrikas (1990–1999).* [Between Persistence and Change: The Dutch Reformed Church in South Africa's Transition Process (1990–1999).] Munster: Waxmann, 2007.

Gensicke, Matthias. "Religiosity of Students Within the Drc : Preliminary Empirical Findings." *Scriptura: International Journal of Bible, Religion and Theology in Southern Africa.* 83 (2003): 276–286.

Giliomee, Hermann B. *The Afrikaners: Biography of a People.* Charlottesville: University of Virginia Press, 2003.

Goba, Bonganjalo. "The Kairos Document and Its Implications for Liberation in South Africa." *Journal of Law and Religion* 5.2 (1987): 313–325

Goldberg, Michelle. *Kingdom Coming: The Rise of Christian Nationalism.* New York: W.W. Norton & Co, 2006.

Goldschmidt, Henry and Elizabeth A. McAlister. *Race, Nation, and Religion in the Americas.* New York: Oxford University Press, 2004.

Goodwin, June, and Benjamin N. Schiff. *Heart of Whiteness: Afrikaners Face Black Rule in the New South Africa.* New York: Scribner, 1995

Gordon, Steven, Benjamin Roberts and Jarè Struwig. "The state of the union? Attitudes to South African trade." *Human Science Research Council.* March 2013. Accessed at

19 November 2015. http://www.hsrc.ac.za/en/review/hsrc-review march-2013/the-state-of-the-union#sthash.omwZUabq.

Greenfeld, Liah. *Nationalism: Five Roads to Modernity*. Cambridge, Mass: Harvard University Press. 1992.

Groch, Kate, Karen E. Gerdes, Elizabeth A. Segal & Maureen Groch. "The Grassroots Londolozi Model of African Development: Social Empathy in Action." *Journal of Community Practice* 20:1–2 (2012): 154–177.

Habib, A. "South Africa – The Rainbow Nation and Prospects for Consolidating Democracy". *African Journal of Political Science* Vol. 2, no. 2, 1997: 15–37.

Heelas, Paul, David Martin, and Paul Morris. *Religion, Modernity, and Postmodernity*. Oxford, UK: Blackwell Publishers, 1998.

Hervieu-Léger, Danièle. *Religion As a Chain of Memory*. New Brunswick, N.J: Rutgers University Press, 2000.

Hervieu-Léger, Danièle. "Bricolage Vaut-Il Dissémination? Quelques Réflexions Sur L'Opérationnalite Sociologique D'une Métaphore Problématique" ['Tinkering' Should Be Disseminated? Some Reflections on the Sociological Implications of a Problematic Metaphor]. *Social Compass* 52.3 (2005): 295–308.

Hickel, Jason. *Democracy As Death: The Moral Order of Anti-Liberal Politics in South Africa*. Oakland, California: University of California Press. 2015.

Hill, Lloyd, and Simon Bekker. "Language, residential space and inequality in Cape Town: Broad-brush profiles and trends." *Language* 28, no. 1 (2014).

Hoffman, A.M., D.T. Keta and M.J. Ramolahlehi. *The Story of the NGKA and It's Decisions Concerning Unification*. Presented in abbreviated version at the Achterberg Meeting of the family of DRC churches. November 6–8, 2006.

Hyslop, J. "Why Did Apartheid's Supporters Capitulate? 'Whiteness', Class and Consumption in Urban South Africa, 1985–1995." *Society in Transition* 31 (2000): 36–44

Institute for Justice and Reconciliation. *Confronting Exclusion. Time for Radical Reconciliation*. SA Reconciliation Barometer Survey: 2013 Report. Cape Town. South Africa. 2013.

James, William. *The Varieties of Religious Experience: A Study in Human Nature*. New York: Modern library, 1936.

Johnston, Alexander. *Reinventing the Nation. South Africa*. London / New York: Bloomsbury. 2014.

Juergensmeyer, M. "The Worldwide Rise of Religious Nationalism." *Journal of International Affairs Columbia University*. 50.1 (1996): 1–20.

Keddie, Nikkie, R. "The New Religious Politics: Where, When, and Why Do 'Fundamentalisms' Appear?" *Comparative Studies in Society and History*. 40.4 (1998): 696–723.

Kinghorn, Johann. "Modernization and Apartheid: The Afrikaner Churches." ." In *Christianity in South Africa,* edited by Elphick and Davenport, 135–154.

Kinnvall, Catarina. "Globalization and Religious Nationalism: Self, Identity, and the Search for Ontological Security". *Political Psychology*. Vol. 25, No. 5 (Oct., 2004): 741–767.

Klaaren, Eugene M. "Creation and Apartheid: South African Theology Since 1948." In *Christianity in South Africa,* edited by Elphick and Davenport, 372–374.

Knecht, Annette. *Ein Geheimbund Als Akteur Des Wandels: Der Afrikaner Broederbond Und Seine Rolle Im Transformationsprozess Südafrikas* [A Secret Organization as Actor of Change: The Afrikaner Brotherhood and its role in South Africa's Transition Process]. Frankfurt am Main: Peter Lang, 2007.

Korom, Frank J. *Hosay Trinidad: Muharram Performances in an Indo-Caribbean Diaspora*. Philadelphia: University of Pennsylvania Press, 2003.

Kuperus, Tracy. *State, Civil Society, and Apartheid in South Africa: An Examination of Dutch Reformed Church-State Relations*. New York, N.Y: St. Martin's Press, 1999.

Landau, Loren B. *Exorcising the Demons Within: Xenophobia, Violence and Statecraft in Contemporary South Africa*. Tokyo: United Nations University Press, 2012.

Leavy, Patricia. *Oral History*. Oxford: Oxford University Press, 2011

Lichterman, Paul. "Religion and the Construction of Civic Identity." *American Sociological Review*. 73.1 (2008): 83–104.

Louw, Alberts and Frank Chikane. *The Road to Rustenburg: The Church Looking Forward to a New South Africa*. Cape Town: Struik Christian Books, 1991.

Marais, Hein. *South Africa Pushed to the Limit: The Political Economy of Change*. London: Zed, 2011.

Marx, Anthony W. *Faith in Nation: Exclusionary Origins of Nationalism*. Oxford: Oxford University Press, 2003.

Marx, Christoph. "Ubu and Ubuntu: on the Dialectics of Apartheid and Nation Building." *Politikon: South African Journal of Political Studies* 29.1 (2002): 49 69.

Marx, Christoph *Im Zeichen Des Ochsenwagens: Der Radikale Afrikaaner-Nationalismus in Südafrika Und Die Geschichte Der Ossewabrandwag* [Oxwagon Sentinel radical Afrikaner Nationalism and the history of the 'Ossewabrandwag']. Münster: Lit, 1998.

Maserumule. M. H. "Politics of Transition in South Africa and the Post-1994 Democratic State." *Journal of Asian and African Studies* 47.3 (2012): 301–314.

Manzo, Kate and Pat McGowan. "Afrikaner Fears and the Politics of Despair: Understanding Change in South Africa." *International Studies Quarterly* 36.1 (1992): 1–24.

Maxwell, Patrick, Alleyn Diesel and Thillay Naidoo. "Hinduism in South Africa." In *Living Faiths in South Africa*, edited by Martin Prozesky and J. W. De Gruchy, 177–201. New York: St. Martin's Press, 1995.

Maylam, Paul. "Unraveling South Africa's racial order: the historiography of racism, segregation, and apartheid." In *Situating "race" and Racisms in Space, Time, and Theory: Critical Essays for Activists and Scholars*, edited by Jo A. Lee and John S. Lutz, 138–160. Montréal: McGill-Queen's University Press, 2005.

Meiring, Piet. *Chronicle of the Truth Commission: A Journey Through the Past and Present-into the Future of South Africa*. Vanderbijlpark: Carpe Diem Books, 1999.

Merwe, van der, J. M. "Kerk En Samelewing 25 Jaar Later: Was Die Kool Die Sous Werd?" [Church and Society 25 years later: was it worthwhile?] *Christelike Lektuurfonds in collaboration with Stellenbosch University* 22 (2012), 571. Accessed 12 April 2015. http://ngtt.journals.ac.za/pub/article/view/65.

Mitchell, Claire. *Religion, Identity and Politics in Northern Ireland: Boundaries of Belonging and Belief.* Aldershot, Hants, England: Ashgate Pub, 2006.

Moodie, T D. *The Rise of Afrikanerdom: Power, Apartheid, and the Afrikaner CivilReligion*. Berkeley: University of California Press, 1975.

Naudé, Piet. *Neither Calendar nor Clock: Perspectives on the Belhar Confession*. Grand Rapids, Mich. u.a.: Eerdmans, 2010.

Nayak, Anoop. "After Race: Ethnography, Race and Post-Race Theory." *Ethnic and Racial Studies*. 29.3 (2006): 411–430.

Neumann, Peter. "Was the Irish Republican Army motivated by religion?" Paper presented at *UCSIA Summer School: Is Faith-based Violence Religious?* 27 August 2015.

Pauw, J C. *Anti-apartheid Theology in the Dutch Reformed Family of Churches: A Depth-Hermeneutical Analysis*. PhD Diss. Vrije Universiteit Amsterdam, 2007.

Plaatjies van Huffel, Mary-Anne. "Remembering reformed documents: Reading the *Belhar Confession* as a historical text." In *Reformed Churches in South Africa and the Struggle for Justice: Remembering 1960–1990*, edited by Vosloo and Plaatjies Van Huffel, 329–345. African SUN MeDIA, 2013.

Plaatjies van Huffel, Mary-Anne and Robert Vosloo, eds. *Reformed churches in South Africa and the struggle for justice: Remembering 1960–1990*. African SUN MeDIA, 2013.

Plaatjies van Huffel, Mary-Anne *Die Doleansiekerkreg en die kerkreg en kerkregering van die Nederduitse Gereformeerde Sendingkerke en die Verenigende Gereformeerde Kerk in Suider Afrika* [The Doleansie Church Polity and the Church Law and Church Order of the Dutch Reformed Mission Churces and the Uniting Reformed Church of Southern Africa]. PhD Diss. University of Pretoria. Pretoria, 2013. Accessed at 8 September 2014. http://upetd.up.ac.za/thesis/available/etd-04022009-190218/.

Plaatjies van Huffel, Mary-Anne and Johan M. van der Merwe. "Die reis met kerkeenwording tussen die Verenigende Gereformeerde Kerk in Suider-Afrika en die Nederduitse Gereformeerde Kerk in Afrika" [Journey towards church unification between the Uniting Reformed Chuch of Southern Africa and the Dutch Reformed Church in Africa]. *Verbum et Ecclesia* 33.1 (2012): 7 pages. Accessed at 5 September 2014, http://www.ve.org.za/index.php/VE/article/view/724.

Pollack, Detlef and Daniel V. A. Olson. *The Role of Religion in Modern Societies*. New York: Routledge, 2008.

Powell, D.M., M. O'Donovan and J. De Visser. *Civic Protest Barometer 2007–2014*. Cape Town MLGI, 2014.

Prozesky, Martin, and Gruchy J. W. De. *Living Faiths in South Africa*. New York: St. Martin's Press, 1995.

Puukka, Jaana, Patrick Dubarle, Holly McKiernan, Jairam Reddy, and Philip Wade. "Higher education in regional and city development: the Free State, South Africa. OECD (2012).

Ramsamy, Edward. "Between Non-Racialism and Multiculturalism: Indian Identity and Nation Building in South Africa." *Tijdschrift Voor Economische En Sociale Geografie* 98.4 (2007): 468–481.

Ratuva, Steven. *The Politics of Preferential Development: Trans-global Study of Affirmative Action and Ethnic Conflict in Fiji, Malaysia and South Africa*. Acton, A.C.T. ANU E Press, 2013.

Rastogi, Pallavi. *Afrindian Fictions: Diaspora, Race, and National Desire in South Africa*. Columbus: Ohio State University Press, 2008.

Ries, J, and H. Jurgens Hendriks. " 'n Evaluering Van Drie Interkulturele Gemeenskapsprojekte" [An Evaluation of Three Intercultural CommunityProjects]. *HTS Teologiese Studies / Theological Studies* 69.2 (2013): 1–9.

Riesebrodt, Martin. *The Promise of Salvation: A Theory of Religion*. Chicago: University of Chicago Press, 2010.

Robinson, Phil. and Johan Botha (red.). *Wat is sending? 'n Werkswinkel vir die familie van NG kerke* [What is mission? A workshop for the DRC family]. Swartland Drukpers (Edms) Bpk: Malmsbury, 1986.

Schoeman, Kobus and Carin van Schalkwyk. "Klein plattelandse gemeentes as ruimtes om brûe na die hele gemeenskap te bou: 'n Prakties-teologiese ondersoek"[Small rural congregations as spaces to build bridges to the entire community: A practical theologocal research]. *LitNet Akademies* 10(3) (2013): 781–799.

Schoeman, W.J. "The racial discourse and the Dutch Reformed Church: Looking through a descriptive-empirical lens ... towards a normative task." *Acta Theologica* 30 (2) (December 2010): 130–151.

Shore, Megan. *Religion and Conflict Resolution: Christianity and South Africa's Truth and Reconciliation Commission*. Farnham, England: Ashgate Pub. Ltd, 2009.

Smit, Dirkie. "What does it mean to live in South Africa and to be Reformed?" In *Essays on Being Reformed: Collected Essays 3*, edited by Dirkie Smit and Robert Vosloo, 239–258. Stellenbosch: SUN Press, 2009.

Smit, Dirkie "Challenges for Reformed Churches in Africa: a Contemporary Narrative." *International Journal for the Study of the Christian Church* 8.4 (2008): 319–336.

Smith, Anthony D. *Chosen Peoples*. Oxford: Oxford University Press, 2003.

Smith, Anthony D "The Sacred Dimension of Nationalism." *Millennium. Journal of International Studies* Vol. 29, no. 3 (2000): 791–814.

Somers, Margaret R. "The Narrative Constitution of Identity: a Relational and Network Approach." *Theory and Society : Renewal and Critique in Social Theory* 23.5 (1994): 605–649.

Strauss, P.J. "Belydenis, Kerkverband En Belhar" [Confession, Church Association and Belhar]. *Dutch Reformed Theological Journal = Nederduitse Gereformeerde Teologiese Tydskrif* 46 (2005): 560–575.

Suzman, Mark. *Ethnic Nationalism and State Power: The Rise of Irish Nationalism, Afrikaner Nationalism, and Zionism.* New York: St. Martin's Press, 1999.

Thesnaar, Christo. "Reformed churches' struggle for justice. Lessons learnt from their submissions before the TRC." In *Reformed Churches in South Africa and the Struggle for Justice: Remembering 1960–1990,* edited by Vosloo and Plaatjies- Van Huffel, 385–399. African SUN MeDIA, 2013.

Tranby, Eric and Douglass Hartman. "Critical Whiteness Theories and the Evangelical "race Problem": Extending Emerson and Smith's *Divided by Faith." Journal fo rthe Scientific Study of Religion* 47.3 (2008): 341–359.

Tshaka, Rothney and Peter M. Maruping."'The hastening that waits': A critical assessment of the tangebility of unity within the Uniting Reformed Church in Southern Africa."*Verbum et Ecclesia* 31.1 (2010): 10 pages. Accessed at September 5, 2014. http://www.ve.org.za/index.php/VE/article/view/426/467.

"Under the Radar. Pentecostalism in South Africa and its potential social and economic role." *Center for Development and Enterprise.* March 2008. Accessed 18 October 2015. http://www.cde.org.za/wpcontent/uploads/2013/02/Under%20the%20rada%20-%20Pentecostalism%20in%20SA.pdf.

Vansina, Jan. *Oral Tradition As History.* Madison, Wis: University of Wisconsin Press, 1985.

Vatter, Miguel E. *Crediting God: Sovereignty and Religion in the Age of Global Capitalism.* New York: Fordham University Press, 2011.

Veer, Peter van der and Hartmut Lehmann. *Nation and Religion: Perspectives on Europe and Asia.* Princeton, N.J: Princeton University Press, 1999.

Veer, Peter van der. *Religious Nationalism: Hindus and Muslims in India.* Berkeley, CA: University of California Press, 1994.

Venter, Jan. "Skep ruimte vir ander se standpunt" [Create space for other person's point of view]. *Beeld.* 3 October 13. Accessed at 20 October 2013 http://www.beeld.com/opinie/2013-10-03-brief-skep-ruimte-vir-ander-se standpunt.

Villiers, de, D.E. "The interdependence of public witness and institutional unity in the Dutch Reformed family of churches." *Verbum et Ecclesia* 29 (3) (2008): 728–743.

Villiers, de, J. "NGK-lidmate 20.000 minder in een jaar" [DRC members 20,000 less in a year]. *Rapport.* 18 February 2012.

Vosloo, R. "The presbytery and church reunification in the Dutch reformed family of churches in South Africa : the story of the United Presbytery of Stellenbosch." Janssen, Allan J. A *Collegial Bishop?: Classis and Presbytery at Issue.* Grand Rapids, Mich: W.B. Eerdmans Pub. Co, 2010. [Article received from author without page numbers].

Waal, Cees van der. "Essentialism in a South African discussion of language and culture". In *Power, Politics and Identity in South African Media: Selected Seminar Papers*, edited by Adrian Hadland, 52–72. Cape Town, South Africa: HSRC Press.

Wagner, C.P. *Our Kind of People: The Ethical Dimensions of Church Growth in America.* Atlanta: J. Knox Press, 1979.

Wale, Kim. "Policing Racial Boundaries: University Students' Interpretations of Race Relations in South Africa." *MMG Working Paper* 10-10. Göttingen: Max Planck Institute for the Study of Religious and Ethnic Diversity, 2010. 1–30.

Walshe, Peter. *Prophetic Christianity and the Liberation Movement in South Africa.* Pietermaritzburg: Cluster Publications, 1995.

Warner, Stephen. "Religion, Boundaries and Bridges," *Sociology of Religion* 58:3, (1997): 217–238.

Watt van der, Gideon. "Die sendingpraktyk van die Ned.Geref. Kerk: Enkele tendense vanaf 1952 tot met die eeuwenteling" [Mission practices in the Dutch Reformed Church: Some trends from 1952 until the turn of the century." *Verbum et Ecclesia* Volume 24 (1) (2003): 2.

Weber, Max, Hans H. Gerth, and C W. Mills. *From Max Weber: Essays in Sociology.* New York: Oxford University Press, 1958.

Weisse, Wolfram, and C.A. Anthonissen. *Maintaining Apartheid or Promoting Change?: The Role of Dutch Reformed Church in a Phase of Increasing Conflict in South Africa. Religion and society in transition*, v. 5. Munster: Waxmann, 2004.

Werbner, Pnina and Tariq Modood. *Debating Cultural Hybridity: Multi-cultural Identities and the Politics of Anti-Racism.* London: Zed Books, 1997.

Welsh, David. *The Rise and Fall of Apartheid.* Charlottesville: University of Virginia Press, 2009.

Westhuizen, Carlene van der. "Country Snapshot South Africa: Economic Growth, Poverty and Equality." *Brookings Institute.* January 5, 2012. 2. Accessed at 6 February 2013. http://www.brookings.edu/research/reports/2012/01/priorities foresight-africa/snapshot_southafrica_vanderwesthuizen.

Westhuizen, M.A. Van der, W. Van der Merwe and R. Van Velde. "Multicultural churches in intercultural ministries." Report presented at the *Multicultural Conference* at Belville, South Africa. 22–23 July 2014. Accessed at 3 March 2015. http://communitas.co.za/taakspanne/gks/multikulturele-konferensie/.

Whitehead, Andrew L. "Gendered Organizations and Inequality Regimes: Gender, Homosexuality, and Inequality Within Religious Congregations." *Journal for the Scientific Study of Religion* 52.3 (2013): 476–493.

Whitehead, K.A. "Racial Categories As Resources and Constraints in Everyday Interactions: Implications for Racialism and Non-Racialism in Post-Apartheid South Africa." *Ethnic and Racial Studies* 35.7 (2012): 1248–1265.

Wodak, Ruth, and Teun A. Dijk. *Racism at the Top: Parliamentary Discourses on Ethnic Issues in Six European States*. Klagenfurt: Drava Verlag, 2000.

Wuthnow, Robert. *After Heaven: Spirituality in America Since the 1950s*. Berkeley: University of California Press, 1998.

Wyngaard, Cobus van. "The language of diversity in reconstructing whiteness in the Dutch Reformed Church," *Churches, Blackness and Contested Multiculturalism*, edited by R. Drew Smith, William Ackah and Anthony G. Reddie, 157–170. New York NY, 2014.

Yancey, George and Ye Yung Kim. "Racial Diversity, Gender Equality, and SES Diversity in Christian Congregations: Exploring the Connections of Racism, Sexism, and Classism in Multiracial and Nonmultiracial Churches." *Journal for the Scientific Study of Religion* Vol. 47, No. 1 (Mar., 2008): 103–111.

Index